Sunset

Quick & Easy

COOK BOOK

By the Editors of Sunset Books and Sunset Magazine

The recipes in this book are also published as part of **Sunset Quick Cuisine**,
Sunset Less Than 7 Ingredients Cook Book, and **Sunset Quick Meals with Fresh Foods**.

Sunset Publishing Corporation ■ **Menlo Park, California**

Research & Text
Tori Bunting
Cynthia Scheer

Contributing Editor
Joan Griffiths

Coordinating Editor
Cornelia Fogle

Design
Joe di Chiarro

Illustrations
Sandra Popovich

Photographers
Victor Budnik: 174, 182. **Peter Christiansen:** 35. **Kevin Sanchez:** 163, 166. **Nikolay Zurek:** 3, 6, 11, 14, 19, 22, 27, 30, 38, 43, 46, 51, 54, 59, 62, 67, 70, 75, 78, 83, 86, 91, 94, 99, 102, 107, 110, 115, 118, 123, 126, 131, 134, 139, 142, 147, 150, 155, 158, 171, 179, 187, 190, back cover.

Photo Stylists
Karen Hazarian: 174. **Susan Massey-Weil:** 6, 11, 14, 19, 30, 51, 78, 86, 107, 147, 158, 163, 166, 179, 190. **Lynne B. Tremble:** 27, 38, 54, 62, 75, 94, 155. **JoAnn Masaoka Van Atta:** 3, 22, 43, 46, 59, 67, 70, 83, 91, 99, 102, 110, 115, 118, 123, 126, 131, 134, 139, 142, 150, 171, 182, 187, back cover.

Cover: Special enough for company, Linguine & Smoked Salmon (recipe on page 80) can be ready for the table in less than half an hour. Smoke fresh salmon briefly in your oven; then serve it warm over tender pasta tossed with a tangy cream sauce. Design by Susan Bryant. Photography by Kevin Sanchez. Photo styling and food styling by Susan Massey-Weil.

Great Meals in Minutes

If you're like most busy cooks, you enjoy good food but prefer to limit your time in the kitchen. You want quick and easy recipes—dishes that go together with little work, yet don't sacrifice flavor and appearance.

The recipes in this collection are designed to save you time and effort. Many dishes call for just a half-dozen ingredients or so, making shopping, preparation, and assembly convenient. We've also emphasized the speediest cooking methods: grilling, broiling, stir-frying, and sautéing. And throughout the book, you'll find a variety of tips and shortcuts—hints for efficient kitchen organization, directions for crisping salad greens, a collection of savory uses for fresh herbs, and more.

For their generosity in sharing props for use in our photographs, we extend special thanks to Best of All Worlds, Biordi Art Imports of San Francisco, S. Christian of Copenhagen, Inc., Crate & Barrel, Menlo Park Hardware, and Williams-Sonoma.

For our recipes, we provide a nutritional analysis (please see page 5) prepared by Hill Nutrition Associates, Inc., of Florida.

Editor, Sunset Books: Elizabeth L. Hogan

First printing September 1991

About the Recipes
All of the recipes in this book were tested and developed in the Sunset test kitchens.

Food and Entertaining Editor
Sunset Magazine
Jerry Anne Di Vecchio

Contents

Veal with Olives & Dried Tomatoes (page 148)

Special Features

Cooking Quick & Easy

Cooks today are increasingly on the lookout for quick and easy recipes—dishes that taste delicious, look attractive, and go together in short order. Lack of time is one factor boosting the popularity of minimum-effort meals: given the pressure of jobs, classes, family activities, and other commitments, many of us just don't have much space in our schedules for cooking. Lack of inclination is another consideration. It may be that you love good food, but not long hours in the kitchen; you'd rather spend the precious "windows" in your day on gardening, reading, or some other hobby.

Whatever the source of your interest in quick cuisine, this book is for you. Among our more than 280 recipes, you'll find many choices calling for just a half-dozen ingredients or so—and a scaled-down ingredient list tends to cut assembly, preparation, and cleanup time accordingly. We've also focussed on the speediest cooking methods: grilling, broiling, stir-frying, and sautéing. And on these two pages, we offer some advice on the basics of quick and easy cookery—efficient kitchen organization, thoughtful meal planning, and smart shopping.

The quick & easy kitchen

If you've ever visited a restaurant kitchen, you may have wondered how so many dishes could emerge so quickly from its often cramped quarters. The secret is organization.

Most tasks in cooking involve three work centers: the refrigerator area, the range area, and the vicinity of the sink. You can make these areas more efficient by storing your utensils and materials near the work center where they'll most often be needed. For example, you'll want to keep plastic bags, foil, and storage containers handy to the refrigerator; spoons, spatulas, pans, and pot holders should be easily reached from the range. Locate a chopping block, colander, knives, and cleanup materials near the sink.

Meal-planning strategy

Planning menus on a day-to-day basis is inefficient. You'll usually spend extra time simply standing in the middle of the kitchen trying to decide what to cook—and you may end up making eleventh-hour dashes to the market (or simply throwing up your hands and calling out for pizza).

It's wiser to plot out a week's worth of menus at a time and, whenever possible, do all your shopping at once (see "Shopping tips," on the facing page). When planning menus, always keep simplicity in mind, but also consider the flavor, texture, appearance, and nutritional content of the food. Remember the following pointers:

■ Provide a good variety of color, shape, flavor, temperature, and texture in the foods you arrange together in a menu.

■ If you're planning to cook two or three dishes at once, choose cooking techniques wisely. It's fine to bake potatoes and game hens in the same oven or to grill lamb chops and skewered vegetables side by side; but you wouldn't want to serve sautéed fish with stir-fried vegetables, since there'd be too much simultaneous activity on the range, all just before serving time. Instead, pair the stir-fried vegetables with baked fish.

■ Plan ahead for leftovers. If you have time to roast a chicken on Sunday, roast two; later in the week, use the leftover meat in a main-dish salad.

- Prepare ingredients ahead of time if you can. Shred cheese and keep it refrigerated in glass jars; rinse and dry salad greens as soon as you bring them home from the market.

- Schedule your meals for smooth serving, with everything ready at once. Base your schedule on the time you'll serve the meal—then figure backward to create a workable plan.

Time-saving tools

Using well-designed utensils correctly and appropriately increases your efficiency in the kitchen. Sharp knives are a must; store them in a protected place, such as in a wooden block or on a magnetic rack. Hone your chopping and slicing skills so you can use knives to the greatest advantage—and save time.

Your food processor is also a great time-saver (see page 24). Let it speed up the chopping, slicing, and shredding of vegetables, cheeses, and other foods. Often, it's not necessary to wash the processor between tasks; just start with the ingredient that makes the least mess.

The microwave oven is another boon for the busy cook; on page 133, you'll find a review of some of the many ways it can help hasten meal preparation.

Another valuable tool (one you may have overlooked) is a pair of helping hands. When you're in a rush, enlist an assistant for any possible job—even if it's just setting the table, getting out serving dishes, slicing bread, or opening a bottle of wine.

Staples for quick meals

Always keep a well-stocked larder and replenish your supplies *before* they run out. These foods should always be in stock: sugar, flour, salt, and rice in your pantry; a variety of spices and herbs conveniently arranged in a cool place away from direct light; and eggs, dairy products, mustard, and mayonnaise in the refrigerator. You'll also want to keep basic vegetables such as onions, carrots, and potatoes in good supply.

Other handy ingredients include versatile hard-cooked eggs; flavored butters to season simply cooked meats, poultry, seafood, and vegetables (see page 149); toasted nuts to include in salads or desserts; and seasoned bread crumbs to sprinkle on casseroles or use for coating various foods.

Though our recipes generally specify fresh ingredients, we do frequently rely on certain canned goods: tomatoes and tomato sauce; tuna; and regular-strength chicken and beef broth. A tube of tomato paste in the refrigerator also comes in handy; you can squeeze out a teaspoon or tablespoon at a time, as needed.

Shopping tips

For many of us, a quick stop at the supermarket after work has become part of life's routine. However, making just one trip each week can actually save time, energy, and money and may even result in less wasted food.

Approach shopping as an adventure. Choose a conveniently located store that has high standards of quality, a wide selection of fresh and packaged foods, and a polite and helpful staff. Learn the store's floor plan, then structure your shopping list according to its departments.

For even easier menus, shop in a supermarket that has a good deli. Many such stores sell easy-to-cook or no-cook items, from assorted salads to succulent roast chickens.

A word about our nutritional data

For our recipes, we provide a nutritional analysis stating calorie count; grams of protein, carbohydrates, and total fat; and milligrams of cholesterol and sodium. Generally, the analysis applies to a single serving, based on the number of servings given for each recipe and the amount of each ingredient. If a range is given for the number of servings and/or the amount of an ingredient, the analysis is based on an average of the figures given.

The nutritional analysis does not include optional ingredients or those for which no specific amount is stated. If an ingredient is listed with a substitution, the information was calculated using the first choice.

Two kinds of onion—shallot and chives—give bold emphasis to the wine–vinegar dip in Shrimp with Tart Dipping Sauce (recipe on page 12). A chive tie decorates each shrimp.

Appetizers

When you really want an appetizer in no time, it's easiest just to open a box of crisp crackers and slice some good cheese. But if you have a few extra minutes, you can serve up an impressive variety of starters: spicy toasted peanuts, crunchy vegetable sticks with a savory dip or spread, skewered meatballs to sizzle on the hibachi, even chilled shrimp tied with fresh chive bows. The following pages offer over a dozen choices—some simple, some more sophisticated, but none that requires more than half an hour in the kitchen.

Prosciutto & Pea Bundles

Preparation time: About 20 minutes
Cooking time: About 30 seconds

Filled with seasoned cream cheese and carrot slivers, then wrapped in salty prosciutto, these crunchy sugar snap peas make bright, pretty appetizers that are low in calories, too.

- 60 sugar snap peas, ends and strings removed
- 2 medium-size carrots
- 2 to 3 ounces thinly sliced prosciutto or cooked ham
- 1 package (4 oz.) onion-flavored spreadable cream cheese

In a wide frying pan, bring 2 inches water to a boil over high heat. Add peas and boil gently until bright green (about 30 seconds). Drain peas, plunge into ice water, and stir until cool. Drain again and set aside.

Cut carrots crosswise into thirds; cut each third into 10 matchstick-size pieces. Cut prosciutto into 60 strips.

With a sharp knife, slice each pea along outside seam. Open slightly and push about ½ teaspoon of the cheese into each, smoothing cheese with back of a knife. Position a carrot stick on filling, hold in place, and wrap prosciutto in a band around carrot and pea to secure. Makes 60 appetizers (10 to 12 servings).

Per appetizer: 11 calories, 0.5 g protein, 0.6 g carbohydrates, 0.7 g total fat, 2 mg cholesterol, 28 mg sodium

Lime- & Chili-spiked Vegetables

Preparation time: 10 to 15 minutes

Here's a simple, spicy starter for a Mexican-style meal. To make it, you just dip crisp jicama slices and whole radishes first into a tart lime-tequila blend, then into nippy chili powder.

- 24 radishes
- 1 pound jicama, peeled
- 3 tablespoons *each* lime juice and tequila (or all lime juice)
- 2 tablespoons chili powder
- 1 teaspoon salt

Remove roots and all but a few leaves from each radish. Cut jicama into ½-inch-wide, ½-inch-thick sticks. Arrange vegetables in a dish or basket. (At this point, you may cover and refrigerate until next day.) In a small bowl, mix lime juice and tequila. In another bowl, mix chili powder and salt. To eat, dip vegetables into lime mixture, then into chili mixture. Makes 8 to 10 servings.

Per serving: 39 calories, 0.9 g protein, 6 g carbohydrates, 0.4 g total fat, 0 mg cholesterol, 268 mg sodium

Chili Peanuts

Preparation time: About 5 minutes
Baking time: About 25 minutes

The lively flavors of cumin and chiles make these peanuts irresistible. To sip alongside, offer ice-cold beer, margaritas, or tomato juice.

- 2 cups (about 11 oz.) raw peanuts
- 2 teaspoons chili powder
- 1 teaspoon ground cumin
- 3 small dried hot red chiles
- 1 tablespoon salad oil
  Salt

Place peanuts in a large rimmed baking pan. Bake in a 350° oven, stirring occasionally, until pale golden (about 15 minutes). Remove from oven. Add chili powder, cumin, chiles, and oil to pan; mix well. Return to oven and continue to bake, stirring once, until peanuts are golden brown (8 to 10 more minutes). Season to taste with salt. Serve warm or cool. Makes 8 to 10 servings.

Per serving: 214 calories, 9 g protein, 6 g carbohydrates, 19 g total fat, 0 mg cholesterol, 12 mg sodium

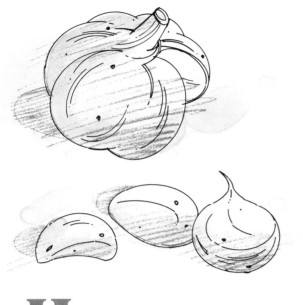

Hummus with Pita Crisps

Preparation time: About 10 minutes
Cooking time: 5 to 10 minutes

Popular in the Middle East, this wholesome and satisfying garbanzo dip fits any informal occasion. Serve it with crisp-baked wedges of pita bread.

- 6 pita breads (*each* about 6 inches in diameter)
- ½ cup olive oil
  Salt and pepper
- ¼ cup sesame seeds
- 1 can (about 15 oz.) garbanzo beans, drained (reserve liquid)
- 3 tablespoons lemon juice
- 1 or 2 cloves garlic

Split pita breads and brush split sides with ¼ cup of the oil; season to taste with salt and pepper. Stack breads; cut stack into 6 to 8 wedges. Place wedges in a single layer on 2 large baking sheets. Bake in a 400° oven until crisp and golden (5 to 10 minutes). Set aside.

Meanwhile, toast sesame seeds in a small frying pan over medium heat until golden (3 to 5 minutes), shaking pan often. Transfer seeds to a blender or food processor and add garbanzos, 2 tablespoons of the oil, lemon juice, garlic, and 6 tablespoons of the reserved garbanzo liquid. Whirl, adding more liquid if needed, until hummus is smooth but still thick enough to hold its shape. Season to taste with salt and pepper.

Transfer hummus to a serving bowl and drizzle with remaining 2 tablespoons oil. Offer pita wedges to scoop up dip. Makes 6 to 8 servings.

Per serving: 390 calories, 9 g protein, 47 g carbohydrates, 19 g total fat, 0 mg cholesterol, 495 mg sodium

Asparagus Spears with Watercress Mayonnaise

Preparation time: 10 to 15 minutes
Cooking time: 5 to 7 minutes

Few finger foods can match the elegance of fresh asparagus. These spears are lightly cooked, then served with a boldly seasoned green mayonnaise for dipping.

- 1 egg
- 1 tablespoon white wine vinegar
- 1 teaspoon *each* Dijon mustard and anchovy paste
- ⅓ cup packed watercress leaves
- 1 small clove garlic (optional)
- 1 cup salad oil
- 24 to 36 asparagus spears, tough ends removed

In a blender or food processor, combine egg, vinegar, mustard, anchovy paste, watercress, and, if desired, garlic. Whirl until smooth. With motor running, add oil in a thin, steady stream; continue to whirl until mayonnaise is smooth. (At this point, you may cover and refrigerate mayonnaise for up to 2 days.)

In a wide frying pan, bring 1 inch water to a boil over high heat. Add asparagus, reduce heat, cover, and boil gently just until tender when pierced (5 to 7 minutes). Drain, immerse in cold water, and drain again. Serve asparagus at room temperature or chilled; offer watercress mayonnaise for dipping. Makes 10 to 12 servings.

Per serving of asparagus: 9 calories, 1 g protein, 1 g carbohydrates, 0.1 g total fat, 0 mg cholesterol, 0.8 mg sodium

Per tablespoon of mayonnaise: 84 calories, 0.3 g protein, .06 g carbohydrates, 9 g total fat, 9 mg cholesterol, 18 mg sodium

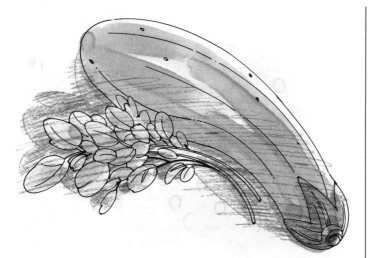

Basil Meatballs

Pictured on facing page

Preparation time: About 30 minutes
Grilling time: 10 to 15 minutes

Serve these basil-wrapped meatballs hot off the grill, with sliced baguettes and Beaujolais.

- 1 pound bulk pork sausage
- 1 cup minced fresh basil
- 1 teaspoon crushed fennel seeds
- 20 to 25 large fresh basil leaves

Soak 7 to 12 long bamboo skewers in hot water to cover for about 30 minutes. Meanwhile, combine sausage, minced basil, and fennel seeds. Shape into 1-inch balls. Wrap a basil leaf around each meatball, lightly pressing it into meat so it sticks (leaf need not cover entire meatball). Thread meatballs closely together on skewers, allowing 2 or 3 per skewer.

Lay skewers on a grill 2 to 4 inches above a solid bed of medium to low coals (extinguish any flares with a spray of water). Grill, turning every 2 to 3 minutes, until meatballs are no longer pink in center; cut to test (10 to 15 minutes). Serve on skewers. Makes 8 servings.

Per serving: 109 calories, 6 g protein, 2 g carbohydrates, 9 g total fat, 22 mg cholesterol, 349 mg sodium

Eggplant & Goat Cheese Rolls

Pictured on facing page

Preparation time: About 15 minutes
Baking time: About 13 minutes

Begin a wide-awake brunch with spicy Bloody Marys, sesame breadsticks, and tender roasted eggplant slices rolled around goat cheese and watercress. (If you can find long, slender Oriental eggplants, use them—they generally taste sweeter and have smaller seeds than regular eggplant.)

- 1 pound Oriental or regular eggplant, stems removed
- 1½ tablespoons olive oil
- 3 ounces soft goat cheese, such as Montrachet
- 12 to 16 watercress sprigs, rinsed and crisped

Cut eggplants lengthwise into ¼- to ⅓-inch-thick slices (if using regular eggplant, cut slices in half lengthwise). Brush both sides of slices with oil; place slices in a single layer on large baking sheets. Bake in a 450° oven for 8 minutes; turn over and continue to bake until very soft when pressed (about 5 more minutes). Remove from pans and let cool.

Divide cheese equally among eggplant slices, placing it at end of each slice. Top cheese on each slice with a sprig of watercress, letting leaves hang over edges of eggplant. Roll up and arrange on a platter. Makes 12 to 16 appetizers (4 to 6 servings).

Per appetizer: 122 calories, 4 g protein, 7 g carbohydrates, 9 g total fat, 16 mg cholesterol, 111 mg sodium

Nachos

Preparation time: About 5 minutes
Baking time: About 10 minutes

Heaped with cheese, chiles, and smooth sour cream, these crunchy nachos are sure to please just about everyone.

- 4 cups tortilla chips
- 1 cup (4 oz.) shredded jack cheese
- 1 cup (4 oz.) shredded Cheddar cheese
- 2 tablespoons *each* diced green chiles and sliced ripe olives
  About ⅓ cup sour cream

Arrange tortilla chips in a 9-inch square baking pan. Sprinkle evenly with cheeses, chiles, and olives. Bake in a 350° oven until cheese is melted (about 10 minutes). Top with sour cream and serve immediately. Makes 4 servings.

Per serving: 494 calories, 18 g protein, 33 g carbohydrates, 34 g total fat, 63 mg cholesterol, 683 mg sodium

Hot and cool hors d'oeuvres are (clockwise from top)
Basil Meatballs (recipe on facing page), Eggplant &
Goat Cheese Rolls (recipe on facing page), and Snow
Peas with Mint Sauce (recipe on page 12).

Shrimp with Tart Dipping Sauce

Pictured on page 6

Preparation time: About 25 minutes
Cooking time: 3 to 4 minutes

Plump pink shrimp, tied with vivid chive sashes, taste as delicious as they look. Offer them with a peppery wine-and-vinegar dipping sauce.

- **1 pound medium-size raw shrimp (30 to 32 per lb.), shelled and deveined**
- **30 to 32 whole chives (*each* about 7 inches long)**
- **Tart Dipping Sauce (recipe follows)**

In a 2-quart pan, bring about 4 cups water to a boil over high heat. Add shrimp. Reduce heat, cover, and simmer until shrimp are opaque in center; cut to test (3 to 4 minutes). Drain, immerse in cold water, and drain again. Set aside.

In a wide frying pan, bring about 1 inch water to a boil over high heat. Add chives and cook just until wilted (about 5 seconds); remove immediately with tongs. Tie a chive around center of each shrimp; set aside.

Prepare Tart Dipping Sauce and pour into a small bowl. Arrange shrimp on a platter and offer sauce alongside. If made ahead, cover and refrigerate for up to 4 hours. Makes about 8 servings.

Tart Dipping Sauce. In a small bowl, stir together ¼ cup *each* **dry white wine** and **white wine vinegar**, 1 tablespoon *each* minced **shallot** and minced **chives**, and ½ teaspoon **pepper**.

Per serving: 18 calories, 3 g protein, 0.4 g carbohydrates, 0.3 g total fat, 22 mg cholesterol, 22 mg sodium

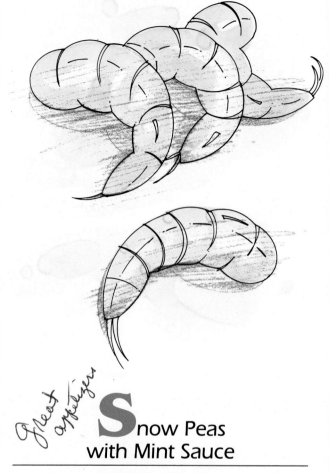

Snow Peas with Mint Sauce

Pictured on page 11

Preparation time: About 15 minutes
Cooking time: About 30 seconds

Here's a fresh choice for springtime patio entertaining. Arrange blanched snow peas on a pretty platter; serve with cool, creamy mint dip.

- **1 pound Chinese pea pods (also called snow peas), ends and strings removed**
- **¼ cup *each* sour cream and mayonnaise**
- **2 tablespoons coarsely chopped fresh mint**
- **Mint sprigs (optional)**

In a wide frying pan, bring 2 inches water to a boil over high heat. Add pea pods and boil gently until bright green (about 30 seconds). Drain pea pods, plunge into ice water, and stir until cool. Drain again and set aside.

In a food processor or blender, whirl sour cream, mayonnaise, and the 2 tablespoons mint until mint is finely chopped. Transfer to a small bowl, place in center of a platter, and surround with pea pods. Garnish with mint sprigs, if desired. Makes 6 servings.

Per serving: 117 calories, 2 g protein, 6 g carbohydrates, 9 g total fat, 10 mg cholesterol, 60 mg sodium

Simple Dips & Spreads

Appetizers make any meal more festive—and there's no need to reserve them for company dinners and special occasions. The quick-to-fix dips and spreads on this page let you dress up everyday suppers with surprising ease. We offer suggestions for dippers with each recipe, but feel free to make other choices—try our curry dip with chilled cooked shrimp, for example, or offer crisp cucumber slices with the salmon spread.

Quick Curry Dip

Preparation time: 2 to 3 minutes

1 cup mayonnaise
1 tablespoon curry powder
1 teaspoon lemon juice
Crisp raw vegetables

In a small bowl, stir together mayonnaise, curry powder, and lemon juice until well combined. Serve with vegetables for dipping. Makes about 1 cup.

Per tablespoon: 100 calories, 0.2 g protein, 0.6 g carbohydrates, 11 g total fat, 8 mg cholesterol, 78 mg sodium

Guacamole

Preparation time: About 10 minutes

2 large ripe avocados
2 to 3 tablespoons lime or lemon juice
1 clove garlic, minced or pressed
1 tomato, seeded and chopped
Salt (optional)
Liquid hot pepper seasoning
Tortilla or corn chips

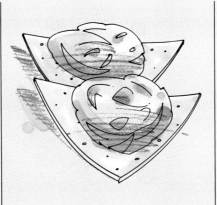

Cut avocados in half, remove pits, and scoop pulp into a bowl. With a fork, mash pulp coarsely while blending in lime juice. Add garlic and tomato; season to taste with salt (if desired) and hot pepper seasoning. Serve with chips for dipping. Makes about 2 cups.

Per tablespoon: 26 calories, 0.3 g protein, 1 g carbohydrates, 2 g total fat, 0 mg cholesterol, 2 mg sodium

Brandied Blue Cheese Spread

Preparation time: 3 to 5 minutes

3 ounces blue-veined cheese
2 tablespoons butter or margarine, at room temperature
1 small package (3 oz.) cream cheese, at room temperature
2 tablespoons brandy
Red or Golden Delicious apple wedges (coated with lemon juice), celery sticks, or unsalted crackers

In small bowl of an electric mixer, beat blue-veined cheese, butter, cream cheese, and brandy until smooth. (Or whirl in a food processor until smooth.) Spread on apple wedges. Makes about 1 cup.

Per tablespoon: 55 calories, 2 g protein, 0.3 g carbohydrates, 5 g total fat, 14 mg cholesterol, 105 mg sodium

Baked Camembert

Preparation time: 2 to 3 minutes
Baking time: 12 to 15 minutes

1 whole Camembert cheese (about 4 oz.)
Olive oil
Fine dry bread crumbs
Sliced crusty bread or crackers

Brush cheese with oil on all sides; then roll in crumbs until completely coated. Place on an ovenproof plate or in a small baking dish and bake in a 350° oven until cheese just begins to melt (12 to 15 minutes). Spread on bread. Makes 4 servings.

Per serving: 257 calories, 8 g protein, 5 g carbohydrates, 23 g total fat, 28 mg cholesterol, 364 mg sodium

great- but cut up salmon + leave by itself

Smoked Salmon Spread

Preparation time: 3 to 5 minutes

1 large package (8 oz.) cream cheese, at room temperature
3 ounces smoked salmon, chopped
1 teaspoon dry dill weed
Cocktail-size bagels, pumpernickel squares, or unsalted crackers

leave c. cheese by itself

In small bowl of an electric mixer, beat cream cheese, salmon, and dill weed until smooth. (Or whirl in a food processor until smooth.) Spread on cocktail-size bagels. Makes about 1¼ cups.

Per tablespoon: 45 calories, 2 g protein, 0.3 g carbohydrates, 4 g total fat, 13 mg cholesterol, 67 mg sodium

*Easy to make and smooth to sip, Creamy Potato
Watercress Bisque (recipe on page 18) owes its
velvety texture to sour cream, its assertiveness to green
onions. A sprinkling of ham adds substance.*

Soups

othing's more soothing than a bowl of soup. A chilled gazpacho or cool, smooth cucumber purée provides the perfect refreshment for sultry days; a chunky chowder quickly warms up winter weather. Soups are versatile, too; depending on the portion size and the accompaniments you select, the same recipe can often serve as either first course or main dish. And many soups—both light and robust—go together in very little time. Using the choices here, you'll find it easy to create comforting menus even on busy days.

Cold Avocado Soup

Preparation time: About 7 minutes

You'll find this velvety green soup a perfect starter for warm-weather meals. Try it with grilled chicken or a juicy steak at dinner time, or serve it with sandwiches for lunch.

- 1 large ripe avocado
- ½ cup chilled half-and-half or whipping cream
- 1½ cups chilled regular-strength chicken broth
- 1 tablespoon lemon juice
  Salt
  Snipped chives or watercress sprigs (optional)

Pit and peel avocado; cut into chunks. In a blender, whirl avocado, half-and-half, broth, and lemon juice until smooth. (To prepare in a food processor, whirl avocado with half-and-half until puréed; add broth and lemon juice and whirl until smooth.) Season to taste with salt.

Ladle soup into wide, shallow bowls. Garnish each portion with chives, if desired. Makes 4 servings.

Per serving: 151 calories, 3 g protein, 7 g carbohydrates, 14 g total fat, 11 mg cholesterol, 389 mg sodium

Cold Cucumber & Dill Soup

Preparation time: About 15 minutes

Top a cool cucumber purée with delicate pink shrimp for an easy no-cook first course. You might follow the soup with sweet cracked crab or lobster.

- 2 large European-style cucumbers (about 1 lb. *each*), peeled
- 1 cup regular-strength chicken broth
- 1 cup plain yogurt
- ¼ cup lightly packed chopped fresh dill
- 3 tablespoons lime juice
  Salt
- ½ pound small cooked shrimp
  Dill sprigs (optional)

Cut cucumbers into ½-inch chunks. Place half the cucumber chunks in a blender or food processor, add ½ cup of the broth, and whirl until puréed. Pour into a large bowl. Place remaining cucumbers, remaining ½ cup broth, yogurt, chopped dill, and lime juice in blender; whirl until puréed. Pour into bowl and stir to blend, then season to taste with salt. (For a smoother texture, rub soup through a fine sieve.)

Ladle soup into bowls and top with shrimp. Garnish each portion with dill sprigs, if desired. Makes 4 servings.

Per serving: 130 calories, 17 g protein, 11 g carbohydrates, 2 g total fat, 114 mg cholesterol, 428 mg sodium

Italian Tomato-Basil Soup

Preparation time: About 10 minutes
Cooking time: 12 to 17 minutes

Celebrate summer! Ripe tomatoes, fresh basil, and a little cream and broth add up to a deliciously fragrant soup you can make in under half an hour.

> 2 **pounds ripe pear-shaped tomatoes**
> 2 **tablespoons olive oil or salad oil**
> ½ **cup lightly packed fresh basil leaves**
> ½ **cup** *each* **regular-strength chicken broth and whipping cream**
> **Salt and pepper**

Core tomatoes, cut into chunks, and place in a 3- to 4-quart pan along with oil and ¼ cup of the basil. Cook over medium-high heat, stirring, until tomatoes mash easily (10 to 15 minutes).

In a blender or food processor, whirl tomato mixture, broth, and cream, a portion at a time, until puréed. Season to taste with salt and pepper.

Return soup to pan and stir over medium heat just until hot. Ladle soup into bowls. Sliver remaining ¼ cup basil and sprinkle over soup. Makes 4 servings.

Per serving: 195 calories, 3 g protein, 11 g carbohydrates, 17 g total fat, 33 mg cholesterol, 151 mg sodium

Gazpacho

Preparation time: 15 to 20 minutes
Chilling time: At least 30 minutes

This light, fresh Spanish soup is served in countless versions. Here, we offer two: a classic all-vegetable rendition and a heartier dish made with cooked ham or chicken.

> 4 **cups tomato juice**
> 3 **tablespoons olive oil or salad oil**
> 2 **tablespoons white wine vinegar**
> ½ **teaspoon dry oregano**
> 1 **small onion, chopped**
> ½ **green bell pepper, seeded and chopped**
> 1 **cucumber, peeled, seeded, and chopped**
> 2 **tomatoes, seeded and diced**
> 1 **avocado, pitted, peeled, and diced**
> **Seasoned croutons (optional)**

In a large bowl, combine tomato juice, oil, vinegar, and oregano; stir well. Add onion, bell pepper, cucumber, tomatoes, and avocado; stir until well combined. Cover and refrigerate for at least 30 minutes or up to 2 days. Ladle chilled soup into bowls; if desired, pass croutons at the table to top individual servings. Makes 4 servings.

Per serving: 239 calories, 4 g protein, 20 g carbohydrates, 18 g total fat, 0 mg cholesterol, 895 mg sodium

Gazpacho with Ham or Chicken

Follow directions for **Gazpacho**, but stir in 1½ cups diced or matchstick-size strips **cooked ham** or cooked chicken after adding avocado. Makes 4 servings.

Per serving with ham: 339 calories, 17 g protein, 20 g carbohydrates, 23 g total fat, 33 mg cholesterol, 1,745 mg sodium

Per serving with chicken: 338 calories, 19 g protein, 20 g carbohydrates, 22 g total fat, 47 mg cholesterol, 940 mg sodium

Carrot & Cilantro Soup

Pictured on facing page

Preparation time: About 10 minutes
Cooking time: About 25 minutes

Flavorful bursts of curry and cilantro accent the natural sweetness of fresh carrots in this tantalizing soup. Pair it with Golden Onion & Ham Sandwiches (page 65) for a winning lunch or supper combination.

- 1½ **pounds carrots**
- 4 **cups regular-strength chicken broth**
- ¾ **teaspoon curry powder**
- 2 **tablespoons lemon juice**
  Ground red pepper (cayenne)
- ¼ **cup lightly packed chopped fresh cilantro (coriander)**

Cut carrots into ½-inch-thick slices and place in a 3- to 4-quart pan. Add broth and curry powder and bring to a boil over high heat; reduce heat, cover, and simmer until carrots are very soft (about 20 minutes). Stir in lemon juice.

In a blender or food processor, whirl soup, a portion at a time, until puréed. Season to taste with red pepper. Ladle soup into bowls and sprinkle cilantro over each portion. Makes 4 servings.

Per serving: 96 calories, 5 g protein, 17 g carbohydrates, 2 g total fat, 0 mg cholesterol, 1,042 mg sodium

Creamy Potato Watercress Bisque

Pictured on page 14

Preparation time: About 15 minutes
Cooking time: 20 to 25 minutes

A garnish of chopped ham adds contrasting color and flavor to this substantial soup. Serve it with crusty bread, cheese, and a crisp salad for a satisfying cool-weather lunch.

- 3 **cups regular-strength chicken broth**
- 2 **large white thin-skinned potatoes (about 1 lb. *total*), peeled and cut into 1-inch chunks**
- 2 **cups lightly packed watercress sprigs, rinsed and drained**
- 1 **cup sour cream**
- 3 **green onions (including tops), thinly sliced**
  Salt and ground white pepper
- ¼ **pound thinly sliced cooked ham, chopped**

In a 3- to 4-quart pan, bring broth and potatoes to a boil over high heat; reduce heat, cover, and simmer until potatoes are tender when pierced (15 to 20 minutes).

Reserve 4 of the watercress sprigs for garnish. In a blender or food processor, whirl sour cream, onions, broth mixture, and remaining watercress, a portion at a time, until puréed. Season to taste with salt and white pepper.

Return soup to pan and stir over medium heat just until hot. Ladle soup into wide, shallow bowls. Top each serving with a mound of ham and a watercress sprig. Makes 4 servings.

Per serving: 280 calories, 13 g protein, 22 g carbohydrates, 16 g total fat, 42 mg cholesterol, 1,211 mg sodium

In brisk autumn weather, warm up with
steaming Carrot & Cilantro Soup (recipe on facing page)
and savory Golden Onion & Ham Sandwiches
(recipe on page 65).

Mushroom-Tarragon Bisque

Preparation time: About 10 minutes
Cooking time: About 15 minutes

Partner this comforting soup with Chicken & Cheese Subs (page 58) or other hearty sandwiches for Sunday supper.

- 1 pound mushrooms
- 4 cups regular-strength chicken broth
- ¼ cup lightly packed fresh tarragon
- ½ cup whipping cream

Set aside 2 of the mushrooms for garnish. In a blender or food processor, whirl half the remaining mushrooms, 2 cups of the broth, and 2 tablespoons of the tarragon until mushrooms are finely chopped. Pour into a 3- to 4-quart pan. Repeat to purée remaining mushrooms with remaining 2 cups broth; pour into pan.

Bring broth mixture to a boil over high heat. Reduce heat, cover, and simmer until mushrooms are soft (about 10 minutes).

Add cream and stir just until hot. Ladle soup into bowls. Slice reserved mushrooms; sprinkle mushroom slices and remaining 2 tablespoons tarragon over soup. Makes 4 servings.

Per serving: 145 calories, 6 g protein, 7 g carbohydrates, 11 g total fat, 33 mg cholesterol, 1,002 mg sodium

Garlic & Eggplant Soup

Preparation time: About 15 minutes
Cooking time: 10 to 15 minutes

A simple purée of oven-browned eggplant, broth, and mellow sautéed garlic makes a marvelous first course for a meal of lamb chops and roasted potatoes.

- 1 large eggplant (1¼ to 1½ lbs.), peeled
  About ¼ cup olive oil or salad oil
- 3 or 4 cloves garlic, peeled
- ½ cup whipping cream
- 2½ cups regular-strength chicken broth
  Salt and pepper
- ¼ cup chopped parsley

Cut eggplant crosswise into ¾-inch-thick slices. Place slices in a single layer on a large baking sheet; brush liberally with oil. Broil 4 inches below heat, turning once, until eggplant is soft and browned on both sides (10 to 15 minutes).

Meanwhile, cook garlic in a small, uncoated frying pan over medium heat, turning as needed, until richly browned all over (about 10 minutes).

Cut eggplant into chunks. In a blender or food processor, whirl eggplant, garlic, and cream until puréed. Add broth and whirl until smooth.

Transfer soup to a 3- to 4-quart pan and stir over medium heat just until hot. Season to taste with salt and pepper. Ladle soup into bowls and sprinkle parsley over each portion. Makes 4 servings.

Per serving: 259 calories, 4 g protein, 10 g carbohydrates, 24 g total fat, 33 mg cholesterol, 633 mg sodium

Oriental Noodle & Pea Broth

Preparation time: About 10 minutes
Cooking time: About 7 minutes

Star anise and ginger infuse this light, fresh soup with Asian flavor. To carry out the Chinese theme, serve the soup with Stir-fried Shrimp with Green Onions (page 103).

¼ pound sugar snap peas or Chinese pea pods (also called snow peas), ends and strings removed
6 cups regular-strength chicken broth
2 whole star anise; or ¼ teaspoon crushed anise seeds and 2 cinnamon sticks (broken into pieces), tied in a cheesecloth bag
¾ teaspoon grated fresh ginger
1 ounce thin dry pasta strands, such as spaghettini or vermicelli

Cut peas diagonally into ¼- to ½-inch-thick slices; set aside.

In a 4- to 5-quart pan, bring broth, star anise, and ginger to a boil over high heat. Add pasta; return to a boil and cook just until *al dente* (about 3 minutes).

With a slotted spoon, remove star anise from soup; discard anise. Add peas and return to a boil. Ladle soup into bowls. Makes 4 to 6 servings.

Per serving: 66 calories, 5 g protein, 8 g carbohydrates, 2 g total fat, 0 mg cholesterol, 1,185 mg sodium

Corn Chowder

Preparation time: About 10 minutes
Cooking time: About 35 minutes

This all-American classic goes well with another national favorite—grilled hamburgers with all the fixings. Because our chowder is made with canned cream-style corn, you can enjoy it any time of year.

8 slices bacon
1 large onion, chopped
4 cups *each* water and peeled, diced thin-skinned potatoes
2 cans (about 1 lb. *each*) cream-style corn
4 cups milk or 2 cups *each* milk and half-and-half
Salt and pepper
2 tablespoons butter or margarine (optional)

In a 5- to 6-quart pan, cook bacon over medium heat until crisp (about 8 minutes). Drain, crumble, and set aside; discard all but about 2 tablespoons of the drippings.

Add onion to drippings in pan and cook, stirring, until soft (about 10 minutes). Add water, potatoes, and corn. Bring to a boil over high heat; reduce heat, cover, and simmer until potatoes are tender when pierced (about 15 minutes).

Stir in milk and season to taste with salt and pepper. Heat chowder until steaming; stir in butter, if desired. Ladle into deep bowls and sprinkle bacon over each portion. Makes 8 servings.

Per serving: 282 calories, 10 g protein, 41 g carbohydrates, 10 g total fat, 25 mg cholesterol, 506 mg sodium

*Thin strands of angel hair pasta mingle with colorful
vegetables in Chicken & Capellini Soup (recipe on facing
page). Each ingredient goes into the pot at just the
right moment to keep color and flavor intact.*

Chicken & Capellini Soup

Pictured on facing page

Preparation time: About 15 minutes
Cooking time: About 30 minutes

Tender strands of capellini swirl through this appetizing chicken–vegetable soup. Enjoy it with a loaf of crusty Italian bread, a selection of cheeses, and sliced ripe pears or crisp apples.

- 2 tablespoons butter or margarine
- ¼ cup finely chopped shallots
- 1 clove garlic, minced or pressed
- ½ teaspoon salt
- ¼ teaspoon dry thyme
- ⅛ teaspoon ground white pepper
- 2 whole chicken breasts (about 1 lb. *each*), skinned, boned, and cut into ½-inch cubes
- 1 can (14½ oz.) regular-strength chicken broth
- 1½ cups water
- ½ cup dry white wine
- 1 medium-size carrot, thinly sliced
- 2 ounces dry capellini
- 2 cups shredded Swiss chard leaves
- 1 medium-size tomato, seeded and chopped
  Grated Parmesan cheese

Melt butter in a 3½- to 4-quart pan over medium heat. Add shallots and cook, stirring often, until soft but not browned (2 to 3 minutes). Stir in garlic, salt, thyme, white pepper, and chicken. Cook, stirring often, until chicken looks opaque (about 3 minutes). Add broth, water, wine, and carrot. Bring to a boil over high heat; reduce heat, cover, and boil gently until carrot is tender to bite (about 15 minutes).

Break capellini strands in half; add capellini to soup and return to a boil. Cook, uncovered, stirring often, until pasta is *al dente* (4 to 5 minutes). Add chard and tomato; cover, remove from heat, and let stand just until tomato is heated through (about 2 minutes). Ladle into bowls; offer cheese to add to individual portions. Makes 4 servings.

Per serving: 305 calories, 38 g protein, 17 g carbohydrates, 9 g total fat, 101 mg cholesterol, 926 mg sodium

Chinese Chicken & Shrimp Soup

Preparation time: About 15 minutes
Cooking time: About 5 minutes

This Asian-style soup is ready to serve almost as soon as it boils. Once you've prepared the nourishing ingredients—chicken, shrimp, tofu, and vegetables—there's little left to do but combine and heat them, then savor the result.

- 5 cups regular-strength chicken broth
- 2 tablespoons finely chopped fresh ginger
- 2 to 3 teaspoons soy sauce
- 1 whole chicken breast (about 1 lb.), skinned, boned, and cut into ½-inch cubes
- 6 ounces mushrooms, sliced
- 3 cups thinly sliced bok choy
- 1 cup cubed firm tofu (about ½-inch cubes)
- ½ cup sliced green onions (including tops)
- ½ pound small cooked shrimp
- ¼ cup chopped fresh cilantro (coriander)
  Ground red pepper (cayenne) or chili oil (optional)

In a 4- to 5-quart pan, bring broth, ginger, and soy sauce to a boil over high heat. Add chicken, mushrooms, bok choy, tofu, and onions. Cook until chicken is no longer pink in center; cut to test (about 2 minutes). Remove pan from heat and stir in shrimp and cilantro. Season to taste with red pepper, if desired. Makes 4 to 6 servings.

Per serving: 230 calories, 36 g protein, 7 g carbohydrates, 7 g total fat, 123 mg cholesterol, 1,335 mg sodium

Processor Tips

The food processor has many uses, and all of them will save you time and energy. Here are just a few of the tasks your processor can do for you.

Shredding & grating cheese

Shredded and grated cheeses are staple ingredients that can be prepared ahead, refrigerated or frozen, and kept on hand for use in recipes. A 4-ounce piece of jack, Swiss, Cheddar, or other firm cheese will yield 1 cup shredded cheese; for best results, shred these cheeses when they're cold, using the shredding disk. Grate harder cheeses, such as Asiago, Parmesan, and Romano, at room temperature. Cut away and discard the tough, hard edges; then cut the cheese into 1-inch cubes. Place the metal blade in the work bowl, turn the motor on, and drop the cheese, a few pieces at a time, into the feed tube. Continue until all cheese is processed (grated); a 5-ounce wedge will yield about 1 cup of finely grated cheese. To store shredded or grated cheese, transfer it to glass jars, then cover and refrigerate for up to a week; for longer storage, freeze in jars, freezer containers, or airtight plastic bags.

Making bread crumbs

You can prepare fine dry bread crumbs from crisp dry bread, soft crumbs from fresh bread. Place the metal blade in the work bowl, turn the motor on, and drop torn or broken slices of bread, a few pieces at a time, into the feed tube. One sandwich-size slice of crisp dry bread yields ¼ cup crumbs; one slice of fresh bread yields ½ cup crumbs. Soft crumbs should be used soon after processing; fine dry crumbs can be stored airtight at room temperature for several months.

Chopping parsley in quantity

For perfectly chopped parsley, remove the stems, then rinse and thoroughly dry the sprigs (wet parsley turns to mush). Using the metal blade, process the sprigs continuously until finely chopped. Store chopped parsley, covered, in the refrigerator for up to a week.

Chopping vegetables

A few seconds can make the difference between vegetables that are chopped and those that are watery and puréed. Using the on-off processing technique will always give you evenly chopped vegetables; each time you turn the motor off, the food drops to the bottom of the work bowl, so it will be in the path of the blade when the motor is restarted. After 2 or 3 on-off bursts, scrape down the sides of the work bowl. After 2 or 3 more on-off bursts, the vegetables will be finely chopped.

Chicken & Vegetable Soup

Preparation time: 15 to 20 minutes
Cooking time: About 25 minutes

Clear broth, plenty of vegetables, and a generous helping of cooked chicken or turkey make a quick main dish that's brimming with lively flavor. You might serve it with a fruit salad and crisp crackers.

- 6 **cups regular-strength chicken broth**
- ½ **cup long-grain white rice**
- 3 **medium-size carrots, cut into ⅛-inch-thick slices**
- 3 **stalks celery, cut into ¼-inch-thick slices**
- 2 **small zucchini, cut into ¼-inch-thick slices**
- 6 **tablespoons butter or margarine**
- 6 **tablespoons all-purpose flour**
- 2 **cups half-and-half or milk**
- 3 **cups bite-size pieces cooked chicken or turkey**
- ½ **cup thinly sliced green onions (including tops)**
  Salt and pepper
  Minced parsley

In a 5-quart pan, bring broth to a boil over high heat. Add rice; reduce heat, cover, and simmer for 10 minutes. Add carrots, celery, and zucchini; cover and continue to simmer until vegetables are tender-crisp to bite (about 10 more minutes).

Meanwhile, melt butter in a small pan over medium heat. Stir in flour and cook, stirring, until bubbly. Remove from heat and gradually stir in half-and-half; then stir in about 1 cup of the broth from soup mixture. Return to heat and cook, stirring, until sauce is smooth and thickened. Stir sauce into soup mixture.

Stir in chicken and onions; season to taste with salt and pepper. Cook until heated through. Ladle into bowls and sprinkle with parsley. Makes 4 to 6 servings.

Per serving: 572 calories, 34 g protein, 34 g carbohydrates, 33 g total fat, 148 mg cholesterol, 1,475 mg sodium

Autumn Vegetable & Turkey Chowder

Preparation time: About 15 minutes
Cooking time: About 30 minutes

Leftover roast turkey gives a delectable repeat performance in a colorful, creamy soup enriched with golden Cheddar cheese. Bake a pan of buttermilk biscuits to serve alongside.

- 3 tablespoons butter or margarine
- 1 medium-size onion, chopped
- 1 cup thinly sliced carrots
- ½ cup thinly sliced celery
- 2 cups diced potatoes
- 1 can (about 14½ oz.) tomatoes
- 2 beef bouillon cubes
- 1½ teaspoons Worcestershire
- 2 cups diced cooked turkey
- 2 cups milk
  Salt and pepper
- 1½ cups (6 oz.) shredded sharp Cheddar cheese
  Chopped parsley

Melt butter in a 3-quart pan over medium heat. Add onion and cook, stirring, until soft (about 10 minutes). Stir in carrots, celery, potatoes, tomatoes (break up with a spoon) and their liquid, bouillon cubes, and Worcestershire. Bring to a boil; reduce heat, cover, and boil gently, stirring occasionally, until vegetables are tender to bite (about 15 minutes). Mix in turkey.

Gradually stir in milk; heat, stirring often, just until soup is steaming. Season to taste with salt and pepper; then add 1¼ cups of the cheese, stirring until cheese is melted. Ladle soup into bowls; sprinkle with parsley and remaining ¼ cup cheese. Makes 4 to 6 servings.

Per serving: 440 calories, 31 g protein, 25 g carbohydrates, 24 g total fat, 111 mg cholesterol, 870 mg sodium

Soup Serving Ideas

Though the classic soup server is a lidded tureen, any handsome pot, bowl, or casserole will do if the size is appropriate. For a smooth, pourable soup, a pitcher is a handy dispenser. For individual servings, consider offering hot soups in cups or mugs, or chilled ones in pretty glasses. Deep bowls are best for soups that cool quickly; wide, shallow containers suit thick soups. Be sure to use ovenproof bowls for any soups with a broiled or baked topping.

Chili Beef Soup

Preparation time: About 10 minutes
Cooking time: About 40 minutes

Serve up a fiesta of flavor when you offer this thick and hearty soup. Squares of cornbread and a tossed salad nicely round out the meal.

- 1 pound lean ground beef
- 1 large onion, chopped
- 3 cups regular-strength beef broth
- 1 can (about 15 oz.) tomato purée
- 1 tablespoon chili powder
- ½ teaspoon *each* ground cumin and dry oregano
- ¼ teaspoon garlic powder
- 2 cans (about 15 oz. *each*) kidney beans, drained
- 1 can (about 11 oz.) whole-kernel corn or whole-kernel corn with red and green bell peppers, drained
  Salt and pepper
- ¼ to ½ cup shredded Cheddar cheese

Crumble beef into a 5-quart pan. Add onion and cook over medium-high heat, stirring occasionally, until meat loses its pink color and onion is soft; spoon off and discard fat. Stir in broth, tomato purée, chili powder, cumin, oregano, garlic powder, beans, and corn. Bring to a boil; then reduce heat, cover and simmer for 30 minutes.

Season to taste with salt and pepper. Ladle into bowls; pass cheese at the table to spoon over individual servings. Makes 4 servings.

Per serving: 542 calories, 39 g protein, 49 g carbohydrates, 22 g total fat, 80 mg cholesterol, 1,458 mg sodium

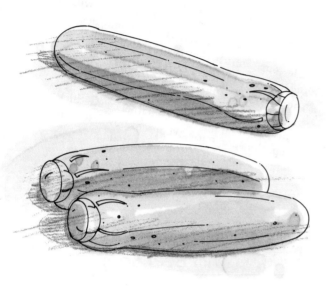

Sausage & Kale Soup

Preparation time: About 15 minutes
Cooking time: About 25 minutes

Accompany this robust soup with buttered pumpernickel bread and apple cider—and you have a speedy, simple supper for a chilly day.

- 1 **pound linguisa sausage, cut diagonally into ¼-inch-thick slices**
- 1 **large onion, chopped**
- 2 **large carrots, chopped**
- 10 **cups regular-strength chicken broth**
- ¾ **pound kale, tough stems removed**
  Salt and pepper

In a 5- to 6-quart pan, cook sausage over high heat until browned (8 to 10 minutes), stirring. Discard all but 2 tablespoons of the drippings.

Add onion and carrots to drippings in pan and cook, stirring, until onion is soft (about 10 minutes). Add broth. Cover and bring to a boil.

Meanwhile, rinse and drain kale. Cut crosswise into ½-inch-wide strips. Add to boiling soup and cook, stirring, until limp and bright green (3 to 5 minutes). Season soup to taste with salt and pepper, then transfer to a large tureen or ladle into bowls. Makes 6 to 8 servings.

Per serving: 233 calories, 14 g protein, 11 g carbohydrates, 15 g total fat, 39 mg cholesterol, 1,649 mg sodium

Italian Sausage Soup

Pictured on facing page

Preparation time: About 20 minutes
Cooking time: About 40 minutes

A medley of vegetables mingles with morsels of sausage in this savory supper soup. Serve it with breadsticks, a green salad, and tumblers of robust red wine.

- 1½ **pounds mild Italian sausages, cut into ½-inch-thick slices**
- 2 **cloves garlic, minced or pressed**
- 2 **large onions, chopped**
- 1 **large can (about 28 oz.) pear-shaped tomatoes**
- 3 **cans (14½ oz. *each*) regular-strength beef broth**
- 1½ **cups dry red wine or water**
- ½ **teaspoon dry basil**
- 3 **tablespoons chopped parsley**
- 1 **medium-size green bell pepper, seeded and chopped**
- 2 **medium-size zucchini, cut into ½-inch-thick slices**
- 5 **ounces medium-size pasta bow ties (about 3 cups)**
  Grated Parmesan cheese

In a 5-quart pan, cook sausage slices over medium-high heat until lightly browned on the outside and no longer pink inside; cut to test. Remove from pan with a slotted spoon, drain on paper towels, and set aside. Spoon off and discard all but 2 tablespoons of the drippings. Add garlic and onions and cook, stirring occasionally, until onions are soft (about 10 minutes).

Stir in tomatoes (break up with a spoon) and their liquid; then add sausage slices, broth, wine, and basil. Bring to a full rolling boil; reduce heat, cover, and simmer for 20 minutes. Stir in parsley, bell pepper, zucchini, and pasta. Cover and simmer, stirring occasionally, until pasta is *al dente* (9 to 11 minutes). Skim off and discard fat. Ladle soup into bowls; pass cheese at the table to spoon over individual servings. Makes 6 servings.

Per serving: 487 calories, 25 g protein, 32 g carbohydrates, 29 g total fat, 92 mg cholesterol, 1,775 mg sodium

To warm your bones on a wintry night, try hearty
Italian Sausage Soup (recipe on facing page). It goes well
with breadsticks and a big green salad with Creamy
Mustard Dressing (recipe on page 44).

Riviera Fish Soup

Preparation time: About 10 minutes
Cooking time: About 30 minutes

Fragrant with garlic and herbs, this tomato-based soup is both hearty and easy.

- 1 pound Greenland turbot or rockfish fillets
- 1 tablespoon olive oil or salad oil
- 1 small onion, sliced
- 1 clove garlic, minced or pressed
- ¼ cup sliced celery
- 2 tablespoons chopped parsley
- ½ teaspoon Italian herb seasoning or ⅛ teaspoon *each* dry basil, dry oregano, dry thyme, and dry marjoram
  Dash of ground red pepper (cayenne)
- 1 can (10¾ oz.) condensed tomato soup
- 2 tablespoons tomato paste
- 1¼ cups hot water
- 1 can (about 6½ oz.) chopped or minced clams
- ¼ pound small cooked shrimp
  Salt and black pepper

Rinse fish, pat dry, and cut into 1½-inch squares. Set aside.

Heat oil in a 3-quart pan over medium heat. Add onion, garlic, and celery; cook, stirring, until onion is soft (about 10 minutes). Stir in parsley, herb seasoning, red pepper, tomato soup, tomato paste, water, and fish; bring to a boil. Then reduce heat, cover, and simmer just until fish is opaque but still moist in center; cut to test (8 to 10 minutes).

Stir in clams and their liquid, then add shrimp. Season to taste with salt and black pepper. Heat through; ladle into wide soup plates. Makes 4 servings.

Per serving: 335 calories, 24 g protein, 13 g carbohydrates, 21 g total fat, 108 mg cholesterol, 758 mg sodium

Mediterranean Fish Stew

Preparation time: About 15 minutes
Cooking time: About 30 minutes

A zesty mayonnaise stirs potent flavor into this fish stew—and can double as a dip for crisp raw vegetables. Be sure there's plenty of warm French bread on the table (and big napkins, too).

  Spicy Hot Mayonnaise (recipe follows)
- 2 tablespoons salad oil
- 1 large onion, chopped
- 1 large green bell pepper, seeded and chopped
- 2 cloves garlic, minced or pressed
- 1 can (about 14½ oz.) pear-shaped tomatoes
- 1½ cups water
- ½ cup dry white wine or water
- 1 bottle (8 oz.) clam juice
- 3 chicken bouillon cubes
- ¼ teaspoon *each* dry basil, dry oregano, and dry thyme
- 2 pounds lean white-fleshed fish fillets, such as rockfish or lingcod

Prepare Spicy Hot Mayonnaise and set aside.

Heat oil in a 5- to 6-quart pan over medium heat. Add onion, bell pepper, and garlic; cook, stirring occasionally, until vegetables are soft (about 10 minutes). Add tomatoes (break up with a spoon) and their liquid, water, wine, clam juice, bouillon cubes, basil, oregano, and thyme. Stir until bouillon cubes are dissolved. Reduce heat, cover, and simmer for 15 minutes.

Rinse fish and pat dry; cut into 1-inch squares. Bring soup to a boil. Add fish, reduce heat, cover, and simmer just until fish is opaque but still moist in center; cut to test (6 to 8 minutes). Ladle into wide, shallow bowls. Pass mayonnaise to stir into individual servings. Makes 4 to 6 servings.

Spicy Hot Mayonnaise. Mix ⅔ cup **mayonnaise;** 2 cloves **garlic,** minced or pressed; ¾ to 1 teaspoon **ground red pepper** (cayenne); 1 tablespoon **white wine vinegar;** and ¼ teaspoon **salt.** If made ahead, cover and refrigerate for up to 1 week. Makes about ⅔ cup.

Per serving of stew: 262 calories, 36 g protein, 9 g carbohydrates, 9 g total fat, 64 mg cholesterol, 1,026 mg sodium

Per tablespoon of mayonnaise: 89 calories, 0.2 g protein, 0.6 g carbohydrates, 10 g total fat, 7 mg cholesterol, 115 mg sodium

Fish Pot-au-Feu

Preparation time: About 15 minutes
Cooking time: About 30 minutes

A classic pot-au-feu simmers slowly all afternoon —but this light, quick contemporary version delivers equally rich flavor after just half an hour. A salad made with radicchio or red cabbage offers a colorful, crunchy contrast to the soup.

- **5 cups regular-strength chicken broth**
- **1 cup dry white wine; or 1 cup regular-strength chicken broth and 3 tablespoons white wine vinegar**
- **½ teaspoon dry tarragon**
- **4 small red thin-skinned potatoes (*each* 1½ to 2 inches in diameter), scrubbed**
- **4 medium-size carrots, cut in half**
- **4 medium-size leeks (about 2 lbs. *total*), roots and most of dark green tops trimmed**
- **1½ pounds lean white-fleshed fish fillets, such as lingcod or sea bass**

In a 5- to 6-quart pan, bring broth, wine, and tarragon to a boil over high heat. Add unpeeled potatoes and carrots and return to a boil; then reduce heat, cover, and boil gently for 10 minutes.

Meanwhile, split leeks lengthwise and rinse well. Add to pan, cover, and boil gently until leeks are tender when pierced (about 10 more minutes). Lift leeks from broth with a slotted spoon, cover, and keep warm.

Rinse fish and pat dry; cut into 4 equal portions. Add to soup, cover, and simmer just until vegetables are tender when pierced and fish is opaque but still moist in thickest part; cut to test (7 to 10 minutes).

With a slotted spatula, carefully lift fish from pan and arrange in 4 wide, shallow bowls. Evenly distribute vegetables alongside fish and ladle broth over all. Makes 4 servings.

Per serving: 349 calories, 37 g protein, 32 g carbohydrates, 4 g total fat, 89 mg cholesterol, 1,385 mg sodium

Yaquina Bay Salmon Chowder

Preparation time: About 10 minutes
Cooking time: About 35 minutes

Chowders are usually hearty, casual dishes, but this one—from the Oregon seacoast—is exceptionally elegant. Succulent salmon chunks and minced vegetables mingle in a rich, delicate broth; a sprinkling of Cheddar cheese tops each serving.

- **2 pounds salmon steaks or fillets (*each* about 1 inch thick)**
- **1 can (10¾ oz.) condensed chicken broth**
- **1 bottle (8 oz.) clam juice**
- **1 cup dry white wine**
- **6 tablespoons butter or margarine**
- **1 medium-size onion, chopped**
- **2 stalks celery, chopped**
- **¼ teaspoon *each* dry basil, dry thyme, and dry marjoram**
- **1½ cups milk**
- **1 large can (about 28 oz.) tomatoes, drained and chopped**
- **1 tablespoon brandy**
  Salt and pepper
  About 1½ cups (6 oz.) shredded Cheddar cheese

Rinse salmon and pat dry. In a wide frying pan, combine broth, clam juice, and wine. Bring to a boil over high heat; reduce heat and place salmon in liquid. Cover and simmer until salmon is opaque but still moist in thickest part; cut to test (10 to 12 minutes). Lift out salmon and let cool slightly; then remove and discard bones, skin, and any gray-brown edges. Flake salmon and set aside; reserve poaching liquid.

Melt butter in a 4- to 5-quart pan over medium heat. Add onion and celery and cook, stirring, until onion is soft (about 10 minutes). Stir in basil, thyme, marjoram, milk, tomatoes, and poaching liquid. Cover and cook gently for 10 minutes. Add salmon, stir in brandy, and season to taste with salt and pepper. Ladle into bowls; offer cheese to add to individual portions. Makes 4 to 6 servings.

Per serving: 631 calories, 52 g protein, 13 g carbohydrates, 40 g total fat, 189 mg cholesterol, 1,228 mg sodium

Elegant dining is only minutes away when you feature
Radicchio Cups with Shrimp & Dill (recipe on page 42)
on the menu. For a light lunch, all you need add are rolls
from the bakery and minted iced tea.

Salads

Do you need a light, colorful first course—or a sturdy main dish? Are you looking for lowfat supper selections? Is it too hot to cook? Are you short on time? In every one of these situations, a salad can give you just what you're looking for. As you leaf through this chapter, you'll find chilled salads and warm ones; light combinations of fruit and greens as well as robust meat-and-vegetable compositions; and new dishes alongside classics such as Salade Niçoise. And of course, every one of these choices is refreshingly quick to prepare!

Preparing Salad Greens

Putting salads together is simpler if you rinse and crisp the greens in advance (up to a few days before use). Each time you make a tossed salad, try to prepare several meals' worth of greens. First discard the coarse outer leaves and stems; then rinse the remaining leaves and dry them in a lettuce spinner (or drain on paper towels or a clean dishtowel). Wrap the leaves loosely in dry paper towels; store in a plastic bag in the crisper of your refrigerator. When you're ready for salad, your greens will be clean, chilled, and crisp. You can even store salad ready-made: just fill plastic bags with torn greens and crisp vegetables such as sliced radishes, celery, and bell pepper.

great! — can we use grapefruit or any kind of citrus fruit

Greens Plus

Preparation time: About 10 minutes
Cooking time: 3 to 5 minutes

Start with a simple green salad—then dress it up with a few added ingredients. This combination of butter lettuce, nuts, and oranges enhances light pasta entrées, poultry, and fish.

- 2 heads butter lettuce, separated into leaves, rinsed, and crisped
- 3 tablespoons pine nuts or slivered blanched almonds
- 2 large oranges
- ¼ cup unseasoned rice vinegar
- 1 tablespoon salad oil
- ½ teaspoon dry basil

Tear lettuce into bite-size pieces and place in a large salad bowl.

Toast nuts in a small frying pan over low heat until golden (3 to 5 minutes), shaking pan often. Let cool.

With a sharp knife, cut peel and all white membrane from oranges. Separate into segments. Add oranges and nuts to lettuce; toss to mix.

In a small bowl, whisk together vinegar, oil, and basil; pour over salad and toss well. Makes 4 servings.

Per serving: 124 calories, 3 g protein, 15 g carbohydrates, 7 g total fat, 0 mg cholesterol, 4 mg sodium

Broiled Avocado Salad

Preparation time: About 15 minutes
Broiling time: 5 to 6 minutes

Why not a serve a hot salad tonight? These shrimp-stuffed avocado halves, crowned with bubbly melted cheese, offer a delicious change of pace.

   Caesar Dressing (recipe follows)
- 3 medium-size ripe avocados
- 4 teaspoons grated Parmesan cheese
- ½ pound small cooked shrimp
- ¼ cup shredded jack cheese
   Salt

Prepare Caesar Dressing; set aside.

Halve and pit avocados. With a small, sharp knife, score avocado flesh lengthwise and crosswise just to shells (not through them), making cuts about ½ inch apart.

Mix Parmesan cheese, shrimp, and dressing; mound mixture into cavities of avocados. Arrange avocados in an 8- or 9-inch-square baking pan. Sprinkle filling with jack cheese.

Broil about 4 inches below heat until jack cheese is melted and avocados are partially warmed (5 to 6 minutes). Season to taste with salt and serve hot. Makes 6 servings.

Caesar Dressing. Mix ¼ cup **salad oil**, 3 tablespoons **red wine vinegar,** 1 tablespoon **lemon juice,** 2 teaspoons **Dijon mustard,** 1 teaspoon **anchovy paste** or drained, minced canned anchovies, and ¼ teaspoon **pepper.**

Per serving: 307 calories, 12 g protein, 8 g carbohydrates, 27 g total fat, 79 mg cholesterol, 216 mg sodium

Preparation time: About 25 minutes
Cooking time: 3 to 4 minutes

Crisp green beans, red onion, and jicama lend an authoritative crunch to this all-vegetable salad. It's great for picnicking on the patio or in the park; try it with fried chicken or sandwiches.

- 5 **tablespoons white wine vinegar**
- ⅔ **cup thinly slivered red onion**
- ¾ **pound green beans, ends removed**
- 1 **pound jicama, peeled**
- ⅓ **cup olive oil or salad oil**
- 2 **teaspoons Dijon mustard**
  Salt and pepper

In a small bowl, combine 1½ cups cold water with 2 tablespoons of the vinegar. Add onion and let stand for 20 minutes.

Meanwhile, pull beans through a French bean cutter or slice into thin strips with a knife. Place beans on a rack above ½ inch boiling water in a 5- to 6-quart pan; cover and steam until tender-crisp to bite (3 to 4 minutes). Plunge beans into ice water and stir until cool; then drain. Cut jicama into matchstick-size pieces.

In a large salad bowl, whisk together oil, mustard, and remaining 3 tablespoons vinegar. Drain onion and add to dressing along with beans and jicama; mix to coat well. Season to taste with salt and pepper. Makes 6 to 8 servings.

Per serving: 136 calories, 2 g protein, 10 g carbohydrates, 10 g total fat, 0 mg cholesterol, 49 mg sodium

atermelon–Mint Salad

Preparation time: About 15 minutes

Crisp, sweet watermelon takes on a new character when mixed with mild onion, cool mint, and a mellow chili dressing.

- 1 **watermelon (about 6 lbs.)**
- ¾ **cup slivered mild white onion**
- ½ **cup minced fresh mint**
- 3 **tablespoons cider vinegar**
- 1 **teaspoon chili powder**
- 6 **tablespoons salad oil**
  Salt

Slice watermelon into 1-inch-thick rounds; remove and discard rind. Cut flesh into 1-inch cubes; remove visible seeds. Place cubes in a large serving bowl, add onion and mint, and mix gently.

In a small bowl, whisk together vinegar, chili powder, and oil. Pour dressing over salad and mix to coat well. Season to taste with salt. Makes 8 servings.

Per serving: 155 calories, 1 g protein, 14 g carbohydrates, 11 g total fat, 0 mg cholesterol, 7 mg sodium

Cherry Tomatoes & Onions Vinaigrette

Preparation time: About 15 minutes

A good tomato and onion salad is always a welcome change from the standard tossed greens. Pungent with garlic and oregano, this bright combination of mild onion rings and cherry tomatoes perks up any casual menu.

- ¼ **cup olive oil or salad oil**
- ⅓ **cup red wine vinegar**
- 1 **small clove garlic, minced or pressed**
- 1 **tablespoon finely chopped fresh oregano or 1 teaspoon dry oregano**
- 7 **to 8 cups cherry tomatoes, halved**
- 1 **medium-size mild white onion, thinly sliced**
  Salt and pepper

In a large salad bowl, whisk together oil, vinegar, garlic, and oregano. Then add tomatoes and onion; mix gently to coat well. Season to taste with salt and pepper. Makes 6 to 8 servings.

Per serving: 95 calories, 1 g protein, 6 g carbohydrates, 8 g total fat, 0 mg cholesterol, 9 mg sodium

Japanese Crab & Radish Salad

Pictured on facing page

Preparation time: About 15 minutes

A food processor will help you prepare this salad especially quickly, but a sharp knife or mandolin slicer also works well. Black sesame seeds (sold in Asian markets) make a pretty garnish for the delicate-hued crab, cucumber, and radishes. Offer Cold Avocado Soup (page 16) as a prelude to this light main dish.

- 1 **small European-style cucumber (about ½ lb.)**
- 1 **green onion (including top), white and green part separated**
- 10 **medium-size radishes**
- ½ **to 1 pound cooked crabmeat**
- ⅓ **to ½ cup seasoned rice vinegar**
- 1 **teaspoon toasted black sesame seeds (optional)**

Cut cucumber in half crosswise; then cut each half lengthwise into quarters. Set aside.

To prepare in a food processor, pack onion (white part only) and as many radishes as will fit into feed tube and slice; repeat to slice remaining radishes. Pack cucumber into feed tube and slice. Remove slicer and spread crabmeat over cucumber. Invert salad onto a large platter, spreading out slightly.

To prepare by hand, slice onion (white part only), radishes, and cucumber as thinly as possible. Spread crabmeat on platter and arrange vegetables in layers on top.

Pour vinegar over salad. Slice green portion of onion into long, thin strands and scatter over salad; sprinkle with sesame seeds, if desired. Makes 4 servings.

Per serving: 116 calories, 18 g protein, 7 g carbohydrates, 2 g total fat, 85 mg cholesterol, 242 mg sodium

Colorful, crunchy, and low in calories, Japanese Crab &
Radish Salad (recipe on facing page) features thinly
sliced radishes and cucumbers topped with crabmeat.
Using a food processor speeds up preparation time.

Carrot Salad with Peppercorns

Preparation time: About 15 minutes
Cooking time: About 2 minutes

Sometime soon, choose this cool carrot salad in place of a hot vegetable side dish. Zesty with tarragon and green peppercorns, it's especially tasty with sautéed fish and parsley-strewn rice.

- 1¼ pounds carrots
- 2 tablespoons chopped fresh tarragon or 2 teaspoons dry tarragon
- 2 tablespoons canned green peppercorns, drained
- ¼ cup olive oil or salad oil
- 2 tablespoons lemon juice
  Salt and pepper

Cut carrots into matchstick-size pieces.

In a 3- to 4-quart pan, bring 6 cups water to a boil over high heat. Add carrots and cook until tender-crisp to bite (about 2 minutes). Drain, plunge into ice water, and stir until cool. Then drain again.

Place carrots, tarragon, peppercorns, oil, and lemon juice in a serving bowl and mix gently. Season to taste with salt and pepper. Makes 4 servings.

Per serving: 186 calories, 2 g protein, 16 g carbohydrates, 14 g total fat, 0 mg cholesterol, 48 mg sodium

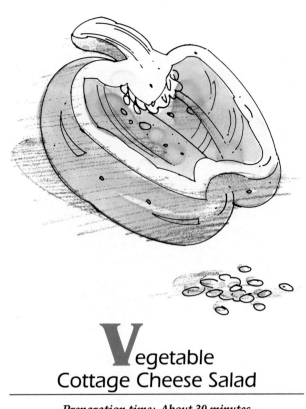

Vegetable Cottage Cheese Salad

Preparation time: About 30 minutes

To transform plain cottage cheese into an elegant warm-weather salad, lace it with colorful bits of raw vegetables and mound it in bell pepper halves. The cheese mixture is also a superb appetizer spread for wheat crackers or celery sticks.

- 2 cups small-curd cottage cheese
- 2 tablespoons chopped parsley
- ½ cup thinly sliced green onions (including tops)
- ¼ cup chopped green or red bell pepper
- ⅓ cup chopped celery
- ½ cup *each* chopped radishes and shredded carrot
- ½ teaspoon *each* garlic salt, dry dill weed, and dry mustard
- 2 red or green bell peppers
  Spinach or lettuce leaves, rinsed and crisped
  Paprika
- 2 hard-cooked eggs, cut into wedges

Combine cottage cheese, parsley, onions, chopped bell pepper, celery, radishes, carrot, garlic salt, dill weed, and mustard; mix lightly. Cover and refrigerate.

Cut bell peppers into halves; discard seeds. Line 4 salad plates with spinach. Mound cottage cheese mixture in peppers. Place a stuffed pepper half on each plate and sprinkle lightly with paprika. Garnish with eggs. Makes 4 servings.

Per serving: 175 calories, 17 g protein, 9 g carbohydrates, 8 g total fat, 122 mg cholesterol, 713 mg sodium

Shanghai Tofu & Peanut Salad

Preparation time: 20 to 25 minutes
Cooking time: About 20 minutes

Crunchy peanuts contrast with mild, tender tofu in this protein-rich salad. To complete a vegetarian menu, just add crisp crackers, fresh fruit, and jasmine tea.

1 package (about 1 lb.) medium-firm tofu
Salad oil
Sesame Dressing (recipe follows)
¾ pound bean sprouts
1 medium-size cucumber
⅔ cup shredded carrot
3 green onions (including tops), thinly sliced
¾ cup coarsely chopped salted peanuts

Cut tofu crosswise into 1-inch-thick slices. Place in a colander; rinse with cold water and let drain for 10 minutes, then place between paper towels and gently press out excess water. Place tofu on a wire rack in a shallow baking pan and brush all surfaces with oil.

Bake in a 350° oven for 20 minutes. Let cool, then cut into small, thin strips (about ¼ by ¼ by 1 inch). Prepare Sesame Dressing; add tofu, stirring gently to coat. Set aside.

Drop bean sprouts into a 5- to 6-quart pan half filled with boiling water. Cook until water returns to a full rolling boil; then drain, rinse with cold water, and drain again.

Peel cucumber, if desired, and cut in half lengthwise. Scoop out and discard seeds; cut cucumber into thin slices. Just before serving, add bean sprouts, cucumber, carrot, onions, and peanuts to tofu mixture; toss gently. Makes 4 to 6 servings.

Sesame Dressing. In a large salad bowl, stir together ¼ cup **white wine vinegar**, 2 tablespoons *each* **sugar** and **salad oil**, 1 tablespoon **soy sauce**, 1½ teaspoons **Oriental sesame oil**, and ¼ teaspoon **ground red pepper** (cayenne).

Per serving: 357 calories, 15 g protein, 19 g carbohydrates, 27 g total fat, 0 mg cholesterol, 413 mg sodium

Plan-ahead Salads

Advance planning can provide you with leftover meat and poultry for main-dish salads. If you're roasting one chicken for Sunday dinner, roast a second one alongside—and use the extra meat in a salad later in the week. Keep in mind that a 3-pound frying chicken will yield about 3 cups meat; a 1-pound whole chicken breast will yield about 1½ cups meat. A half pound of cooked boneless ham, beef, or turkey will yield about 2 cups meat. Keep hard-cooked eggs in the refrigerator (marked to distinguish them from raw eggs). A common ingredient in main-dish salads, they also add extra flavor and a protein boost to side-dish salads. Slice or chop the eggs coarsely and toss them with the salad; or cut into wedges and use as a garnish.

Catalan Avocado & Tomato Platter

Preparation time: About 15 minutes

Northeastern Spain is famous for its robust cuisine—and this colorful salad is a good example of the region's flavorful dishes. Feature it at a buffet, along with cold sliced meats, crusty bread, and crisp white wine.

2 medium-size firm-ripe tomatoes
2 medium-size firm-ripe avocados
12 large fresh basil leaves
1 can (2 oz.) anchovy fillets, drained
3 tablespoons balsamic or red wine vinegar
1 tablespoon olive oil
½ teaspoon pepper

Core tomatoes, then cut each into 6 equal-size wedges. Pit, peel, and quarter each avocado; set 2 quarters aside. On a platter, arrange tomatoes, basil leaves, and remaining avocado quarters.

In a blender or food processor, whirl reserved avocado quarters, anchovies, vinegar, oil, and pepper until smooth. Transfer dressing to a small bowl and offer with vegetables. Makes 4 to 6 servings.

Per serving: 188 calories, 5 g protein, 10 g carbohydrates, 16 g total fat, 5 mg cholesterol, 343 mg sodium

*A colorful display of juicy summer fruits is the secret
to Fruit Salad Platter (recipe on facing page), a light and
luscious entrée for brunch, lunch, or supper. Orange
Yogurt Dressing complements both fruit and ham.*

Stir-fried Napa Cabbage Salad

Preparation time: About 10 minutes
Cooking time: 2 to 3 minutes

Taking its cue from pickled vegetable dishes popular in Asia, this salad blends wilted napa cabbage with a tart-sweet dressing. Enjoy it with brown rice and barbecued spareribs or chicken for a satisfying meal.

- 2 tablespoons unseasoned rice vinegar or white wine vinegar
- 2 tablespoons sugar
- 1 tablespoon soy sauce
- ¼ teaspoon ground red pepper (cayenne)
- 1 medium-size head napa cabbage (about 1¼ lbs.)
- 3 tablespoons salad oil

Stir together vinegar, sugar, soy sauce, and red pepper; set aside.

Discard any wilted outer leaves from cabbage. Then rinse cabbage; cut off and discard base. Slice cabbage in half lengthwise and chop coarsely.

Heat oil in a wide frying pan or wok over high heat; add cabbage and cook, stirring, until it begins to wilt (2 to 3 minutes). Add vinegar mixture, stir well, and remove from heat. Transfer salad to a serving dish. Makes 4 to 6 servings.

Per serving: 113 calories, 2 g protein, 9 g carbohydrates, 8 g total fat, 0 mg cholesterol, 216 mg sodium

Fruit Salad Platter

Pictured on facing page

Preparation time: 20 to 25 minutes

Guests will enjoy this pretty finger-food salad. Arrange thinly sliced ham and juicy chunks of fresh fruit on each plate, then offer individual cups of honey-sweetened yogurt dressing for dipping.

- Orange Yogurt Dressing (recipe follows)
- 1 basket strawberries, unhulled
- 1 small cantaloupe, seeds and rind removed, cut into 8 wedges
- 1 small pineapple (about 3 lbs.), peeled, cored, and cut into spears
- 2 medium-size peaches or nectarines
- Lemon juice
- 1 pound thinly sliced cooked ham or turkey (or a combination)
- Orange zest (optional)

Prepare Orange Yogurt Dressing; set aside. Just before serving, evenly divide strawberries, cantaloupe, and pineapple among 4 dinner plates. Peel peaches; pit and slice, then coat with lemon juice and divide among plates. Roll up ham slices and arrange next to fruit on each plate.

Pour dressing evenly into 4 cups or small bowls; place one on each plate. Garnish with orange zest, if desired. At the table, dip fruit and ham into dressing as you eat. Makes 4 servings.

Orange Yogurt Dressing. Mix ¾ cup **plain yogurt,** ½ cup **sour cream,** 3 tablespoons **honey,** ½ teaspoon **grated orange peel,** and ¼ teaspoon **ground nutmeg.**

Per serving: 476 calories, 31 g protein, 51 g carbohydrates, 18 g total fat, 82 mg cholesterol, 1,759 mg sodium

Egg Salad Boats

Preparation time: About 15 minutes

Tomatoes filled with dill-seasoned egg salad make a stylish luncheon entrée. Alongside, you might serve an assortment of crisp crackers or crunchy breadsticks and a pitcher of iced tea or chilled fruit juice.

- 12 hard-cooked eggs, coarsely chopped
- ½ cup mayonnaise
- 1 cup thinly sliced celery
- 3 green onions (including tops), thinly sliced
- ¾ teaspoon dry dill weed
- ½ teaspoon lemon juice
- 6 large tomatoes
  Lettuce leaves, rinsed and crisped

In a large bowl, gently stir together eggs, mayonnaise, celery, onions, dill weed, and lemon juice until well combined; set aside. Core tomatoes; then cut each tomato almost to the base into 8 wedges (don't slice all the way through).

Place each tomato on a lettuce-lined plate, carefully spread wedges open, and spoon egg salad into center. Makes 6 servings.

Per serving: 320 calories, 14 g protein, 9 g carbohydrates, 26 g total fat, 436 mg cholesterol, 258 mg sodium

Cheddar Cheese Potato Salad

Preparation time: 10 to 15 minutes
Cooking time: About 18 minutes

At your next picnic or barbecue, try a potato salad with something extra—hearty Cheddar cheese chunks and crumbled crisp bacon. (You can make and chill the salad a day in advance, if you like.)

- ½ cup chopped bacon
- 1 medium-size onion, chopped
- 1 pound thin-skinned potatoes, boiled, peeled (if desired), and cut into ½-inch cubes
- 4 hard-cooked eggs, chopped
- ½ cup cubed Cheddar cheese (about ¼-inch cubes)
- ½ cup mayonnaise
- 2 teaspoons prepared mustard
  Salt and pepper

Cook bacon in a wide frying pan over medium heat until crisp (about 8 minutes), stirring occasionally. Remove with a slotted spoon and transfer to a large bowl; reserve drippings in pan.

Add onion to pan and cook, stirring often, until soft (about 10 minutes). Remove with a slotted spoon and add to bacon; then add potatoes, eggs, cheese, mayonnaise, and mustard. Mix lightly. Season to taste with salt and pepper. If made ahead, cover and refrigerate until next day. Makes 6 servings.

Per serving: 384 calories, 10 g protein, 17 g carbohydrates, 31 g total fat, 173 mg cholesterol, 343 mg sodium

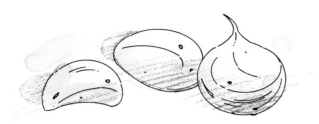

Italian-style Vermicelli Salad

Preparation time: 20 to 25 minutes
Cooking time: 10 to 12 minutes

Salami strips, artichoke hearts, and garlic give this room-temperature salad its zesty flavor. For a light warm-weather meal, serve with breadsticks, steamed green beans, and red wine.

 8 ounces dry vermicelli or spaghetti
 1 jar (8 oz.) marinated artichoke hearts
 ⅓ cup olive oil or salad oil
 2 tablespoons white wine vinegar
 1 teaspoon *each* dry oregano and dry basil
 ¼ teaspoon *each* dry rosemary and pepper
 2 cloves garlic, minced or pressed
1½ teaspoons dry mustard
 1 medium-size carrot, finely diced
 1 small zucchini, finely diced
 1 package (3 oz.) sliced salami, cut into julienne strips
 2 cups (8 oz.) shredded mozzarella cheese
 ⅓ cup grated Parmesan cheese
    Lettuce leaves, rinsed and crisped

In a 5- to 6-quart pan, cook vermicelli in about 3 quarts boiling water just until *al dente* (10 to 12 minutes); or cook according to package directions. Drain thoroughly, rinse with cold water, and drain again.

Drain marinade from artichokes into a large bowl; chop artichokes and set aside. To marinade, add oil, vinegar, oregano, basil, rosemary, pepper, garlic, mustard, and vermicelli. Stir to coat pasta thoroughly. Add carrot, zucchini, salami, mozzarella cheese, Parmesan cheese, and artichokes. Stir well. Line a platter with lettuce leaves and spoon pasta mixture into center. Serve at room temperature. Makes 6 servings.

Per serving: 472 calories, 18 g protein, 34 g carbohydrates, 29 g total fat, 44 mg cholesterol, 640 mg sodium

Shrimp-Rice Salad

Preparation time: About 15 minutes
Baking time: About 6 minutes

A smooth, tart lemon dressing and a topping of toasted almonds make this salad special. There isn't a more elegant use for leftover cooked rice!

 ½ cup sliced almonds
    Creamy Lemon Dressing (recipe follows)
 3 cups cold cooked long-grain white rice
 1 pound small cooked shrimp
 1 cup *each* thinly diced celery and chopped green bell pepper
 1 can (about 8 oz.) sliced water chestnuts, drained
    Salt and pepper
    Lettuce leaves, rinsed and crisped

Spread almonds in a shallow baking pan and toast in a 350° oven, stirring occasionally, until golden (about 6 minutes). Meanwhile, prepare Creamy Lemon Dressing.

In a large bowl, gently stir together rice, shrimp, celery, bell pepper, and water chestnuts; add dressing and stir gently until all ingredients are well coated. Season to taste with salt and pepper. Line a platter or 4 individual plates with lettuce leaves; spoon salad atop lettuce and top with almonds. Makes 4 servings.

Creamy Lemon Dressing. Mix ¾ cup **mayonnaise**, 1 teaspoon **grated lemon peel**, 1 tablespoon **lemon juice**, 2 teaspoons **prepared horseradish**, and ¼ teaspoon **garlic powder**. Then stir in ½ cup thinly sliced **green onions** (including tops), ¼ cup chopped **parsley**, and 1 jar (2 oz.) **sliced pimentos** (drained).

Per serving: 696 calories, 31 g protein, 52 g carbohydrates, 41 g total fat, 246 mg cholesterol, 533 mg sodium

Cashew, Shrimp & Pea Salad

Pictured on facing page

Preparation time: About 20 minutes

Summer is the time for no-cook entrées. Here's one good choice: a refreshing salad of tiny pink shrimp, green peas, and crisp cashews.

Dill Dressing (recipe follows)
1½ cups salted or unsalted roasted cashews
 1 package (about 1 lb.) frozen tiny peas, thawed and drained
 1 cup thinly sliced green onions (including tops)
 2 large stalks celery, cut diagonally into thin slices
 ¾ pound small cooked shrimp
 Salt and pepper
 6 to 8 large butter lettuce leaves, rinsed and crisped
 Dill sprigs (optional)

Prepare Dill Dressing; set aside.

Set aside 2 tablespoons of the cashews. In a large bowl, combine remaining cashews, peas, onions, celery, and shrimp. Add dressing and mix lightly. Season to taste with salt and pepper.

Line a platter or serving bowl with lettuce. Spoon salad into center; garnish with reserved 2 tablespoons cashews and, if desired, dill sprigs. Makes 4 servings.

Dill Dressing. Mix ¼ cup *each* **mayonnaise** and **sour cream,** 1 tablespoon **lemon juice,** and 1 tablespoon minced **fresh dill** or 1 teaspoon dry dill weed.

Per serving: 602 calories, 34 g protein, 34 g carbohydrates, 39 g total fat, 180 mg cholesterol, 798 mg sodium

Radicchio Cups with Shrimp & Dill

Pictured on page 30

Preparation time: About 15 minutes
Cooking time: About 5 minutes

Just a few simple ingredients, artfully arranged, make an attractive light lunch or supper. Round out the menu with rolls and minted iced tea.

 1 head radicchio (4 to 5 inches in diameter)
 1 to 2 tablespoons slivered Black Forest ham, Westphalian ham, or prosciutto
 ⅓ cup olive oil or salad oil
 1 pound small cooked shrimp
 2 tablespoons red wine vinegar
1½ tablespoons chopped fresh dill or 2½ teaspoons dry dill weed
 Salt and pepper
 Dill sprigs (optional)

Remove 4 large outer leaves from radicchio (reserve remainder of head for other uses). Rinse leaves, wrap in paper towels, and refrigerate.

In a small frying pan, stir ham and oil over low heat until oil picks up ham flavor (about 5 minutes). Transfer to a medium-size bowl; stir until cool. Stir in shrimp, vinegar, and chopped dill. Season to taste with salt and pepper.

Place a radicchio leaf on each of 4 dinner plates. Spoon shrimp mixture equally into center of each leaf. Garnish with dill sprigs, if desired. Makes 4 servings.

Per serving: 284 calories, 25 g protein, 2 g carbohydrates, 19 g total fat, 223 mg cholesterol, 309 mg sodium

*A cool candidate for warm summer weather, our
Cashew, Shrimp & Pea Salad (recipe on facing page)
demands no cooking and very little preparation time. Its
creamy dill dressing adds a Scandinavian touch.*

Salad Dressings

Enhance main-course and side-dish salads alike with your own homemade dressings—fresh tasting, free of artificial ingredients, and simple enough to prepare in minutes. Leftover dressing can be refrigerated and used the next time you serve salad.

The dressings below are good on a variety of salads. Keep in mind, though, that thick dressings such as Creamy Mustard Dressing (or Chili-spiced Thousand Island Dressing, page 53) are more appropriate for crunchier greens, while the lighter choices go well with delicate, leafy greens. And remember that dressings made with oil and refrigerated should be brought to room temperature, then stirred to blend, before being added to a salad.

Basic Vinaigrette

Preparation time: 2 to 3 minutes

In a jar, combine ½ cup **white wine vinegar**, ¾ teaspoon **salt**, a dash of **pepper**, and 1½ cups **salad oil** or olive oil (or a combination). Close jar tightly and shake to mix thoroughly. Makes about 2 cups.

Per tablespoon: 91 calories, 0 g protein, 0.1 g carbohydrates, 10 g total fat, 0 mg cholesterol, 51 mg sodium

Creamy Mustard Dressing

Preparation time: 2 to 3 minutes

In a bowl, stir together 1¾ cups **commercial mayonnaise**, 2 tablespoons **red wine vinegar**, 2 tablespoons **Dijon mustard**, and 1 teaspoon **dry tarragon**. Stir until dressing is thoroughly mixed. Makes about 2 cups.

Per tablespoon: 88 calories, 0.1 g protein, 0.5 g carbohydrates, 10 g total fat, 7 mg cholesterol, 97 mg sodium

Honey-Yogurt Dressing

Preparation time: 4 to 7 minutes

Stir together 1½ tablespoons grated **orange peel**, 1 teaspoon minced **fresh ginger**, 1 cup **plain lowfat yogurt**, 2 tablespoons **honey**, and 1 tablespoon **lemon juice** until smooth. Stir in 2 teaspoons **poppy seeds,** if desired. If made ahead, cover and refrigerate for up to 1 week. Makes about 1¼ cups.

Per tablespoon: 14 calories, 0.6 g protein, 3 g carbohydrates, 0.2 g total fat, 0.7 mg cholesterol, 8 mg sodium

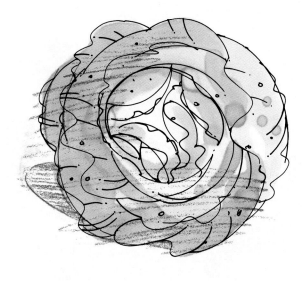

Tuna Chutney Salad

Preparation time: 15 to 20 minutes

Sweet pineapple, your choice of salad greens, and chunks of tuna are tossed together in a creamy curry dressing; a sprinkling of crunchy Spanish peanuts goes on top. (Another time, you might try cooked chicken or turkey in place of the tuna.)

- ½ cup **mayonnaise**
- ⅓ cup **finely chopped Major Grey's chutney**
- 1 teaspoon **curry powder**
- 1 tablespoon **white wine vinegar**
- ¼ teaspoon **ground ginger**
- 8 cups bite-size pieces **spinach, red leaf lettuce, butter lettuce, or romaine lettuce** (or a combination), rinsed and crisped
- 2 cups thinly sliced **celery**
- ½ cup thinly sliced **green onions** (including tops)
- 1 can (about 8 oz.) **pineapple chunks** in their own juice, drained
- 2 cans (6⅛ oz. *each*) **chunk light tuna** in water, drained and flaked; or 2 to 3 cups diced **cooked chicken or turkey**
- ⅔ cup **Spanish peanuts**

In a small bowl, stir together mayonnaise, chutney, curry powder, vinegar, and ginger; set aside. In a large salad bowl, combine greens, celery, onions, pineapple, and tuna. Just before serving, pour dressing over salad and toss to coat greens thoroughly; sprinkle peanuts over top. Makes 4 to 6 servings.

Per serving: 456 calories, 28 g protein, 27 g carbohydrates, 28 g total fat, 41 mg cholesterol, 546 mg sodium

alade Niçoise for Two

Preparation time: 10 to 15 minutes
Cooking time: About 20 minutes

Salade Niçoise is a French classic, always popular for summertime meals; our recipe is scaled down to make just two servings. You line individual plates with crisp spinach leaves, then top each with a single-serving-size can of light tuna, quartered hard-cooked eggs, and cool cooked potatoes and green beans.

- 4 **small thin-skinned potatoes (***each* 1½ to 2 inches in diameter**), scrubbed**
- ¼ **pound green beans, ends removed**
  Spinach leaves, rinsed and crisped
- 2 **cans (3½ oz.** *each***) solid light tuna in water, drained**
- 4 **anchovy fillets**
  Pitted ripe olives or Niçoise olives
- 2 **hard-cooked eggs, cut into quarters**
- ¼ **cup olive oil or salad oil**
- 2 **tablespoons red wine vinegar**
- 1 **clove garlic, minced or pressed**
- ½ **teaspoon Dijon mustard**
  Dash *each* **of salt and pepper**

Place unpeeled potatoes in a 2-quart pan; add water to cover. Bring to a boil over high heat; cover and boil for 15 minutes. Add beans and continue to boil until potatoes are tender throughout when pierced and beans are just tender-crisp to bite (about 6 more minutes). Drain vegetables and rinse under cold running water until cool enough to handle; drain again. Peel potatoes, if desired; then cut into ¼-inch-thick slices.

Line 2 salad plates with spinach leaves. Invert one can of tuna onto each plate; arrange anchovies in a crisscross pattern over tuna. Arrange potatoes, beans, olives, and eggs around tuna.

In a small bowl, stir together oil, vinegar, garlic, mustard, salt, and pepper. Drizzle dressing evenly over salads. Makes 2 servings.

Per serving: 562 calories, 38 g protein, 26 g carbohydrates, 34 g total fat, 254 mg cholesterol, 785 mg sodium

Fresh-looking Fruit Salads

Soon after slicing, fruits such as apples, apricots, avocados, bananas, peaches, and pears begin to darken as the cut surfaces are exposed to air. To prevent such darkening, brush the sliced fruit with lemon or lime juice or an ascorbic acid (vitamin C) powder used to preserve the color of frozen fruits. Treated fruits will be protected for up to 4 hours in the refrigerator, up to 2 hours at room temperature.

San Diego Salad

Preparation time: About 25 minutes

This colorful composition displays ingredients popular in Mexican cuisine: chicken, cheese, oranges, avocado, and—in the creamy dressing—cumin and salsa.

- **Creamy Cumin Dressing (recipe follows)**
- 1 **head romaine lettuce, separated into leaves, rinsed, and crisped**
  About 3 cups bite-size pieces cooked chicken breast
- 3 **to 4 ounces jack cheese, cut into bite-size strips**
- 12 **thin slices salami**
- 2 **oranges, peeled and sliced**
- 1 **firm-ripe avocado**
  Pitted ripe olives
  Tortilla chips

Prepare Creamy Cumin Dressing; set aside.

Arrange large outer lettuce leaves on 4 dinner plates. Finely chop inner leaves and arrange over whole leaves. Top with chicken, cheese, salami, and orange slices. Pit, peel, and slice avocado; add to salads. Garnish with olives and tortilla chips. Offer dressing at the table to add to taste. Makes 4 servings.

Creamy Cumin Dressing. Mix ⅓ cup *each* **sour cream** and **mayonnaise,** 1½ tablespoons **lemon juice,** ¼ teaspoon *each* **dry mustard** and **garlic salt,** ½ teaspoon **ground cumin,** and 3 tablespoons **prepared green or red chile salsa.** Makes about 1 cup.

Per serving of salad: 498 calories, 48 g protein, 16 g carbohydrates, 27 g total fat, 130 mg cholesterol, 625 mg sodium

Per tablespoon of dressing: 44 calories, 0.2 g protein, 0.6 g carbohydrates, 5 g total fat, 5 mg cholesterol, 74 mg sodium

Festively garnished with orange zest, oven-smoked chicken teams with mixed greens in Smoked Chicken Breast Salad (recipe on facing page). Complete the menu with crusty bread and a glass of white Zinfandel.

Smoked Chicken Breast Salad

Pictured on facing page

Preparation time: About 15 minutes
Cooking time: 20 to 25 minutes

Fresh orange juice adds a sweet-tart accent to mellow oven-smoked chicken breasts in this main-dish salad; buttery toasted pecans add a rich, nutty crunch.

- 3 **tablespoons liquid smoke**
- 2 **whole chicken breasts (about 1 lb. *each*), skinned, boned, and split**
  Orange Vinaigrette (recipe follows)
- 1 **tablespoon butter or margarine**
- ¾ **cup pecan halves**
- 6 **cups mixed salad greens, such as butter lettuce, romaine lettuce, and watercress, rinsed and crisped**
  Orange zest
  Orange wedges

Pour liquid smoke into a 5- to 6-quart pan. Set a rack in pan. Arrange chicken breasts in a single layer on rack and cover pan tightly. Bake in a 350° oven until meat in thickest part is no longer pink; cut to test (20 to 25 minutes). If made ahead, let cool; then cover and refrigerate for up to 2 days.

While chicken is baking, prepare Orange Vinaigrette; set aside. Also melt butter in a medium-size frying pan over low heat. Add pecans and stir until nuts are slightly darkened and have a toasted flavor (about 6 minutes). Drain on paper towels.

Arrange salad greens on 4 dinner plates and sprinkle with pecans. Cut each chicken breast into ¼-inch-thick slanting slices; arrange on plates beside greens. Spoon Orange Vinaigrette over greens and chicken. Garnish with orange zest and orange wedges. Makes 4 servings.

Orange Vinaigrette. Mix ¼ cup **orange juice,** 2 tablespoons *each* **white wine vinegar** and **salad oil,** 1 tablespoon thinly slivered or shredded **orange peel,** 2 teaspoons *each* **honey** and **Dijon mustard,** and ½ teaspoon **coarsely ground pepper.**

Per serving: 420 calories, 37 g protein, 12 g carbohydrates, 25 g total fat, 93 mg cholesterol, 213 mg sodium

Curry & Fruit Chicken Salad

Preparation time: About 30 minutes

Its flavors inspired by East Indian cuisine, this spicy chicken and fruit combination is just right for a special lunch or supper. Choose either sour cream or yogurt as the base for the dressing.

  Dill-Curry Dressing (recipe follows)
- 1 **medium-size red apple**
- 3 **cups ½-inch-wide strips of cooked chicken**
- 2 **cups thinly sliced celery**
- ¾ **cup salted roasted peanuts**
- ½ **cup raisins**
- 1 **small pineapple (about 3 lbs.)**
- 8 **to 10 large lettuce leaves, rinsed and crisped**
- 2 **tablespoons minced candied or crystallized ginger (optional)**

Prepare Dill-Curry Dressing; set aside.

Core apple and cut lengthwise into thin slivers. Combine apple, chicken, celery, ½ cup of the peanuts, raisins, and dressing; mix gently.

Peel and slice pineapple. Arrange lettuce leaves on 4 dinner plates; place pineapple on lettuce and top with chicken salad. Sprinkle salads with remaining ¼ cup peanuts and, if desired, ginger. Makes 4 servings.

Dill-Curry Dressing. Mix 1 cup **sour cream** or plain yogurt, 2 tablespoons **lemon juice,** 1½ teaspoons **curry powder,** and ½ teaspoon **dry dill weed.**

Per serving: 656 calories, 41 g protein, 54 g carbohydrates, 34 g total fat, 119 mg cholesterol, 421 mg sodium

Chicken Salad with Sesame Dressing

Preparation time: About 30 minutes

Crisp celery, juicy kiwi fruit, creamy avocado, and tender shredded chicken combine in this bright main course. A lemony sesame seed dressing brings all the flavors together.

> Sesame Dressing (recipe follows)
> 8 cups bite-size pieces leaf lettuce, rinsed and crisped
> 4 large kiwi fruit
> 1 large firm-ripe avocado
> 2 cups shredded cooked chicken
> 1 cup thinly sliced celery
> ⅓ cup thinly sliced green onions (including tops)

Prepare Sesame Dressing; set aside.

Spread lettuce in a wide salad bowl. Peel kiwi fruit and thinly slice crosswise. Pit, peel, and slice avocado. Arrange kiwi fruit, avocado, chicken, celery, and onions over lettuce. Pour dressing over salad and mix lightly. Makes 4 servings.

Sesame Dressing. Heat ⅓ cup **salad oil** in a small frying pan over low heat. Add 3 tablespoons **sesame seeds** and cook, stirring often, until golden (about 5 minutes). Remove from heat and let cool for 10 minutes. Stir in ½ teaspoon *each* grated **lemon peel** and **dry mustard**, ¼ cup **lemon juice,** and 1 tablespoon *each* **sugar** and **soy sauce.** Season to taste with **salt.**

Per serving: 545 calories, 27 g protein, 32 g carbohydrates, 37 g total fat, 62 mg cholesterol, 374 mg sodium

Grecian Chicken Salad Plates

Preparation time: About 30 minutes

For a carefree summer menu, offer a whole-meal salad featuring rice-stuffed grape leaves, deli-roasted or barbecued chicken, and an assortment of greens and fresh vegetables. Serve with crusty rolls and chilled dry white wine or fruity rosé.

> 1 jar (6 oz.) marinated artichoke hearts
> 1 teaspoon grated lemon peel
> 1 tablespoon lemon juice
> 1 clove garlic, minced or pressed
> ½ teaspoon dry oregano
> 2 tablespoons chopped fresh mint or 2 teaspoons dry mint
> 3 tablespoons olive oil
> 1 tablespoon drained capers
> 1 small cucumber
> 1 head romaine lettuce, separated into leaves, rinsed, and crisped
> 2 cups cherry tomatoes, cut in half
> 1 yellow or green bell pepper, seeded and cut into thin strips
> 1 cooked (rotisseried or barbecued) chicken (2 to 2½ lbs.), cut into quarters
> 2 to 3 ounces feta cheese, crumbled Greek olives
> 1 small can (6½ oz.) stuffed grape leaves, drained

Drain artichokes, reserving marinade in a small bowl; set artichokes aside. To marinade, add lemon peel, lemon juice, garlic, oregano, and mint; whisk in oil until well combined. Stir in capers. Set dressing aside.

Peel cucumber and cut in half lengthwise, then scoop out and discard seeds. Slice each cucumber half crosswise into ⅛-inch-thick slices. Set aside large outer lettuce leaves; tear inner leaves into bite-size pieces. Combine cucumber, torn lettuce leaves, tomatoes, bell pepper, and artichokes. Reserve 2 tablespoons of the dressing; mix salad lightly with remaining dressing.

Coarsely sliver large lettuce leaves and arrange on 4 dinner plates. Place a chicken quarter on one side of each plate; mound salad mixture on other side. Sprinkle salads with cheese. Drizzle chicken with reserved dressing and garnish each salad with olives and stuffed grape leaves. Makes 4 servings.

Per serving: 499 calories, 38 g protein, 14 g carbohydrates, 33 g total fat, 115 mg cholesterol, 646 mg sodium

Sichuan Chicken Salad

Preparation time: About 20 minutes
Cooking time: About 10 minutes

Won ton skins, cut into strips and crisply fried, accent this Chinese chicken salad. Peanut butter combines with hot chili oil to season the piquant dressing.

- 2 **tablespoons creamy peanut butter**
- 3 **tablespoons soy sauce**
- ¼ **cup unseasoned rice vinegar**
- 2 **teaspoons sugar**
  About ¼ teaspoon hot chili oil or ground red pepper (cayenne)
- 2 **tablespoons sesame seeds**
  Salad oil
- 6 **won ton skins (each about 3 inches square), cut into ¼-inch-wide strips**
- 8 **cups finely shredded iceberg lettuce**
- 2 **green onions (including tops), thinly sliced**
- 2 **to 3 cups shredded cooked chicken**
- 2 **tablespoons chopped fresh cilantro (coriander)**

Place peanut butter in a small bowl; with a fork, smoothly mix in soy sauce, a little at a time, until well blended. Stir in vinegar and sugar; season to taste with chili oil.

Toast sesame seeds in a small frying pan over medium heat until golden (3 to 5 minutes), shaking pan frequently; set seeds aside. Pour salad oil into pan to a depth of ¼ inch; increase heat to medium-high. When oil is hot, add won ton strips, about half at a time. Cook, stirring, until lightly browned (1½ to 2 minutes). With a slotted spoon, lift out strips and drain on paper towels.

Place lettuce in a large salad bowl; top with onions, chicken, and dressing. Sprinkle with sesame seeds, fried won ton strips, and cilantro. Mix lightly. Makes 4 to 6 servings.

Per serving: 267 calories, 22 g protein, 13 g carbohydrates, 15 g total fat, 50 mg cholesterol, 707 mg sodium

Curried Turkey Salad with Papaya

Preparation time: About 25 minutes

Golden papaya spears and deep green romaine leaves make an exceptionally pretty garnish for cashew-sprinkled, curry-seasoned turkey salad.

- **Curry Dressing (recipe follows)**
- 3 **cups diced cooked turkey or chicken**
- 1 **cup thinly sliced celery**
- ½ **cup thinly sliced green onions (including tops)**
  Salt and ground red pepper (cayenne)
- 8 **to 12 large romaine lettuce leaves, rinsed and crisped**
- 2 **large papayas, peeled, seeded, and sliced lengthwise**
- ¼ **cup salted roasted cashews**
- 1 **lemon, cut into wedges**

Prepare Curry Dressing; set aside. Combine turkey, celery, and onions; mix lightly with dressing. Season to taste with salt and red pepper. Arrange lettuce on 4 dinner plates. Mound turkey salad on each plate; arrange papaya slices alongside. Sprinkle cashews over salad. Offer lemon wedges to squeeze over salad and fruit. Makes 4 servings.

Curry Dressing. Mix 1 cup **sour cream**; 2 tablespoons minced **candied or crystallized ginger;** 1 tablespoon *each* **curry powder, lemon juice,** and **Dijon mustard;** and ½ teaspoon **cumin seeds.**

Per serving: 473 calories, 36 g protein, 35 g carbohydrates, 22 g total fat, 106 mg cholesterol, 314 mg sodium

Turkey, Red Pepper & Blue Cheese Salad

Follow directions for **Curried Turkey Salad with Papaya,** but omit Curry Dressing, celery, ground red pepper, papayas, cashews, and lemon wedges.

For dressing, mix ½ cup *each* **sour cream** and **mayonnaise,** 1 tablespoon *each* **prepared horseradish** and **lemon juice,** and ⅛ teaspoon **pepper.**

For salad, combine turkey, onions, and 1 large **red bell pepper,** seeded and chopped. Mix lightly with dressing and ½ cup crumbled **blue-veined cheese.** Season to taste with salt. Arrange lettuce leaves and turkey salad on plates as directed. Sprinkle with ½ cup **salted roasted peanuts.** Makes 4 servings.

Per serving: 614 calories, 41 g protein, 10 g carbohydrates, 47 g total fat, 122 mg cholesterol, 652 mg sodium

Steak & Vegetable Salad

Preparation time: 20 to 25 minutes
Cooking time: About 25 minutes

Let steak-and-potato fans enjoy their favorite
dinner in a new guise: a hearty main-dish salad.
Complete the meal with warmed French rolls and
a light red wine.

- 1½ **pounds flank steak, trimmed of fat; or 3½ cups thinly sliced roast beef**
- 2 **tablespoons white wine vinegar**
- 6 **tablespoons salad oil**
- 1 **tablespoon Dijon mustard**
- ¼ **teaspoon *each* salt and pepper**
- 1 **pound small thin-skinned potatoes (*each* 1½ to 2 inches in diameter), scrubbed**
- ½ **pound green beans, ends removed**
- 1 **jar (6 oz.) marinated artichoke hearts, drained**
- 1 **can (7 oz.) whole pimentos, drained and cut into strips**
- ¼ **pound mushrooms, sliced**
- 5 **green onions (including tops), sliced**

Place steak on greased rack of a broiler pan. Broil
4 inches below heat, turning once, until browned
on outside but still rare in center; cut to test (about
10 minutes). Meanwhile, in a large bowl, combine
vinegar, oil, mustard, salt, and pepper; whisk until
well mixed.

Cut steak across the grain into thin, slanting
slices. Cut each slice into 2-inch lengths and add to
mustard dressing in bowl; stir until steak is well
coated.

While steak is broiling, place unpeeled potatoes in a 3-quart pan; add water to cover. Bring to a
boil over high heat; cover and boil for 15 minutes.
Add beans and continue to boil until potatoes are
tender throughout when pierced and beans are just
tender-crisp to bite (about 6 more minutes). Drain
vegetables and rinse under cold running water
until cool enough to handle; drain again. Peel potatoes, if desired; then cut into ¼-inch-thick slices.
Cut beans into 2-inch lengths. Add potatoes and
beans to steak; then add artichoke hearts, pimentos, mushrooms, and onions. Toss until all ingredients are thoroughly coated with dressing. Serve at
room temperature. Makes 6 servings.

*Per serving: 367 calories, 22 g protein, 19 g carbohydrates, 23 g total
fat, 49 mg cholesterol, 339 mg sodium*

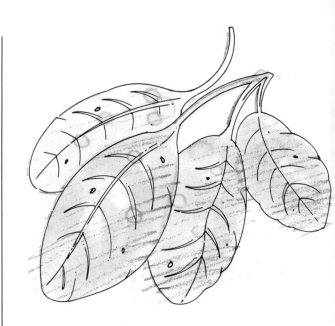

Warm Spinach & Sausage Salad

Pictured on facing page

Preparation time: About 15 minutes
Cooking time: About 10 minutes

This substantial combination of spinach, bell pepper, and sausage offers delicious proof that not all
salads are cool, delicate dishes. Try it for brunch,
with cheese omelets and fresh fruit.

- ¾ **pound spinach, stems removed, leaves rinsed and crisped**
- 1 **large red or yellow bell pepper, seeded**
- 3 **green onions (including tops)**
- ½ **pound mild or hot Italian sausages, casings removed**
- ½ **teaspoon fennel seeds**
- ⅓ **cup balsamic or red wine vinegar Salt and pepper**

Tear spinach leaves into bite-size pieces. Cut bell
pepper lengthwise into thin strips. Cut onions into
3-inch lengths and sliver lengthwise. Place vegetables in a large salad bowl and set aside.

In a wide frying pan, cook sausage over medium-high heat, stirring and breaking up with a
spoon, until crumbly and browned (about 10
minutes). Add fennel seeds and vinegar, stirring
to scrape browned bits free.

Pour sausage mixture over vegetables and toss
well. Season to taste with salt and pepper. Makes
4 servings.

*Per serving: 223 calories, 10 g protein, 5 g carbohydrates, 18 g total
fat, 49 mg cholesterol, 465 mg sodium*

*Bold ingredients are quickly transformed into simple
yet showy Warm Spinach & Sausage Salad (recipe on
facing page). A splash of balsamic vinegar and a
sprinkling of fennel seeds add extra bursts of flavor.*

Red Cabbage & White Sausage Salad

Preparation time: About 15 minutes
Cooking time: About 10 minutes

If you have an electric wok or frying pan, you can prepare this sturdy cold-weather salad right at the table. Serve it with caraway rye bread and mugs of dark beer.

- ¼ cup salad oil
- 1 to 1¼ pounds white veal sausage, such as bratwurst, bockwurst, or weisswurst, cut into ¼-inch-thick slices
- 3 tablespoons white wine vinegar
- 2 tablespoons sugar
- 1½ teaspoons *each* Dijon mustard, celery seeds, and Worcestershire
- 1 clove garlic, minced or pressed
- 1 cup thinly sliced green onions (including tops)
- 6 cups finely shredded red cabbage
  Salt and pepper

Heat oil in a wok or wide frying pan over medium-high heat. Add sausage slices and cook, turning often, until browned. Add vinegar, sugar, mustard, celery seeds, Worcestershire, and garlic; stir until sugar is dissolved. Bring mixture to a boil over high heat; add onions and cabbage, then turn off heat. Lift and turn onions and cabbage with 2 forks or spoons until coated with dressing. Season to taste with salt and pepper. Serve immediately. Makes 6 servings.

Per serving: 395 calories, 14 g protein, 15 g carbohydrates, 32 g total fat, 51 mg cholesterol, 542 mg sodium

Salad Olé

Preparation time: About 25 minutes
Cooking time: About 10 minutes

Spicy chorizo, kidney beans, chiles, and cumin add a Mexican accent to this warm salad. Choose simple accompaniments—perhaps just corn chips or hot buttered tortillas. (If you prefer a milder flavor, omit the chorizo and use a pound of ground beef in the salad.)

  Avocado Dressing (recipe follows)
- 4 cups shredded iceberg lettuce
- 1 can (2¼ oz.) sliced ripe olives, drained
- 1 medium-size cucumber, peeled and sliced
- 1 cup shredded carrots
- 1 can (about 15 oz.) kidney beans, drained
- 1 cup (4 oz.) shredded jack cheese
- ½ pound *each* lean ground beef and chorizo sausage
- 1 large onion, chopped
- 12 cherry tomatoes, halved

Prepare Avocado Dressing; cover and refrigerate.

In a large salad bowl, combine lettuce, olives, cucumber, carrots, beans, and cheese; set aside.

Crumble beef into a wide frying pan. Remove chorizo casings and crumble meat into pan. Add onion and cook over medium heat, stirring occasionally, until beef and sausage are browned and onion is soft. Spoon off and discard fat; then spoon meat mixture over lettuce mixture. Toss gently and garnish with tomatoes. Serve immediately. Pass dressing to spoon over individual portions. Makes 4 to 6 servings.

Avocado Dressing. Pit and peel 1 large ripe **avocado.** Place in a small bowl; mash thoroughly. Stir in 1 tablespoon **lime juice,** 1 can (4 oz.) **diced green chiles,** ¼ teaspoon **ground cumin,** 1 teaspoon **garlic salt,** and ⅓ cup **regular-strength beef broth.** Mix until smooth.

Per serving: 473 calories, 27 g protein, 27 g carbohydrates, 30 g total fat, 73 mg cholesterol, 1,088 mg sodium

Chef's Salad

Preparation time: About 25 minutes

This big, hearty salad is brimming with crunch and color. You might offer garlic bread alongside, then finish the meal with Spirited Chocolate Fondue (page 178).

Chili-spiced Thousand Island Dressing (recipe follows)
1 medium-size head iceberg lettuce, shredded
1 cup julienne strips cooked ham
1½ cups (about 6 oz.) julienne strips Cheddar or jack cheese
½ cup sliced green onions (including tops)
1 basket cherry tomatoes, halved
2 hard-cooked eggs, chopped
1 can (3½ oz.) pitted ripe olives, drained

Prepare Chili-spiced Thousand Island Dressing; cover and refrigerate.

Place lettuce in a large salad bowl. Arrange ham, cheese, onions, tomatoes, and eggs on top of lettuce in separate wedge-shaped sections; place olives in center.

Present salad at the table; just before serving, add dressing and toss gently. Makes 4 servings.

Chili-spiced Thousand Island Dressing. Mix ¾ cup **mayonnaise**, 3 tablespoons **tomato-based chili sauce**, 1 tablespoon **sweet pickle relish**, 1½ teaspoons **lemon juice**, and ¼ to ½ teaspoon **chili powder**.

Per serving: 669 calories, 27 g protein, 16 g carbohydrates, 57 g total fat, 200 mg cholesterol, 1,602 mg sodium

Sliced Steak Salad with Blue Cheese Dressing

Preparation time: About 15 minutes
Broiling time: About 10 minutes

Steak and salad are traditional dinner partners—and they taste even better when they share the same mustard–garlic dressing. You use some of the dressing as a baste for the meat, then mix the rest with blue cheese and toss it with romaine lettuce, avocado, and red onion.

Mustard-Garlic Dressing & Baste (recipe follows)
1½ pounds flank steak, trimmed of fat
½ cup crumbled blue-veined cheese
8 cups bite-size pieces romaine lettuce, rinsed and crisped
1 small red onion, thinly sliced
1 large firm-ripe avocado
1 large tomato, cut into wedges

Prepare Mustard-Garlic Dressing & Baste. Brush about 1 tablespoon of the mixture over each side of steak; set remaining mixture aside. Place steak on rack of a broiler pan. Broil about 4 inches below heat, turning once, until browned on outside but still rare in center; cut to test (about 10 minutes).

Meanwhile, stir cheese into remaining dressing-baste mixture. In a large bowl, combine lettuce and onion. Pit, peel, and thinly slice avocado. Add to lettuce mixture along with dressing and mix lightly. Arrange salad on 4 dinner plates.

Cut steak across the grain into thin, slanting slices. Arrange meat over each salad. Garnish with tomato wedges. Makes 4 servings.

Mustard-Garlic Dressing & Baste. With a whisk, mix 1 tablespoon *each* **red wine vinegar, lemon juice,** and **Dijon mustard;** 1 large clove **garlic,** minced or pressed; ¼ teaspoon **dry dill weed;** ⅛ teaspoon *each* **salt** and **ground white pepper;** and 5 tablespoons **olive oil** or salad oil.

Per serving: 700 calories, 46 g protein, 12 g carbohydrates, 53 g total fat, 111 mg cholesterol, 556 mg sodium

*Spilling over the sides of this open-faced entrée is an
ocean of succulent small shrimp. Along with chips, hot
soup, and a tall glass of beer, Shrimp Stack Sandwiches
(recipe on page 60) make a satisfying meal.*

Sandwiches & Pizza

For the busy cook, sandwiches soon become a favorite standby. These hearty, casual entrées—along with sandwich-type specialties like pizza, burritos, and piroshkis—owe their perennial appeal to the unbeatable combination of great flavor, good nutrition, and ease of preparation. They also lend themselves readily to creative experimentation. Feel free to use the cheese you already have on hand, or try a different kind of bread or roll. Just pick one of the many recipes we offer, then add your own personal touches.

Garden Vegetable Pockets

Preparation time: 15 to 20 minutes

A nutritious blend of lettuce, carrots, tomatoes, and cheese makes a tasty stuffing for warmed pita breads. If you prefer heartier sandwiches, try adding diced meat, seafood, or hard-cooked eggs to the filling.

- 2 cups lightly packed shredded lettuce
- 1 cup shredded carrots
- 1 cup (4 oz.) shredded jack cheese
- ⅓ cup chopped green onions (including tops)
- 1 tomato, seeded and diced
- 1 avocado, pitted, peeled, and diced
- ¼ cup mayonnaise
- 3 tablespoons tomato-based chili sauce
- 1 tablespoon sweet pickle relish
- 3 pita breads (*each* about 6 inches in diameter), halved

In a bowl, combine lettuce, carrots, cheese, onions, tomato, and avocado. In a cup, stir together mayonnaise, chili sauce, and relish; pour over vegetables and toss gently to blend. Fill bread halves evenly with vegetable mixture, packing gently. Makes 3 servings.

Per serving: 612 calories, 18 g protein, 56 g carbohydrates, 37 g total fat, 44 mg cholesterol, 961 mg sodium

Garden Vegetable Pockets with Ham, Turkey, or Chicken

Follow directions for **Garden Vegetable Pockets,** but add about 1 cup diced **cooked ham,** turkey, or chicken along with the avocado. Makes 3 servings.

Per serving with ham: 697 calories, 29 g protein, 56 g carbohydrates, 41 g total fat, 72 mg cholesterol, 1,681 mg sodium

Garden Vegetable Pockets with Shrimp or Crab

Follow directions for **Garden Vegetable Pockets,** but add ¼ pound **small cooked shrimp** or cooked crabmeat along with the avocado. Makes 3 servings.

Per serving with shrimp: 649 calories, 26 g protein, 56 g carbohydrates, 37 g total fat, 118 mg cholesterol, 1,046 mg sodium

Turkey & Cheese Burgers

Preparation time: About 10 minutes
Baking time: About 15 minutes

Here's a cheeseburger that's just right for health-conscious dining. You make the moist meat patties from ground turkey, cottage cheese, and—for lively flavor—green chiles, taco sauce, and cumin. Serve with all your favorite burger trimmings.

- 1 pound ground turkey
- 1 can (4 oz.) diced green chiles
- 1 cup small-curd cottage cheese
- ¼ cup fine dry bread crumbs
- 1 tablespoon prepared red taco sauce
- ½ teaspoon ground cumin
  Salt and pepper
- 5 hamburger buns, split and toasted

In a bowl, mix turkey, chiles, cottage cheese, bread crumbs, taco sauce, and cumin until well combined. Heat a broiler pan with a rack in a 500° oven for 10 minutes.

Meanwhile, divide turkey mixture into 5 equal portions and shape each into a patty about 3½ inches in diameter. With a spatula, slide patties onto rack of broiler pan, spacing well apart. Bake until patties are browned on top and no longer pink in center; cut to test (about 15 minutes). Let stand for 3 minutes to firm slightly; season to taste with salt and pepper. Place patties, browned sides up, on toasted buns. Makes 5 servings.

Per serving: 341 calories, 26 g protein, 28 g carbohydrates, 14 g total fat, 55 mg cholesterol, 625 mg sodium

Broiled Tarragon-Turkey Sandwiches

Preparation time: About 10 minutes
Broiling time: 5 to 8 minutes

Turn a casual supper into a special occasion—serve these hot open-faced sandwiches made with mustard-flavored turkey salad. Offer potato chips and crisp raw vegetables to complete the menu.

- ⅓ cup mayonnaise
- ¼ cup Dijon mustard
- 2 teaspoons dry tarragon
- ⅛ teaspoon ground red pepper (cayenne)
- 2 cloves garlic, minced or pressed
- 2 cups shredded cooked turkey
- ½ cup drained, chopped pickled sweet cherry peppers
- 3 English muffins, split
- 6 thin slices tomato
- 6 thin slices jack cheese (*each* about 2½ inches square)

In a bowl, stir together mayonnaise, mustard, tarragon, red pepper, and garlic. Add turkey and peppers; mix lightly. Set aside.

Place muffins, cut sides up, on a baking sheet. Broil about 4 inches below heat until golden (3 to 5 minutes). Spread each muffin half with turkey mixture and top with a tomato slice, then a cheese slice.

Return sandwiches to oven and broil until cheese is melted (2 to 3 minutes). Makes 3 servings.

Per serving: 610 calories, 39 g protein, 34 g carbohydrates, 35 g total fat, 111 mg cholesterol, 1,797 mg sodium

Swiss Ham & Turkey Melt

Follow directions for **Broiled Tarragon-Turkey Sandwiches,** but omit 1 clove of the garlic, cherry peppers, English muffins, tomato, and jack cheese.

To turkey mixture, add 1 tablespoon chopped **pickled onions.** Substitute split sandwich-size **croissants** for muffins; broil until browned (2 to 3 minutes). Spread croissants with turkey mixture and top with 6 thin slices **cooked ham** and 6 thin slices **Swiss cheese** (*each* 3 to 4 inches square). Broil as directed. Makes 3 servings.

Per serving: 737 calories, 53 g protein, 24 g carbohydrates, 47 g total fat, 170 mg cholesterol, 2,015 mg sodium

A Touch of Relish

A colorful, piquant relish adds extra zest to a sandwich supper. Chutney, corn relish, and sweet or dill pickles are good tucked into sandwiches or served alongside. Other favorite accompaniments include spiced peaches, cinnamon apple rings, green or ripe olives, marinated vegetables (such as artichoke hearts, mushrooms, and baby corn on the cob), and pickled beets, onions, and peppers.

Turkey & Bacon Salad Sandwiches

Preparation time: About 15 minutes

These open-faced treats feature sliced turkey, crisp bacon, and your choice of creamy dressings atop a base of shredded lettuce and sliced green onions. To round out the meal, just add tall glasses of iced tea.

- 8 slices firm-textured white, whole wheat, or rye bread
  Butter, margarine, or mayonnaise
- 4 cups lightly packed shredded lettuce
- ¼ cup sliced green onions (including tops)
- 1 pound thinly sliced cooked turkey
- ¼ cup sliced radishes
- 12 slices bacon, crisply cooked and drained
- 1 avocado, pitted, peeled, and sliced
  Salt and pepper
  Cherry tomatoes
  Chili-spiced Thousand Island Dressing (page 53) or purchased green goddess dressing

Toast both sides of bread slices; spread one side of each slice with butter. Place 2 slices, buttered sides up, side by side on each of 4 salad plates; cover evenly with lettuce and sprinkle with onions. Evenly distribute turkey, radishes, bacon, and avocado atop lettuce. Season to taste with salt and pepper; garnish with tomatoes. At the table, pass dressing to spoon over sandwiches. Eat sandwiches with knife and fork. Makes 4 servings.

Per serving: 592 calories, 45 g protein, 31 g carbohydrates, 32 g total fat, 126 mg cholesterol, 721 mg sodium

Chicken & Cheese Subs

Preparation time: 10 to 15 minutes
Cooking time: 20 to 25 minutes

For a snack of Dagwoodian proportions, enjoy these hefty French rolls stuffed with shredded chicken breast and Camembert.

- 1 **whole chicken breast (about 1 lb.), split**
- 4 **slices bacon**
- 4 **unsliced French sandwich rolls (*each* about 3 by 6 inches)**
- 8 **ounces Camembert, fontina, or jack cheese, cut into 16 equal chunks**
- 2 **tablespoons butter or margarine, melted**

In a 3- to 4-quart pan, bring 4 cups water to a boil over high heat. Add chicken. Reduce heat, cover, and simmer until meat in thickest part is no longer pink; cut to test (about 15 minutes). Drain; let cool slightly. Discard skin and bones; shred meat.

While chicken is simmering, cook bacon in a wide frying pan over medium heat until crisp (about 8 minutes); drain.

Slice off ends of rolls. With a knife, carefully scoop out insides, leaving a ¼-inch-thick shell (reserve soft bread for other uses). Fill each roll with one slice of the bacon, 4 chunks of the cheese, and an equal portion of the chicken. Lay roll on a large rimmed baking sheet and brush with butter.

Bake sandwiches in a 450° oven until rolls are crisp and browned (6 to 8 minutes). To serve, slice rolls diagonally across center. Makes 4 servings.

Per serving: 512 calories, 35 g protein, 32 g carbohydrates, 26 g total fat, 110 mg cholesterol, 1,006 mg sodium

Avocado-Chicken Rolls

Pictured on facing page

Preparation time: About 10 minutes
Broiling time: 6 to 8 minutes

Quick to put together when you have cooked chicken on hand, these multilayered sandwiches satisfy even the heartiest appetite.

- 4 **round crusty rolls (*each* 4 to 5 inches in diameter)**
- 2 **tablespoons butter or margarine, at room temperature**
- ½ **cup sour cream**
- 2 **teaspoons Dijon mustard**
  About 1½ cups shredded cooked chicken
  About ⅔ cup prepared chile salsa
- 4 **canned whole green chiles, split lengthwise and seeded**
- 2 **small firm-ripe avocados**
  About 4 ounces jack cheese, thinly sliced

Split rolls in half and spread cut sides with butter. Place roll halves, buttered sides up, on a baking sheet. Broil about 4 inches below heat until golden (3 to 5 minutes). Set aside top halves of rolls.

Spread bottoms of rolls with sour cream and mustard. Mix chicken with about ⅓ cup of the salsa and mound evenly on rolls; top each with a chile.

Halve, pit, and peel avocados; place on a cutting board, cut sides down. Cut each half from wide, round end to within about 1 inch of narrow top, making slices about ¼ inch thick. Lay knife across slices and press gently to fan out. Carefully lift each avocado with a wide spatula and place atop chile on a roll half. Cover avocados with cheese.

Broil 6 inches below heat until cheese is melted (about 3 minutes). Serve with tops of rolls and remaining salsa to add to taste. Makes 4 servings.

Per serving: 634 calories, 31 g protein, 45 g carbohydrates, 38 g total fat, 102 mg cholesterol, 1,252 mg sodium

For short-order sandwiches with spirited south-of-the-border flavor, stack up Avocado-Chicken Rolls (recipe on facing page). Salsa-seasoned chicken is topped with whole chiles, avocado, cheese, and still more salsa.

Seafood Sandwiches

When it comes to seafood sandwiches, tuna isn't the only fish in the sea—and there's certainly more to this long-time favorite than the standard tuna-on-white. The three recipes on this page present tuna, shrimp, and crab in appetizing sandwiches you'll enjoy for lunch or supper.

Hearty onion rolls stuffed with tuna and Cheddar are great for a casual cool-weather meal; for warmer days and more elegant occasions, try cool, dilly shrimp stacks. And when you want an easy light supper, sample creamy open-faced crab sandwiches, bubbly hot from the broiler.

Tuna Buns

Preparation time: 10 to 15 minutes
Baking time (optional): 15 to 20 minutes

⅔ cup mayonnaise
3 tablespoons sweet pickle relish
2 teaspoons prepared mustard
1 large can (12½ oz.) chunk light tuna in water, drained and flaked
1 cup (4 oz.) shredded Cheddar cheese
½ cup *each* chopped celery and green onions (including tops)
4 onion or kaiser-style rolls, split

In a bowl, stir together mayonnaise, relish, and mustard. Add tuna, cheese, celery, and onions; stir until well combined. Spread tuna mixture

evenly over bottom halves of rolls; top with remaining roll halves. Serve. Or, to heat, wrap each sandwich in foil; place sandwiches on a baking sheet and heat in a 350° oven until cheese is melted (15 to 20 minutes). Unwrap and serve immediately. Makes 4 servings.

Per serving: 661 calories, 36 g protein, 36 g carbohydrates, 41 g total fat, 86 mg cholesterol, 1,107 mg sodium

Shrimp Stack Sandwiches

Pictured on page 54

Preparation time: About 10 minutes

¼ cup *each* mayonnaise and sour cream
1 teaspoon *each* lemon juice and dry dill weed
½ teaspoon prepared horseradish
4 slices firm-textured white or whole wheat bread
1 large tomato, thinly sliced
1 pound small cooked shrimp
1 avocado, pitted, peeled, and thinly sliced
Dill sprigs (optional)
Lemon wedges (optional)

In a small bowl, stir together mayonnaise, sour cream, lemon juice, dill weed, and horseradish. Spread a little of the dill mixture over each bread slice; top with a few tomato

slices. Evenly distribute shrimp atop tomato slices; spoon remaining dill mixture over shrimp. Top sandwiches with avocado slices. Garnish with dill sprigs and lemon wedges, if desired. Eat with knife and fork. Makes 4 servings.

Per serving: 396 calories, 28 g protein, 19 g carbohydrates, 24 g total fat, 236 mg cholesterol, 471 mg sodium

Hot Crab Sandwiches

Preparation time: 5 to 10 minutes
Broiling time: 3 to 4 minutes

½ pound cooked crabmeat
1 cup (4 oz.) shredded Swiss cheese
1 jar (2 oz.) diced pimentos, drained
⅓ cup *each* mayonnaise and finely chopped green bell pepper
4 slices firm-textured white bread
Butter or margarine, at room temperature

In a bowl, mix crabmeat, cheese, pimentos, mayonnaise, and bell pepper until well blended. Meanwhile, toast bread. Spread each slice lightly with butter; then top evenly with crab mixture, spreading it out to edges. Place sandwiches on a baking sheet and broil 6 inches below heat until bubbly and heated through (3 to 4 minutes). Eat with knife and fork. Makes 4 servings.

Per serving: 399 calories, 22 g protein, 15 g carbohydrates, 28 g total fat, 105 mg cholesterol, 500 mg sodium

Chicken-Artichoke Monte Cristos

Preparation time: About 10 minutes
Cooking time: About 10 minutes

When unexpected guests drop by for dinner, treat them to these French-toasted sandwiches stuffed with shredded chicken, artichokes, and Swiss cheese.

- 1½ cups shredded cooked chicken
- 1 jar (6 oz.) marinated artichoke hearts, drained and chopped
- 1 tablespoon *each* mayonnaise and dry sherry
- ¾ teaspoon dry rosemary
- 8 slices firm-textured white bread
- 4 square slices Swiss or jack cheese (4 oz. *total*)
- 2 eggs
- ¼ cup milk
- About 2 tablespoons butter or margarine

In a bowl, stir together chicken, artichokes, mayonnaise, sherry, and rosemary. Spread chicken mixture evenly over 4 of the bread slices; top each with a slice of cheese, then with one of the remaining 4 bread slices, pressing lightly to hold sandwiches together.

In a pie pan, beat together eggs and milk until well blended. Melt about 1 tablespoon of the butter in a wide frying pan over medium heat. Meanwhile, dip 2 of the sandwiches in egg mixture to coat both sides; drain briefly. Place in frying pan, cheese side down; cook, turning once, until golden brown on both sides (about 5 minutes). Remove from pan and keep warm. Repeat with remaining 2 sandwiches, adding more butter as needed. Serve immediately; eat with knife and fork. Makes 4 servings.

Per serving: 505 calories, 32 g protein, 30 g carbohydrates, 28 g total fat, 200 mg cholesterol, 699 mg sodium

Store Bread in the Freezer

You'll always have fresh bread for sandwiches if you keep a loaf in the freezer. Bread kept at room temperature must be used quickly, and refrigerated bread can dry out rapidly. To thaw frozen bread in a hurry, spread out slices in a single layer and let stand for 10 minutes. If slices are to be toasted, put them right into the toaster.

Quick Flaky Piroshkis

Preparation time: About 10 minutes, plus 25 minutes to thaw patty shells
Cooking time: About 35 minutes

Here's a streamlined version of a Russian favorite. Start out with frozen patty shells instead of homemade pastry; while the shells thaw, fry up an easy beef-onion filling.

- 1 package (about 10 oz.) frozen patty shells
- ½ pound lean ground beef
- 1 medium-size onion, chopped
- 2 cloves garlic, minced or pressed
- ¼ pound mushrooms, chopped
- 2 tablespoons soy sauce
- 2 hard-cooked eggs, chopped
- Pepper
- 1 egg white

Let patty shells thaw at room temperature.

Meanwhile, crumble beef into a wide frying pan; cook over medium-high heat, stirring often, until well browned (about 5 minutes). Add onion, garlic, and mushrooms and continue to cook, stirring often, until onion is soft (about 10 more minutes). Stir in soy sauce, scraping pan to loosen browned bits; remove from heat. Stir in eggs and season mixture to taste with pepper. Let cool.

On a lightly floured board, roll out each shell to a 7-inch circle; spoon a sixth of the meat mixture onto center. Beat egg white lightly, then use to moisten edges of pastry. Bring edges of each pastry circle to center and pinch firmly to seal; flute sealed edge. Place piroshkis on an ungreased baking sheet, seam side up. Pierce tops in several places.

Bake in a 450° oven until golden (about 20 minutes). Serve warm. Makes 6 servings.

Per serving: 353 calories, 13 g protein, 19 g carbohydrates, 25 g total fat, 99 mg cholesterol, 581 mg sodium

Fix a no-fuss fiesta with do-it-yourself *Spicy Beef Burritos* (recipe on facing page). A zesty, Mexican-seasoned beef mixture and colorful condiments are wrapped up in warm flour tortillas to eat out of hand.

picy Beef Burritos

Pictured on facing page

Preparation time: 20 to 25 minutes
Cooking time: About 20 minutes

To keep the beef in these burritos juicy and tender, stir-fry the strips just briefly before enclosing them in soft flour tortillas. Sangría and fresh fruit complete a delightful menu.

Condiments: Shredded lettuce, diced tomatoes, shredded Cheddar or jack cheese, sour cream, sliced avocado (coated with lemon juice), fresh cilantro (coriander) sprigs, and prepared taco sauce

- 6 **large flour tortillas (*each* about 10 inches in diameter)**
- ¼ **cup salad oil**
- 2 **pounds boneless top round steak (about 1 inch thick), thinly sliced, then cut into 2-inch-long strips**
- 1 **large onion, chopped**
- 2 **cloves garlic, minced or pressed**
- 1½ **teaspoons *each* ground cumin and chili powder**
- ¼ **teaspoon dry oregano**
- ⅛ **teaspoon ground red pepper (cayenne)**
  Salt

Prepare condiments and place on a platter or in individual bowls. Stack tortillas, wrap in foil, and place in a 350° oven until heated through (about 15 minutes).

Meanwhile, heat 2 tablespoons of the oil in a wide frying pan over medium-high heat. Add half the beef and cook, stirring, until browned on outside but still pink in center; cut to test (about 5 minutes). Remove from pan. Repeat with remaining 2 tablespoons oil and remaining meat.

To drippings in pan, add onion, garlic, cumin, chili powder, oregano, and red pepper. Reduce heat to medium and cook, stirring, until onion is soft (about 10 minutes). Add meat; stir until well combined, then heat through. Season filling to taste with salt.

To eat, spoon filling onto a warm tortilla, top with condiments, and roll up. Makes 6 servings.

Per serving without condiments: 476 calories, 36 g protein, 27 g carbohydrates, 24 g total fat, 92 mg cholesterol, 293 mg sodium

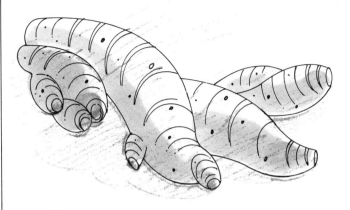

Oriental Pita Sandwiches

Preparation time: About 15 minutes
Cooking time: 5 to 10 minutes

Stir-fries are usually served over rice, but this one—a gingery blend of tender strips of pork and crisp bean sprouts—is a hearty filling for pita bread halves.

- 3 **pita breads (*each* about 6 inches in diameter), halved**
- 1 **tablespoon cornstarch**
- 2 **tablespoons *each* soy sauce and dry sherry**
- 1 **teaspoon sugar**
- ⅓ **cup water**
- 2 **tablespoons salad oil**
- ¾ **pound boneless pork or beef, cut into thin 1- by 3-inch strips**
- 2 **cloves garlic, minced or pressed**
- 2 **teaspoons minced fresh ginger or 1 teaspoon ground ginger**
- ¼ **teaspoon pepper**
- ½ **pound bean sprouts**
- ⅓ **cup thinly sliced green onions (including tops)**

Wrap breads in foil; heat in a 350° oven while preparing filling.

In a small bowl, stir together cornstarch, soy sauce, sherry, sugar, and water; set aside.

Heat oil in a wok or wide frying pan over high heat. Add pork, garlic, ginger, and pepper; cook, stirring, until meat is lightly browned (3 to 4 minutes). Add cornstarch mixture and cook, stirring constantly, until sauce thickens and boils. Gently mix in bean sprouts and onions.

To serve, spoon filling into warm bread halves. Makes 3 servings.

Per serving: 623 calories, 30 g protein, 49 g carbohydrates, 34 g total fat, 79 mg cholesterol, 1,119 mg sodium

Creativity with Leftovers

Leftovers of many kinds are easily transformed into tempting sandwiches. Cold cooked chicken, turkey, ham, beef, lamb, and meat loaf are all popular sandwich fillings; mild fish or hard-cooked eggs, chopped and mixed with mayonnaise and seasonings, are delicious as well. And if you have a bit of sour cream, cream cheese, or thick salad dressing (such as Creamy Mustard Dressing, page 44) to use up, try it as a sandwich spread in place of the usual butter, margarine, or mayonnaise.

To add juiciness, color, and crunch to your sandwiches, add lettuce, sliced tomatoes, and/or alfalfa sprouts.

Roasted Red Pepper & Avocado Melts

Preparation time: 5 to 10 minutes
Broiling time: 5 to 8 minutes

Colorful ingredients stack up in this delectable broiled sandwich. It's a savory choice for lunch, perhaps with a cup of vegetable soup.

- 4 whole wheat English muffins, split
- 8 thin slices red onion
- 1 large ripe avocado
- 8 thin slices jack cheese (about 4 oz. *total*)
- 2 jars (7 oz. *each*) roasted red bell peppers or pimentos, drained
- 3 tablespoons grated Parmesan cheese

Arrange muffins, cut sides up, on a baking sheet. Broil about 4 inches below heat until toasted (3 to 5 minutes).

Place an onion slice on each muffin half. Halve, pit, and peel avocado; slice each half into 8 wedges. Top each onion slice with 2 of the avocado wedges, a slice of the jack cheese, and an eighth of the bell peppers. Sprinkle with Parmesan cheese. Return to oven; broil 6 inches below heat until jack cheese is melted (2 to 3 minutes). Makes 4 servings.

Per serving: 384 calories, 15 g protein, 39 g carbohydrates, 21 g total fat, 28 mg cholesterol, 481 mg sodium

Giant Sesame Ham Sandwich

Preparation time: 20 to 25 minutes
Cooking time: About 5 minutes

Offer this hollowed-out, ham salad–filled loaf to hungry sports fans on big game day—or wrap it up to tote to the park for a picnic.

- 6 tablespoons salad oil
- 2 tablespoons sesame seeds
- 1 teaspoon ground ginger
- 3 tablespoons white wine vinegar
- 1½ tablespoons soy sauce
- 1 teaspoon sugar
- 1 clove garlic, minced or pressed
- ½ cup sliced green onions (including tops)
- 1½ cups julienne strips cooked ham
- 1 can (about 8 oz.) sliced water chestnuts, drained
- 1 package (6 oz.) frozen Chinese pea pods, thawed and drained
- 1 cup thinly sliced celery
- ⅓ pound mushrooms, thinly sliced
- 1 round loaf (1½ lbs.) crusty bread

Heat oil in a medium-size frying pan over low heat. Add sesame seeds; cook, stirring often, until seeds are golden (about 5 minutes). Let cool; then stir in ginger, vinegar, soy sauce, sugar, garlic, and onions.

In a bowl, stir together ham, water chestnuts, pea pods, celery, and mushrooms. Reserve 1 to 2 tablespoons of the sesame dressing; add the rest to ham mixture.

Slice off top portion of bread to form a ½- to ¾-inch-thick lid. Pull out soft center of bread, leaving a shell about ⅜ inch thick (reserve soft bread for other uses). Spoon ham mixture into bread bowl. Drizzle reserved sesame dressing over cut side of lid; place on top. To serve, cut into wedges. Makes 6 servings.

Per serving: 584 calories, 22 g protein, 74 g carbohydrates, 22 g total fat, 26 mg cholesterol, 1,506 mg sodium

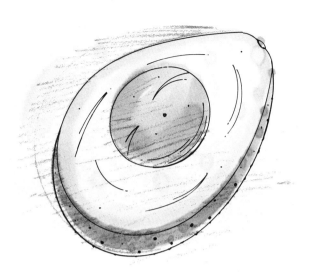

Golden Onion & Ham Sandwiches

Pictured on page 19

Preparation time: About 5 minutes
Cooking time: About 25 minutes

Ham and cheese sandwiches get a new look here. To make these hot deli-style specialties, layer Black Forest ham, Swiss cheese, and lots of golden sautéed onions on slices of dark rye; serve with your favorite pickles.

- 4 large onions
- ¼ cup butter or margarine
- 6 slices dark rye bread
  Dijon or German mustard
- 6 thin slices Black Forest, Westphalian, or baked ham (6 oz. *total*)
- 6 slices Swiss cheese (about 5 oz. *total*)
  Coarsely ground pepper

Thinly slice onions and separate into rings. Melt butter in a wide frying pan over medium heat. Add onions and cook, stirring occasionally, until very soft and golden (about 25 minutes).

About 5 minutes before onions are done, place bread in a single layer on a large baking sheet. Broil about 4 inches below heat, turning once, until toasted (about 2 minutes). Spread each slice with mustard; add one slice each of the ham and cheese. Return to oven and broil until cheese is melted (about 1 minute). Spoon onions equally atop each sandwich. Season to taste with pepper. Makes 6 servings.

Per serving: 304 calories, 17 g protein, 22 g carbohydrates, 17 g total fat, 59 mg cholesterol, 706 mg sodium

Sausage & Salsa Rolls

Preparation time: About 10 minutes
Cooking time: About 10 minutes

Sandwiches, like tacos, benefit from a lively fresh salsa. Here, sautéed slices of Polish sausage, topped with coarse-grained mustard, rest on crusty rolls spread with homemade cilantro-chile salsa.

- Cilantro Salsa (recipe follows)
- 2 Polish or linguisa sausages (4 to 5 oz. *each*)
- 2 round crusty rolls (*each* 4 to 5 inches in diameter), split
  Coarse-grained mustard
  Mayonnaise (optional)

Prepare Cilantro Salsa and set aside.

Cut sausages into ⅜-inch-thick slanting slices. Lay slices in a wide frying pan and cook over medium heat, turning once, until lightly browned on both sides.

Meanwhile, arrange rolls, cut sides up, on a baking sheet; broil about 4 inches below heat until toasted (3 to 5 minutes).

Spoon about 2 tablespoons of the salsa onto bottom half of each roll. Place sausage slices on top and add a dollop of mustard. If desired, spread roll tops with mayonnaise. Offer remaining salsa to add to taste. Serve open-faced or closed; eat with knife and fork. Makes 2 servings.

Cilantro Salsa. In a blender or food processor, combine ¼ cup *each* **lime juice** and **salad oil;** 1 cup lightly packed **fresh cilantro (coriander) leaves;** 1 small **hot fresh or pickled chile,** such as serrano or jalapeño, stemmed and seeded; ¼ cup chopped **onion;** and 1 clove **garlic,** minced or pressed. Whirl mixture until puréed. Season to taste with **salt.** If made ahead, cover and refrigerate until next day. Makes about 1 cup.

Per sandwich: 685 calories, 25 g protein, 42 g carbohydrates, 46 g total fat, 91 mg cholesterol, 1,526 mg sodium

Per tablespoon of salsa: 33 calories, 0.1 g protein, 0.7 g carbohydrates, 3 g total fat, 0 mg cholesterol, 1 mg sodium

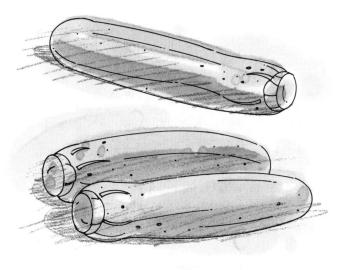

Italian Bell Pepper & Sausage Rolls

Preparation time: 10 to 15 minutes
Cooking time: About 20 minutes

Simple, but so satisfying! For a sturdy, casual lunch, offer buttered rolls filled with fried Italian sausages, bell peppers, and sweet onion rings.

- 6 **mild or hot Italian sausages (about 1¼ lbs.** *total***), casings removed**
- 1 **large onion, thinly sliced**
- 2 **large green or red bell peppers (or 1 of each), seeded and thinly sliced lengthwise**
- ¼ **cup butter or margarine, at room temperature**
- 6 **sandwich rolls (***each* **3 to 4 inches long), split**

Place sausages, one at a time, between sheets of plastic wrap and flatten with your hand into thin patties about the same length as rolls. Cook patties in a wide frying pan over medium-high heat, turning once, until well browned on outside and no longer pink in center; cut to test (about 5 minutes). Lift out and keep warm. Discard all but 2 tablespoons of the drippings.

Add onion and bell peppers to drippings and cook, stirring often, until limp (about 10 minutes). Return sausage patties to pan and cook just until hot (about 2 more minutes).

Meanwhile, spread butter on cut sides of rolls. Arrange rolls, buttered sides up, on a baking sheet; broil about 4 inches below heat until toasted (3 to 5 minutes). Put a sausage patty inside each roll and top each patty equally with onion mixture. Makes 6 servings.

Per serving: 577 calories, 19 g protein, 36 g carbohydrates, 39 g total fat, 94 mg cholesterol, 1,100 mg sodium

Zucchini Pizzas

Pictured on facing page

Preparation time: About 20 minutes
Cooking time: About 30 minutes

Soft ricotta cheese and sautéed zucchini slices may be unusual pizza ingredients—but when they join mozzarella, salami, and olives atop puffy rounds of prebaked, cheese-sprinkled bread, the results are delicious. (Look for the bread in your market's refrigerator or freezer section.)

- 2 **tablespoons olive oil**
- 1 **clove garlic, cut in half**
- ½ **pound medium-size zucchini, cut into ¼-inch-thick slices**
- ½ **cup finely chopped onion**
- 1 **cup whole-milk ricotta cheese**
  Salt and black pepper
- 2 **packages (8 oz.** *each***) prebaked refrigerated or frozen cheese crusts (***each* **6 inches in diameter)**
- ¼ **pound thinly sliced dry salami, slivered**
- 2 **cups (8 oz.) shredded mozzarella cheese**
- 1 **can (2¼ oz.) sliced ripe olives, drained**
  Crushed red pepper flakes (optional)

Heat 1 tablespoon of the oil in a wide frying pan over medium-high heat; add garlic and cook, stirring, just until golden brown. Remove and discard garlic. To oil, add half the zucchini slices. Cook, turning once, until lightly browned (about 5 minutes). Drain on paper towels. To pan, add remaining 1 tablespoon oil and remaining zucchini. Cook until lightly browned; then drain. Reserve drippings in pan.

Add onion to drippings; cook over medium heat, stirring often, until soft (about 10 minutes). Transfer to a bowl and stir in ricotta cheese; season to taste with salt and black pepper.

Place crusts in a single layer on baking sheets; spread ricotta mixture over each, almost to edges. Top with salami, zucchini, mozzarella cheese, and olives.

Bake in a 450° oven until mozzarella is melted and lightly browned (10 to 12 minutes). Season to taste with red pepper flakes, if desired. Makes 4 servings.

Per serving: 798 calories, 36 g protein, 55 g carbohydrates, 48 g total fat, 116 mg cholesterol, 1,613 mg sodium

Here's an appetizing version of pizza presto, based on prebaked rounds of cheese-flavored bread. Single-size Zucchini Pizzas (recipe on facing page) offer a delectable way to make use of your garden's harvest.

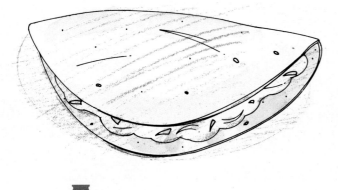

Italian Tortilla Pizzas

Follow directions for **Armenian Tortilla Pizzas**, but substitute 1 pound **lean ground beef** for the lamb, omit paprika and allspice, and add 1 teaspoon **Italian herb seasoning** (or ¼ teaspoon *each* dry basil, dry oregano, dry thyme, and dry marjoram). Makes 6 servings.

Per serving: 316 calories, 21 g protein, 19 g carbohydrates, 18 g total fat, 64 mg cholesterol, 456 mg sodium

Mexican Tortilla Pizzas

Follow directions for **Armenian Tortilla Pizzas**, but in place of lamb, use ½ pound *each* **lean ground beef** and **chorizo,** casings removed (or use 1 pound lean ground beef). Omit paprika and allspice; add 1 teaspoon **chili powder** and ½ teaspoon *each* **ground cumin** and **dry oregano**. Makes 6 servings.

Per serving: 321 calories, 20 g protein, 21 g carbohydrates, 19 g total fat, 63 mg cholesterol, 554 mg sodium

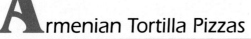

Armenian Tortilla Pizzas

Preparation time: About 10 minutes
Cooking time: 20 to 25 minutes

To make these speedy individual pizzas, you top flour tortilla "crusts" with a spicy tomato-lamb sauce and a sprinkling of mild cheese, then broil briefly. You can vary the recipe to suit your taste; use beef instead of lamb, for example, or substitute other seasonings for the paprika and allspice.

> 1   **pound lean ground lamb**
> 1   **cup finely chopped green or red bell pepper (or a combination)**
> 2   **large cloves garlic, minced or pressed**
> ½   **cup chopped parsley**
> 3   **tablespoons tomato paste**
> 1   **can (about 14½ oz.) pear-shaped tomatoes**
> 1   **teaspoon *each* paprika and ground allspice**
> ¼   **teaspoon pepper**
>   **Salt**
> 6   **flour tortillas (*each* 7 to 8 inches in diameter)**
> 1¼ **cups (5 oz.) shredded mozzarella cheese**

Crumble lamb into a wide frying pan. Add bell pepper and garlic and cook over medium-high heat, stirring often, until meat is browned (5 to 7 minutes); spoon off and discard fat. Stir in parsley, tomato paste, tomatoes (break up with a spoon) and their liquid, paprika, allspice, and pepper. Reduce heat and simmer, uncovered, until liquid has evaporated (about 10 minutes). Season to taste with salt.

Place 3 of the tortillas on a large baking sheet. Spoon about ½ cup of the meat mixture over each tortilla; spread out to within ¼ inch of edges. Sprinkle tortillas evenly with half the cheese; broil about 6 inches below heat until cheese is melted. Repeat with remaining 3 tortillas, meat mixture, and cheese. Eat out of hand or with knife and fork. Makes 6 servings.

Per serving: 328 calories, 22 g protein, 19 g carbohydrates, 19 g total fat, 73 mg cholesterol, 457 mg sodium

Quesadillas

Preparation time: 5 to 10 minutes
Cooking time: 6 to 10 minutes

The addition of green onions and fresh cilantro jazzes up these popular snacks.

> 1   **tablespoon butter or margarine**
> 4   **flour tortillas (*each* 7 to 8 inches in diameter)**
> 1   **cup (4 oz.) shredded Cheddar or jack cheese**
> ¼   **cup *each* thinly sliced green onions (including tops) and chopped fresh cilantro (coriander)**

Melt half the butter in a small frying pan over medium-high heat. Add a tortilla and cook, turning several times, until soft (about 30 seconds). Sprinkle ¼ cup of the cheese over half the tortilla and top with 1 tablespoon each of the onions and cilantro. With tongs, fold tortilla in half.

Cook, turning once, until cheese is melted (1 to 2 minutes); remove and keep warm. Repeat with remaining tortillas and filling, adding more butter as needed. Makes 4 servings.

Per serving: 211 calories, 9 g protein, 13 g carbohydrates, 14 g total fat, 38 mg cholesterol, 346 mg sodium

Fresh Herb Flavors

For fragrance and flavor, not even the best-quality dried herbs can compare to the fresh leaves and sprigs. And today, you can enjoy those intense flavors whether or not you have your own herb garden: many supermarkets sell fresh basil, dill, oregano, and other herbs, either tied in bundles or packaged in clear plastic boxes.

On this page, we offer four ways to put a variety of fresh herbs to good use: in aromatic herb mayonnaise, tangy sour cream or yogurt dip, classic pesto sauce, and delicious whipped butter. Serving suggestions accompany each recipe—but you'll want to come up with your own ideas, as well.

Fresh Herb Mayonnaise

Preparation time: About 5 minutes
Chilling time: At least 8 hours

1 cup mayonnaise
2 teaspoons lemon juice
½ cup chopped fresh herbs, such as basil, dill, marjoram, oregano, savory, or tarragon

In a bowl, mix mayonnaise, lemon juice, and herbs until well blended. Cover and refrigerate for at least 8 hours or up to 1 month.

Serve as a dressing for green salad or sliced tomatoes, as a dip for artichokes, or as a spread for roast beef or turkey sandwiches; or use to make deviled eggs or tuna or chicken salad. Makes about 1 cup.

Per tablespoon: 100 calories, 0.2 g protein, 0.8 g carbohydrates, 11 g total fat, 8 mg cholesterol, 78 mg sodium

Savory Cream Dip

Preparation time: About 5 minutes
Chilling time: At least 1 hour

1 cup sour cream or plain yogurt
¼ cup chopped fresh herbs, such as basil, dill, fennel, or thyme
Salt and pepper

In a bowl, mix sour cream and herbs until well blended. Season to taste with salt and pepper. Cover and refrigerate for at least 1 hour or up to 5 days.

Serve as a dip for fresh vegetables, as a salad dressing, or as a sauce for fish. Makes about 1 cup.

Per tablespoon: 31 calories, 0.5 g protein, 0.8 g carbohydrate, 3 g total fat, 6 mg cholesterol, 8 mg sodium

Pesto

Preparation time: 5 to 10 minutes

2 cups lightly packed fresh basil leaves
1 cup (5 oz.) grated Parmesan cheese
½ to ⅔ cup olive oil
1 or 2 cloves garlic

In a blender or food processor, whirl basil, cheese, ½ cup of the oil, and garlic until smoothly puréed; add more oil, if necessary. If made ahead, divide into small, easy-to-use portions; place in containers and top with a thin layer of oil to prevent darkening. Cover and refrigerate for up to 5 days; freeze for longer storage (thaw in refrigerator overnight before using).

Serve over pasta, tomatoes, or hot cooked vegetables, or on toasted French bread. Makes about 1½ cups.

Per tablespoon: 78 calories, 3 g protein, 1 g carbohydrates, 7 g total fat, 5 mg cholesterol, 111 mg sodium

Whipped Herb Butter

Preparation time: About 5 minutes
Chilling time: At least 8 hours

1 cup (½ lb.) butter or margarine, at room temperature
2 teaspoons lemon juice
⅓ cup finely chopped fresh herbs, such as basil, marjoram, oregano, savory, or chives

In a blender or food processor, combine butter, lemon juice, and herbs. Whirl until thoroughly blended. Cover and refrigerate for at least 8 hours or up to 2 weeks; freeze for longer storage.

Serve over hot cooked vegetables or baked potatoes; use to cook omelets; or spread on hot biscuits or corn muffins. Makes about 1 cup.

Per tablespoon: 103 calories, 0.2 g protein, 0.2 g carbohydrates, 11 g total fat, 31 mg cholesterol, 117 mg sodium

For spur-of-the-moment splendor, wrap up an
Apple & Cheese Omelet (recipe on page 72). Its golden
topping is a blend of spicy sautéed apples
and sharp Cheddar cheese.

Eggs & Cheese

For breakfast, brunch, lunch, or supper, eggs are a long-time favorite. They're satisfying, quick to cook, and easily dressed up—try them scrambled with crisp sprouts and spicy sausage, or sample a plump omelet filled with apples or savory herbed zucchini. Many of our egg specialties are accented with Cheddar, jack, or Parmesan—and we also offer a pair of recipes with cheese in the starring role. One's a zesty fondue; the other's a baked version of classic chiles rellenos. For best results in our recipes, use large eggs.

pple & Cheese Omelet

Pictured on page 70

Preparation time: About 10 minutes
Cooking time: About 15 minutes

Onions sautéed with spiced apples add a savory note to this speedy entrée. Heat muffins in the oven to accompany the omelet.

- **2 large tart apples**
- **1 tablespoon lemon juice**
- **⅛ teaspoon *each* ground nutmeg and ground cinnamon**
- **¼ cup butter or margarine**
- **1 small onion, finely chopped**
- **6 eggs**
- **2 tablespoons water**
- **1 cup (4 oz.) shredded sharp Cheddar cheese**
  Apple slices (optional)
  Parsley sprigs (optional)

Peel and core apples; slice into a bowl. Add lemon juice, nutmeg, and cinnamon; mix lightly.

Melt 2 tablespoons of the butter in a wide frying pan over medium-high heat. Stir in apple mixture and onion. Cook, stirring often, just until apples begin to brown (6 to 8 minutes). Remove from heat and keep warm.

In a bowl, beat eggs with water until well blended. Melt remaining 2 tablespoons butter in a wide nonstick omelet pan over medium heat. Pour in eggs. Cook, gently lifting cooked portion to let uncooked eggs flow underneath, until omelet is set but still moist on top. Remove from heat.

Spoon half each of the apple mixture and cheese down center of omelet. Fold a third of the omelet over filling. Slide unfolded edge onto a warm serving plate; flip folded portion over top. Spoon remaining apple mixture over omelet and sprinkle with remaining cheese. Garnish with apple slices and parsley sprigs, if desired. Makes 3 servings.

Per serving: 500 calories, 22 g protein, 18 g carbohydrates, 38 g total fat, 506 mg cholesterol, 518 mg sodium

ucchini-Basil Omelet for Two

Preparation time: About 10 minutes
Cooking time: About 10 minutes

Dinner for two is ready in no time when you serve a golden omelet filled with zucchini, tomatoes, and basil. Alongside, offer warm pita bread and fresh fruit.

- **¼ cup butter or margarine**
  About ½ pound medium-size zucchini, diced
  Coarsely ground pepper
- **¼ cup chopped fresh basil**
- **5 eggs**
- **2 tablespoons water**
- **¾ cup shredded jack cheese**
- **¼ cup canned crushed tomatoes**

Melt 2 tablespoons of the butter in a 2- to 3-quart pan over medium-high heat. Add zucchini and cook, stirring often, just until tender-crisp to bite (about 3 minutes). Season to taste with pepper. Reduce heat, cover, and continue to cook until zucchini is tender to bite (2 to 3 more minutes). Stir in basil and set aside.

In a bowl, beat eggs with water until well blended. Melt remaining 2 tablespoons butter in a wide nonstick frying pan over medium-high heat; tilt pan to coat bottom and sides. Pour in eggs. Cook, gently lifting cooked portion to let uncooked eggs flow underneath, until omelet is set but still moist on top (about 4 minutes).

Sprinkle cheese over half of omelet and top with zucchini and tomatoes. Remove omelet from heat, loosen from pan, and slide onto a warm large platter, flipping untopped portion over filling. Makes 2 servings.

Per serving: 576 calories, 28 g protein, 8 g carbohydrates, 49 g total fat, 631 mg cholesterol, 673 mg sodium

Eggs in Pepper Sauce

Preparation time: About 25 minutes
Cooking time: About 25 minutes

Typically mild-mannered at breakfast, poached eggs make a lively supper dish when cooked in a spicy sauce of Italian sausages, sweet peppers, and green chiles.

- 1 large red or yellow bell pepper
- 2 large fresh mild green chiles, such as Anaheim (California)
- ½ pound mild or hot Italian sausages, cut into ½-inch-thick diagonal slices
- 2 cloves garlic, minced or pressed
- 1 large onion, thinly sliced
- 1 teaspoon dry basil
- ½ teaspoon crushed anise seeds
- 2 large tomatoes, coarsely chopped
- 4 eggs
  Salt and pepper

Place bell pepper and chiles in a 9-inch pie pan; broil about 4 inches below heat, turning often, until charred (about 10 minutes). Enclose in a plastic bag and let stand for 15 minutes. Pull off and discard skins, seeds, and stems; then thinly slice pepper and chiles and set aside.

In a wide frying pan, cook sausage slices over medium heat, turning occasionally, until browned. With a slotted spoon, remove sausages and set aside. Discard all but 2 tablespoons of the drippings. To remaining drippings, add garlic, onion, basil, and anise seeds. Cook, stirring often, until onion is soft (about 10 minutes).

Return sausage to pan and add bell pepper, chiles, and tomatoes. Bring to a boil, stirring often. Reduce heat so mixture is simmering.

With a large spoon, make 4 hollows in sauce, 3 to 4 inches apart. Carefully break an egg into each hollow. Cover pan and simmer until eggs are done to your liking (4 to 6 minutes for soft yolks). Carefully transfer each egg to a wide soup bowl or rimmed plate; spoon sauce around eggs. Season to taste with salt and pepper. Makes 4 servings.

Per serving: 308 calories, 17 g protein, 13 g carbohydrates, 21 g total fat, 249 mg cholesterol, 488 mg sodium

Easy Does It

Never rush egg and cheese dishes. Eggs are delicate and should be cooked gently, at moderate temperatures, to avoid rubbery results. Cheese, too, becomes tough and stringy when exposed to high temperatures or prolonged cooking. If you're melting cheese atop an omelet or casserole, heat *just* until melted, then serve; when you're making fondue, use medium or low heat—and don't overcook.

Rolled Fresh Corn Frittata

Preparation time: About 5 minutes
Cooking time: About 10 minutes

A French-style omelet encloses its filling—but a frittata's "filling" (here, a mixture of corn and bell pepper) is mixed right into the eggs. Frittatas tend to be pan-browned on both sides or baked, but ours is cooked and rolled in typical omelet fashion.

- 2 tablespoons butter or margarine
- ½ to ¾ cup fresh or thawed frozen corn kernels
- ½ cup diced green bell pepper
- ⅓ cup sliced green onions (including tops)
- 4 eggs
- 2 tablespoons whipping cream or water
- ⅛ teaspoon liquid hot pepper seasoning
  Salt

Melt butter in a wide nonstick frying pan over medium-high heat. Add corn and bell pepper; cook, stirring often, until pepper is tender-crisp to bite (about 3 minutes). Stir in onions and continue to cook until onions are soft (1 to 2 more minutes); reduce heat to medium-low.

In a bowl, beat eggs, cream, and hot pepper seasoning until well blended; season to taste with salt. Pour egg mixture over vegetables in pan. Cook, gently lifting cooked portion to let uncooked eggs flow underneath, until omelet is set but still moist on top. Tilt pan and roll or fold frittata out onto a warm serving plate. Makes 2 servings.

Per serving: 346 calories, 15 g protein, 13 g carbohydrates, 27 g total fat, 473 mg cholesterol, 265 mg sodium

Chiles Rellenos Casserole

Preparation time: About 20 minutes
Baking time: 25 to 30 minutes

While this piquant casserole bakes, you can easily put together the rest of the meal: just prepare a relish tray of raw jicama, carrot, and green or red bell pepper strips, then slice a loaf of crusty sourdough bread.

- 1 **can (7 oz.) diced green chiles**
- 2 **cups (8 oz.) shredded sharp Cheddar cheese**
- 2 **green onions (including tops), thinly sliced**
- 2 **large pear-shaped tomatoes, seeded and chopped**
- 1¼ **cups milk**
- 4 **eggs**
- ½ **cup all-purpose flour**
- 1½ **cups (6 oz.) shredded jack cheese**

Spread half the chiles in a shallow 2-quart baking dish. Cover with half the Cheddar cheese, onions, and tomatoes; repeat layers, using remaining chiles, Cheddar cheese, onions, and tomatoes.

In a blender or food processor, whirl milk, eggs, and flour until smooth. Pour over mixture in baking dish; sprinkle evenly with jack cheese. Bake in a 375° oven until center jiggles only slightly when dish is gently shaken (25 to 30 minutes). Let stand for 1 to 2 minutes; then cut into squares. Makes 4 to 6 servings.

Per serving: 475 calories, 29 g protein, 19 g carbohydrates, 32 g total fat, 256 mg cholesterol, 792 mg sodium

Chunky Cheddar Fondue

Pictured on facing page

Preparation time: About 15 minutes
Cooking time: About 20 minutes

Traditional Swiss fondue is made with Gruyère cheese and white wine, but this Latin-accented version features Cheddar cheese, tomatoes, and green chiles. You'll want to serve a cooling dessert after the meal; Berry Slush (page 181) is a good choice.

   Assorted raw vegetables: Bell pepper strips, carrot sticks or whole baby carrots, zucchini rounds, celery sticks, mushrooms (quartered if large), green onions, cauliflowerets
   Firm French bread cubes, tortilla chips, or breadsticks
- 3 **tablespoons butter or margarine**
- 1 **medium-size onion, chopped**
- 1 **small can (about 8 oz.) stewed tomatoes**
- 1 **can (4 oz.) diced green chiles**
- ¼ **teaspoon dry oregano**
- 4 **cups (1 lb.) shredded Cheddar cheese**

Prepare vegetables and bread; set aside. Melt butter in a wide frying pan over medium heat. Add onion and cook, stirring occasionally, until lightly browned (about 10 minutes). Stir in tomatoes, chiles, and oregano. Reduce heat and simmer, uncovered, for 5 minutes. Add cheese, a handful at a time, stirring until cheese is melted and mixture is well blended.

If desired, transfer to a fondue pot or chafing dish and keep warm over heat source. If serving in frying pan, reheat as necessary over medium heat, stirring occasionally. Use assorted vegetables and bread cubes as dippers. Makes 4 servings.

Per serving: 563 calories, 29 g protein, 8 g carbohydrates, 46 g total fat, 142 mg cholesterol, 1,109 mg sodium

The Swiss invented fondue, but they might not
recognize this one! Chunky Cheddar Fondue (recipe on
facing page) is lively in flavor and boasts a variety
of distinctive dippers.

Unbeatable Brunches

On a lazy weekend morning, nothing could be more delightful than a special brunch for family or friends. On these two pages, you'll find six choices that offer wide-awake new approaches to breakfast eggs—enriched with lox and cream cheese, for example, or whipped into a giant, crisp pancake to top with powdered sugar and lemon juice. Besides pleasing guests, our unbeatable recipes do the cook a favor, too; they're so easy to make that you can probably sleep for an extra hour before you start preparing the meal!

Ham, Egg & Asparagus Brunch

Preparation time: About 10 minutes
Cooking time: 12 to 14 minutes

- 4   large slices sourdough or French bread
- 6   tablespoons olive oil
- 1   medium-size onion, thinly sliced
- 1   pound asparagus, tough ends removed, spears cut diagonally into 2-inch pieces
- ½   pound cooked ham, cut into thin strips
- 4   eggs

Lightly brush both sides of each bread slice with 2 tablespoons of the oil. In a wide frying pan, toast bread over medium-high heat, turning once, until browned on both sides (about 5 minutes). Place a slice on each of 4 dinner plates; keep warm.

Add 2 tablespoons of the oil to pan; then add onion, asparagus, and ham. Cook, stirring often, until asparagus is tender to bite (5 to 7 minutes). Evenly spoon asparagus mixture beside bread on each plate; keep warm.

Add remaining 2 tablespoons oil to pan and tilt to coat. Break eggs into pan and cook until done to your liking (about 2 minutes for firm whites and soft yolks). Place an egg atop asparagus mixture on each plate. Makes 4 servings.

Per serving: 457 calories, 24 g protein, 20 g carbohydrates, 31 g total fat, 247 mg cholesterol, 1,080 mg sodium

Tender Dutch Baby

Preparation time: 5 minutes
Baking time: About 20 minutes

- 3   eggs
- 6   tablespoons all-purpose flour
- 1   tablespoon granulated sugar
- 6   tablespoons milk
- 3   tablespoons butter or margarine
      Powdered sugar
      Lemon wedges (optional)

In a blender or food processor, whirl eggs, flour, granulated sugar, and milk until smooth, scraping edges of container as needed.

Place butter in a wide ovenproof frying pan and set on a rack slightly above center in a 425° oven. When butter is melted (about 4 minutes), remove pan and tilt to coat bottom and sides. Quickly pour in batter, return pan to oven, and bake until pancake is puffed and golden brown (about 15 minutes).

Sprinkle with powdered sugar and cut into wedges. If desired, offer lemon wedges to squeeze over individual portions. Makes 4 servings.

Per serving: 215 calories, 7 g protein, 17 g carbohydrates, 13 g total fat, 186 mg cholesterol, 147 mg sodium

Cream Cheese Eggs with Smoked Salmon

Preparation time: About 5 minutes
Cooking time: About 7 minutes

- 6   eggs
- 4   ounces thinly sliced smoked salmon or lox, cut into thin strips
- 1   green onion (including top), thinly sliced
- 1   tablespoon butter or margarine
- 1   small package (3 oz.) cream cheese, cut into small pieces

In a bowl, beat eggs until blended; stir in salmon and half the onion.

Melt butter in a wide frying pan over medium heat. Pour in egg mixture and cook, stirring often, until eggs are set but still moist (about 5 minutes). Scatter cheese over eggs and continue to cook, stirring often, until set to your liking. Spoon onto warm plates and garnish with remaining onion. Makes 4 servings.

Per serving: 245 calories, 16 g protein, 2 g carbohydrates, 19 g total fat, 356 mg cholesterol, 409 mg sodium

Sprouts & Eggs

Preparation time: About 10 minutes
Cooking time: 15 to 20 minutes

½ pound mild or hot Italian sausages, casings removed

1 large onion, finely chopped

1 clove garlic, minced or pressed

½ teaspoon Italian herb seasoning or ⅛ teaspoon *each* dry basil, dry oregano, dry thyme, and dry marjoram

⅛ teaspoon *each* ground nutmeg and pepper

6 eggs

3 cups alfalfa or other sprouts

3 tablespoons grated Parmesan cheese

Crumble sausages into a wide frying pan. Cook over medium heat, stirring occasionally, until lightly browned. Add onion, garlic, herb seasoning, nutmeg, and pepper. Cook, stirring often, until onion is soft (about 10 minutes).

In a bowl, beat eggs until well blended. Add to pan and cook, stirring gently, just until softly set. Stir in sprouts and sprinkle with cheese. Makes 4 servings.

Per serving: 348 calories, 20 g protein, 6 g carbohydrates, 27 g total fat, 365 mg cholesterol, 584 mg sodium

Egg & Asparagus Gratins

Preparation time: 5 to 10 minutes
Cooking time: 11 to 15 minutes

12 asparagus spears, tough ends removed

¼ cup butter or margarine

8 eggs

½ cup grated Parmesan cheese

In a wide frying pan, bring 2 inches water to a boil over high heat. Add asparagus; cover, reduce heat, and boil gently until tender when pierced (5 to 7 minutes). Drain.

While asparagus is cooking, place 1 tablespoon of the butter in each of 4 small oval baking dishes. Set dishes on a baking sheet and place in a 450° oven just until butter is melted (about 5 minutes).

Remove dishes from oven and quickly lay 3 asparagus spears in each. Carefully break 2 eggs into each dish, return to oven, and bake until set to your liking (5 to 7 minutes for firm whites and soft yolks). Sprinkle with cheese and bake for 1 more minute. Makes 4 servings.

Per serving: 306 calories, 18 g protein, 3 g carbohydrates, 25 g total fat, 464 mg cholesterol, 430 mg sodium

Rocky Mountain Eggs

Preparation time: About 10 minutes
Cooking time: About 20 minutes

¼ cup butter or margarine

1 or 2 small thin-skinned potatoes (*each* 1½ to 2 inches in diameter), peeled and cut into ½-inch cubes (about ¾ cup)

1 small onion, finely chopped

½ cup diced cooked ham, beef, or pork

1 tablespoon chopped parsley

3 eggs

¼ teaspoon salt
Dash of pepper

1 tablespoon milk

½ cup shredded Cheddar or jack cheese

Melt 2 tablespoons of the butter in a wide frying pan over medium heat. Add potatoes, onion, and ham; cover and cook, stirring occasionally, until potatoes are tender when pierced (about 15 minutes). Sprinkle with parsley, add remaining 2 tablespoons butter, and distribute mixture evenly in pan.

In a bowl, beat eggs with salt, pepper, and milk until well blended. Pour egg mixture into pan and cook without stirring. As egg mixture begins to set, gently lift cooked portion to let uncooked eggs flow underneath. Continue to cook until eggs are set but still moist on top. Remove from heat and sprinkle with cheese; cover pan just until cheese is melted. Cut into wedges to serve. Makes 2 servings.

Per serving: 574 calories, 27 g protein, 19 g carbohydrates, 44 g total fat, 433 mg cholesterol, 1,326 mg sodium

*Subtly seasoned with olive oil and pepper,
thin strands of squash and pasta swirl through the rich
egg sauce of Spaghetti with Zucchini Carbonara
(recipe on page 81).*

Pasta & Grains

Fresh or dry, whatever the shape, pasta cooks in mere minutes. If you choose an equally speedy sauce or topping, you can turn out dinner in a jiffy. Quick pasta dishes can be delightfully elegant, too; our combination of linguine and salmon in creamy mustard sauce is a party-perfect entrée you'll select often. Just as satisfying as pasta are hearty rice and cracked wheat. For sturdy one-pan meals, turn to our risotto, pilaf, paella, and fried rice; all combine a generous helping of grain with plenty of meat and vegetables.

Linguine & Smoked Salmon

Pictured on the cover

Preparation time: 5 to 10 minutes
Cooking time: 10 to 12 minutes

Smoke fresh salmon in just 10 to 12 minutes in your oven, then serve it warm over linguine tossed with a tangy cream sauce. Alongside, offer a cucumber and butter lettuce salad with a lemon vinaigrette dressing.

- 3 tablespoons liquid smoke
- ¾ pound salmon fillet, skinned and cut into ½-inch-wide strips
- 12 ounces dry linguine or spaghetti
- 2 tablespoons white wine vinegar
- ½ cup finely chopped onion
- 1 cup whipping cream
- ¾ cup dry white wine
- 1 tablespoon Dijon mustard
- ¼ cup grated Parmesan cheese
  Parsley sprigs
  Salt and pepper

Pour liquid smoke into a 5- to 6-quart pan. Set a rack in pan. Arrange salmon in a single layer on rack and cover pan tightly. Bake in a 350° oven until fish is opaque but still moist in thickest part; cut to test (10 to 12 minutes). Set aside.

Meanwhile, in a 5- to 6-quart pan, cook linguine in 3 quarts boiling water just until *al dente* (about 10 minutes); or cook according to package directions.

While pasta is cooking, combine vinegar and onion in a wide frying pan. Boil over high heat until vinegar has evaporated (about 2 minutes). Add cream, wine, and mustard. Boil, stirring often, until sauce is reduced to 1¾ cups. Drain linguine and add to cream mixture; lift and stir with 2 forks until coated.

Arrange linguine on 4 warm dinner plates; sprinkle each serving with 1 tablespoon of the cheese. Arrange salmon over linguine. Garnish with parsley; season to taste with salt and pepper. Makes 4 servings.

Per serving: 647 calories, 33 g protein, 10 g carbohydrates, 27 g total fat, 117 mg cholesterol, 273 mg sodium

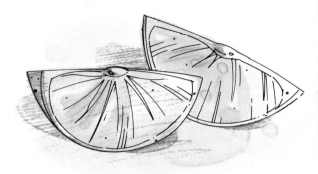

Lemon Scallops with Fusilli

Preparation time: About 10 minutes
Cooking time: About 10 minutes

Gently cook tiny scallops in a light, buttery wine sauce; then catch the sauce's good flavor in the twists and turns of spiral-shaped fusilli (also called rotelle). Complement the creamy-white scallops and golden pasta with bright green, tender-crisp broccoli spears.

- 8 ounces fusilli, rotelle, or other medium-size dry pasta shapes
- ¼ cup dry white wine
- ¼ teaspoon grated lemon peel
- 2 tablespoons lemon juice
- 2 green onions (including tops), thinly sliced
- 2 tablespoons drained capers
- 1 teaspoon dry rosemary
- ½ teaspoon dry basil
- 2 cloves garlic, minced or pressed
- ½ pound bay scallops, rinsed and patted dry
- ¼ cup butter or margarine
  Chopped parsley

In a 5- to 6-quart pan, cook fusilli in 3 quarts boiling water just until *al dente* (8 to 10 minutes); or cook according to package directions.

Meanwhile, in a wide frying pan, combine wine, lemon peel, lemon juice, onions, capers, rosemary, basil, and garlic. Boil over high heat, stirring often, until liquid is reduced by half. Add scallops. Cook, stirring, just until coated with lemon mixture and opaque in center; cut to test (2 to 3 minutes). Remove pan from heat, add butter all at once, and stir until smoothly blended into sauce.

Drain pasta and add to sauce. Lift and stir with 2 forks until coated. Sprinkle with parsley. Makes 3 servings.

Per serving: 493 calories, 23 g protein, 61 g carbohydrates, 17 g total fat, 66 mg cholesterol, 434 mg sodium

Chicken Pasta Italiano

Preparation time: About 15 minutes
Cooking time: About 25 minutes

Choose the reddest, ripest tomatoes for this zesty, fresh-tasting dinner dish. The colorful sauce is laden with strips of chicken, crisp bacon bits, and plenty of garlic.

- ¼ **pound sliced bacon, chopped**
- 4 **cloves garlic, minced or pressed**
- ¾ **pound boneless, skinless chicken breast, cut into ¼-inch-wide strips**
- 4 **medium-size tomatoes, seeded and chopped**
- ½ **cup dry sherry or regular-strength chicken broth**
- 1 **tablespoon Italian herb seasoning or ¾ teaspoon *each* dry basil, dry oregano, dry thyme, and dry marjoram**
- ⅛ **teaspoon ground red pepper (cayenne)**
- 6 **ounces dry spaghetti**
- ½ **cup grated Parmesan cheese**

In a wide frying pan, cook bacon over medium heat, stirring often, until crisp. Lift out, drain, and set aside. Discard all but 2 tablespoons of the drippings.

Add garlic and chicken to drippings in pan. Cook over high heat, stirring, until meat is lightly browned (about 3 minutes). Remove chicken from pan and set aside.

Add tomatoes, sherry, herb seasoning, and red pepper to pan; boil over high heat until mixture is thickened (7 to 10 minutes).

Meanwhile, in a 4- to 5-quart pan, cook spaghetti in 2 quarts boiling water just until *al dente* (10 to 12 minutes); or cook according to package directions.

Return chicken to tomato mixture; stir until heated through. Drain spaghetti and arrange on a warm platter. Spoon chicken mixture over pasta and sprinkle with bacon. Offer cheese to add to taste. Makes 3 servings.

Per serving: 581 calories, 44 g protein, 57 g carbohydrates, 19 g total fat, 91 mg cholesterol, 572 mg sodium

Start Pasta Water First

When you're cooking pasta, your first step should be to heat the water—it takes time for a large quantity of water to boil. If the water comes to a rolling boil before you need to cook your pasta, reduce the heat to keep it at a simmer. Just before you want to cook, increase the heat again; the water will return to a boil fairly rapidly.

Spaghetti with Zucchini Carbonara

Pictured on page 78

Preparation time: About 10 minutes
Cooking time: About 30 minutes

In this unusual vegetarian version of an Italian pasta classic, slivered zucchini stands in for the traditional bacon. The result is a light, meatless—yet protein-rich—meal of superb flavor. Offer Pear Fans with Orange Syrup (page 176) for dessert.

- 12 **ounces dry spaghetti, linguine, or other pasta strands**
- 5 **tablespoons olive oil or salad oil**
- 1 **large onion, chopped**
- 1 **pound zucchini, cut into long, thin strips**
- 4 **eggs, lightly beaten**
- 1 **cup (about 5 oz.) shredded or grated Parmesan cheese**
  Coarsely ground pepper

In a 5- to 6-quart pan, cook spaghetti in 3 quarts boiling water just until *al dente* (10 to 12 minutes); or cook according to package directions. Drain; keep warm.

Heat oil in a wide 3- to 4-quart pan over medium-high heat. Add onion and cook, stirring often, until soft (about 10 minutes). Add zucchini and continue to cook, stirring often, until zucchini is tender to bite (about 8 more minutes).

Add spaghetti and eggs to vegetable mixture. Reduce heat to low and toss until eggs cling to pasta. Add cheese and season to taste with pepper; toss again, then serve. Makes 4 servings.

Per serving: 730 calories, 34 g protein, 72 g carbohydrates, 34 g total fat, 240 mg cholesterol, 733 mg sodium

Linguine with Prosciutto & Olives

Pictured on page 190

Preparation time: About 10 minutes
Cooking time: About 10 minutes

An assertive sauce of prosciutto, onions, and olives complements tender linguine. To complete the meal, offer vinaigrette-dressed green salad.

- 8 ounces dry linguine, spaghetti, or other pasta strands
- 2 ounces thinly sliced prosciutto, cut into ¼-inch-wide strips
- ¼ cup olive oil
- ½ cup thinly sliced green onions (including tops)
- 1 jar (3 oz.) pimento-stuffed green olives, drained
- 1 cup cherry tomatoes, halved
  Grated Parmesan cheese (optional)

In a 5- to 6-quart pan, cook pasta in 3 quarts boiling water just until *al dente* (about 10 minutes); or cook according to package directions. Drain and pour into a warm bowl.

While pasta is cooking, combine prosciutto and oil in a wide frying pan. Cook over medium-high heat, stirring, until prosciutto is lightly browned (about 3 minutes). Add onions and cook, stirring, until soft (about 2 minutes). Add olives and tomatoes and continue to cook, shaking pan often, until olives are hot (about 2 more minutes). Pour prosciutto mixture over pasta and toss well. Transfer to a warm serving bowl. Offer cheese to add to taste, if desired. Makes 3 servings.

Per serving: 516 calories, 16 g protein, 8 g carbohydrates, 25 g total fat, 11 mg cholesterol, 974 mg sodium

Mushroom Risotto with Italian Sausage Sauce

Pictured on facing page

Preparation time: 15 to 20 minutes
Cooking time: 25 to 30 minutes

Moist, creamy risotto is a pleasant change of pace from pasta. This one's laced with mushrooms and crowned with a meaty tomato sauce.

- 2 tablespoons butter or margarine
- 2 tablespoons olive oil
- 1 small onion, finely chopped
- ½ pound small mushrooms, cut into quarters
- 1 small clove garlic, minced or pressed
- ⅛ teaspoon ground white pepper
- 1 cup imported Italian rice or short-grain rice
- 2¾ cups regular-strength chicken broth
- ¼ cup dry white wine
  Italian Sausage Sauce (recipe follows)
- ½ cup whipping cream
- ½ cup grated Asiago or Parmesan cheese

Melt butter in oil in a heavy 2-quart pan over medium heat. Add onion and mushrooms; cook, stirring often, until onion is soft but not browned and liquid has evaporated. Stir in garlic, white pepper, and rice. Cook, stirring, until rice looks opaque (about 2 minutes). Stir in broth and wine; bring to a boil. Then adjust heat so mixture boils gently and cook, uncovered, stirring occasionally, for 15 minutes. Meanwhile, prepare Italian Sausage Sauce.

Add cream to rice mixture. Continue to cook until rice is just tender to bite and almost all liquid has been absorbed (about 5 more minutes; rice should still be *al dente* without tasting starchy). Stir in ¼ cup of the cheese. Spoon rice into a warm serving bowl and top with sauce. Offer remaining ¼ cup cheese to add to taste. Makes 4 servings.

Italian Sausage Sauce. Remove casings from ½ to ¾ pound **mild or hot Italian sausages;** crumble meat into a wide frying pan. Add 1 small **onion,** thinly sliced. Cook over medium-high heat, stirring, until sausage is browned. Spoon off and discard most of the drippings. To pan, add 2 medium-size **pear-shaped tomatoes,** seeded and chopped; ½ teaspoon **dry basil;** ⅛ teaspoon **salt;** 1 tablespoon **tomato paste;** and 1 cup **dry white wine.** Bring to a boil; reduce heat and boil gently, stirring often, until thickened (about 10 minutes). Keep warm.

Per serving: 722 calories, 22 g protein, 49 g carbohydrates, 49 g total fat, 111 mg cholesterol, 1,566 mg sodium

*Occasionally, Italians enjoy a dish of creamy rice
instead of pasta—and once you've tasted parsley-
sprinkled Mushroom Risotto with Italian Sausage Sauce
(recipe on facing page) you'll understand why.*

Quick Paella

Preparation time: About 10 minutes
Cooking time: About 40 minutes

Like many traditional one-pot dinners, Spanish paella—a marvelous mix of chicken, shellfish, sausage, and boldly seasoned rice—can take hours to cook. We've reduced the time by using deli-roasted chicken, heat-and-serve sausages, and canned clams. Accompany with crisp cabbage slaw and lots of crusty bread.

About ½ pound Polish sausages, cut into ¼-inch-thick slices

1 clove garlic, minced or pressed

1 small yellow onion, chopped

1 cup long-grain white rice

1 jar (4 oz.) sliced pimentos, drained

1 can (about 6½ oz.) chopped or minced clams, drained (reserve liquid)

1 can (14½ oz.) regular-strength chicken broth

1 cooked (rotisseried or barbecued) chicken (2 to 2½ lbs.), cut into serving-size pieces

1 or 2 green onions (including tops), thinly sliced

In a wide frying pan, cook sausages briefly over medium-high heat to release some of the fat; add garlic, yellow onion, and rice. Cook, stirring often, until onion is soft (about 10 minutes). Mix in pimentos, liquid from clams, and broth. Bring to a boil; reduce heat to low, cover, and simmer until rice is barely tender to bite (about 15 minutes).

Stir clams into rice mixture; then arrange the chicken pieces over rice. Cover and continue to cook until chicken is heated through (10 to 15 more minutes).

Spread rice mixture on a warm platter and arrange chicken on top; sprinkle with green onions. Makes 4 servings.

Per serving: 734 calories, 56 g protein, 42 g carbohydrates, 36 g total fat, 173 mg cholesterol, 1,090 mg sodium

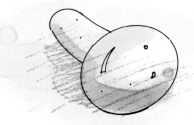

Fried Rice with Ham & Peanuts

Preparation time: About 15 minutes
Cooking time: 12 to 15 minutes

If you have a few cups of leftover meat and rice on hand, you have the makings for a savory, super-fast dinner dish. Serve this Chinese-style entrée with crisp snow peas, cups of hot tea, and purchased almond or fortune cookies.

2 cups cold cooked long-grain white rice

2 eggs

¼ cup salad oil

1 small onion, chopped

1 clove garlic, minced or pressed

1 medium-size green bell pepper, seeded and diced

¼ pound mushrooms, diced

About 1½ cups diced cooked ham, chicken, turkey, or pork

½ cup salted roasted peanuts

2 tablespoons soy sauce

Rub cooked rice with wet hands so all grains are separated; set aside. In a small bowl, lightly beat eggs. Heat 1 tablespoon of the oil in a wok or wide frying pan over medium heat. Add eggs and cook, stirring occasionally, until soft curds form; remove from pan and set aside.

Increase heat to medium-high; add 1 more tablespoon oil to pan. Add onion and garlic and cook, stirring, until onion is soft; then add bell pepper, mushrooms, ham, and peanuts. Cook, stirring, until heated through (about 2 minutes). Remove from pan and set aside.

Heat remaining 2 tablespoons oil in pan. Add rice and cook, stirring, until heated through (about 2 minutes); stir in ham mixture and soy sauce. Add eggs; stir mixture gently until eggs are in small pieces. Makes 4 servings.

Per serving: 475 calories, 24 g protein, 28 g carbohydrates, 31 g total fat, 140 mg cholesterol, 1,559 mg sodium

Wild Rice & Mushroom Pilaf with Grilled Sausages

Preparation time: About 10 minutes
Cooking time: About 40 minutes

With its hearty, toasted flavor and crunchy texture, wild rice pilaf deliciously complements grilled Italian sausages. Complete the menu with butter-steamed baby carrots.

⅔ cup wild rice
1 can (14½ oz.) regular-strength beef or chicken broth
¼ cup water
4 mild or hot Italian sausages (¾ to 1 lb. *total*)
3 tablespoons butter or margarine
1 medium-size onion, chopped
¼ pound mushrooms, sliced
⅛ teaspoon *each* dry thyme and dry marjoram
   Chopped parsley

Place wild rice in a strainer. Rinse with hot running water for about 1 minute; drain well. In a 2-quart pan, combine rice, broth, and water. Bring to a boil over high heat; reduce heat, cover, and simmer until rice is tender to bite and almost all liquid has been absorbed (30 to 40 minutes). Drain off and discard any excess liquid.

Meanwhile, in a wide nonstick frying pan, cook sausages over medium heat, turning often, until skins are browned and juices run clear when sausages are pierced (15 to 20 minutes).

While sausages are cooking, melt butter in a wide frying pan over medium heat; add onion and mushrooms and cook, stirring occasionally, until onion is soft and mushrooms are lightly browned (about 10 minutes).

Stir thyme and marjoram into mushroom mixture. Add rice and stir until heated through. Serve pilaf and sausages sprinkled with parsley. Makes 4 servings.

Per serving: 432 calories, 20 g protein, 24 g carbohydrates, 28 g total fat, 80 mg cholesterol, 1,139 mg sodium

Easy Side Dishes

Plain cooked cracked wheat, rice, couscous, and pasta make great side dishes. Enhance them with a pat of butter, a sprinkling of chopped parsley or toasted almonds, or some sautéed sliced mushrooms; pasta can also be dressed up with a spoonful of pesto sauce (see page 69), or a little olive oil and garlic. (You'll find more ideas for grain side dishes on page 173.)

Lamb & Spinach Pilaf

Preparation time: About 15 minutes
Cooking time: 15 to 20 minutes

Bulgur simmered in beef broth makes a tasty base for a lightly spiced blend of ground lamb, onions, and spinach. Alongside, you might serve sliced tomatoes and cucumbers in minted yogurt dressing.

2¼ cups regular-strength beef broth
1 cup cracked wheat (bulgur)
¾ pound spinach
½ teaspoon salt
1 pound lean ground lamb
1 large onion, chopped
½ teaspoon ground cinnamon
⅓ cup water
½ cup raisins
   Pepper

In a 2-quart pan, bring broth to a boil over high heat. Add wheat, then cover pan. When broth returns to a full rolling boil, reduce heat and simmer until wheat is tender to bite and liquid has been absorbed (15 to 20 minutes). Meanwhile, remove and discard spinach stems; rinse leaves, pat dry, and cut into 1-inch-wide strips. Set aside.

Sprinkle salt into a wide frying pan over medium heat. Crumble lamb into pan; cook, stirring, until meat begins to brown. Discard all but 2 tablespoons of the drippings. Add onion, cinnamon, water, and raisins to pan; cover and simmer for 5 minutes. Stir spinach into meat mixture; cover and cook just until spinach is wilted (1 to 2 minutes). Remove from heat and season to taste with pepper.

Mound hot cracked wheat on a platter and top with meat mixture. Makes 4 to 6 servings.

Per serving: 402 calories, 24 g protein, 37 g carbohydrates, 19 g total fat, 71 mg cholesterol, 693 mg sodium

*Vivid tomatoes, hot jalapeño chile, and zesty
cilantro lend an unmistakably Latin accent to full-
flavored fish in Swordfish Steaks with Salsa
(recipe on page 88).*

Fish & Shellfish

Seafood might have been created just for quick meals: it requires very little preparation, and it cooks in next to no time. In fact, you'll need to guard against overcooking; serve fish and shellfish as soon as they're just opaque in the center, but still moist. Whether you favor thick swordfish steaks, whole trout, or delicate scallops, you'll find recipes to suit you in this chapter. Whatever you choose, remember that freshest is best: buy seafood only from reputable markets, and serve as soon as possible after purchase.

Buying Fresh Fish

Always buy the freshest fish you can find. The flesh of whole fish should spring back when gently pressed, and the eyes should be clear and full, not sunken. Fillets and steaks should look cleanly cut and feel firm and moist. Avoid any fish with a strong, unpleasant odor; truly fresh seafood has a mild and delicate aroma.

Uncooked fish doesn't keep well. To avoid waste, buy only as much as you need, and cook it as soon as possible after purchase—preferably on the same day, within 2 days at the most. To store fish, discard the market wrapping; rinse the fish under cool running water, place it in a container, and cover with wet paper towels. Store in the coldest part of your refrigerator.

Swordfish Steaks with Salsa

Pictured on page 86

Preparation time: About 15 minutes
Cooking time: 10 to 12 minutes

A vivid topping of tomatoes, chile, and cilantro lends zest to pan-fried swordfish. Complete the fiesta with black beans and sliced avocados.

- 4 swordfish steaks (*each about 1 inch thick*)
- 2 tablespoons salad oil
- 2 cloves garlic, minced or pressed
- 1 fresh jalapeño or other small hot chile, stemmed, seeded, and minced
- 5 firm-ripe pear-shaped tomatoes, seeded and diced
- ½ cup packed fresh cilantro (coriander) leaves, chopped

Rinse fish and pat dry. Heat oil in a wide frying pan over medium-high heat. Add fish and cook, turning once, until well browned on outside and just opaque but still moist in thickest part; cut to test (8 to 10 minutes). Transfer to a warm platter; keep warm.

Add garlic and chile to pan and cook, stirring, until fragrant (about 30 seconds). Add tomatoes and cilantro and cook, stirring, until hot (about 2 minutes). Spoon over fish. Makes 4 servings.

Per serving: 349 calories, 46 g protein, 3 g carbohydrates, 16 g total fat, 89 mg cholesterol, 209 mg sodium

Grilled Fish Steaks

Pictured on page 163

Preparation time: About 5 minutes
Grilling time: 8 to 10 minutes

For a speedy yet stylish entrée, grill meaty fish steaks, then dress them up with a mild fresh dill butter or a nippier blend featuring chili powder and cilantro.

Dill Butter (recipe follows) or Cilantro-Chili Butter (page 149)
- 4 salmon, tuna, swordfish, halibut, or sturgeon steaks (*each about 1 inch thick*)
  Olive oil or salad oil
  Salt and pepper

Prepare flavored butter of your choice. Set aside.

Rinse fish, pat dry, and rub with oil. Place on a lightly greased grill 4 to 6 inches above a solid bed of hot coals. Cook, turning once or twice, until fish is just opaque (or tuna is slightly pink) but still moist in thickest part; cut to test (8 to 10 minutes).

Season fish to taste with salt and pepper; offer flavored butter to spoon over individual portions. Makes 4 servings.

Dill Butter. In a small bowl, mix ¼ cup **butter** or margarine (at room temperature) and ¼ cup chopped **fresh dill** (or 2 tablespoons dry dill weed) until well blended. Makes about ¼ cup.

Per serving of fish: 272 calories, 34 g protein, 0 g carbohydrates, 14 g total fat, 94 mg cholesterol, 75 mg sodium

Per tablespoon of Dill Butter: 106 calories, 0.4 g protein, 0.9 g carbohydrates, 12 g total fat, 31 mg cholesterol, 120 mg sodium

Broiled Swordfish with Tomato-Olive Confetti

Pictured on page 187

Preparation time: About 15 minutes
Broiling time: About 10 minutes

A colorful relish made from fresh tomatoes and sliced green olives crowns these swordfish steaks; to give the flavors time to blend, prepare the "confetti" before you slip the fish into the broiler. You might serve buttered tiny red potatoes alongside.

    Tomato-Olive Confetti (recipe follows)
4 **swordfish steaks** (*each* about 1 inch thick)
1 **tablespoon olive oil or salad oil**
3 **cups lightly packed watercress sprigs, rinsed and crisped**
    Lime wedges (optional)

Prepare Tomato-Olive Confetti and set aside.

    Rinse fish, pat dry, and place on oiled rack of a 12- by 14-inch broiler pan; brush fish with oil. Broil about 5 inches below heat for 5 minutes. Turn fish over, brush with oil, and continue to broil until fish is just opaque but still moist in thickest part; cut to test (about 5 more minutes).

    Arrange watercress on 4 dinner plates and place fish on top. Spoon Tomato-Olive Confetti over fish; garnish with lime wedges, if desired. Makes 4 servings.

Tomato-Olive Confetti. Stir together 1 medium-size **tomato,** seeded and finely chopped; ½ cup sliced **pimento-stuffed green olives;** 2 tablespoons drained **capers;** 3 tablespoons *each* sliced **green onions** (including tops) and **lime juice;** and 3 tablespoons **olive oil** or salad oil.

Per serving: 358 calories, 35 g protein, 3 g carbohydrates, 23 g total fat, 66 mg cholesterol, 688 mg sodium

Stuffed Sole Princess

Preparation time: About 20 minutes
Cooking time: 25 to 30 minutes

Here's a quick entrée that's fancy enough for company. You fill thin sole fillets with tiny shrimp, bake them in wine and lemon juice, and then use the pan juices to make a creamy sauce. Serve a green vegetable with the fish; asparagus and steamed broccoli are both good choices.

4 **large sole fillets (about 1½ lbs. *total*)**
¼ **pound small cooked shrimp**
    Salt, pepper, and paprika
1 **tablespoon lemon juice**
¼ **cup dry white wine**
2 **tablespoons sliced green onion (including top)**
1 **clove garlic, minced or pressed**
2 **tablespoons butter or margarine**
1 **tablespoon all-purpose flour**

Rinse fish, pat dry, and place on a work surface. Place a fourth of the shrimp across one end of each fillet; roll each fillet into a cylinder and secure with a wooden pick. Place rolled fillets, seam sides down, in a greased shallow baking dish. Sprinkle with salt, pepper, and paprika.

    In a small bowl, stir together lemon juice, wine, onion, and garlic; pour over fish. Cover and bake in a 350° oven until fish is just opaque but still moist in thickest part; cut to test (20 to 25 minutes). With a slotted spoon, transfer rolled fillets to a warm serving plate; reserve liquid from baking dish. Remove and discard picks from fish; cover fish and keep warm.

    Melt butter in a small pan over medium heat. Stir in flour and cook, stirring, until bubbly. Remove pan from heat and gradually stir in liquid from baking dish. Return to heat and cook, stirring, until thickened. Pour sauce over rolled fillets. Makes 4 servings.

Per serving: 254 calories, 38 g protein, 2 g carbohydrates, 8 g total fat, 153 mg cholesterol, 262 mg sodium

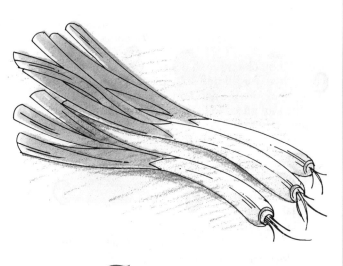

Sand Dabs with Basil-Chili Butter

Preparation time: About 10 minutes
Broiling time: About 4 minutes

Junior members of the sole family, sand dabs are just the right size for individual servings. Here, they're cooked whole, then topped with spoonfuls of spicy chili butter at the table. Choose mild accompaniments, such as cornbread and sautéed sweet peppers.

- ¼ **cup butter or margarine, at room temperature**
- 1 **teaspoon chili powder**
- 1 **tablespoon minced fresh basil or 1 teaspoon dry basil**
- 4 **whole sand dabs (about ½ lb.** *each***), cleaned and trimmed; or 1 pound sole fillets**
   All-purpose flour
- 2 **tablespoons salad oil**

In a small bowl, mix butter, chili powder, and basil until well blended. Set aside.

Rinse fish and pat dry. Dredge in flour; shake off excess. Heat oil in a large rimmed baking pan about 4 inches below broiler. When oil is hot, add fish, carefully turning to coat. Broil until just opaque but still moist in thickest part; cut to test (about 4 minutes).

Transfer fish to warm plates; top each portion with a dollop of the butter mixture. Makes 4 servings.

Per serving: 268 calories, 22 g protein, 4 g carbohydrates, 18 g total fat, 86 mg cholesterol, 216 mg sodium

Sole with Pistachio Butter Sauce

Pictured on facing page

Preparation time: About 10 minutes
Cooking time: 10 to 15 minutes

Chopped pistachios swirl through the butter-vermouth sauce that cloaks these thin sole fillets. Toss a green salad to serve alongside—and you have a memorable meal.

- 1½ **pounds thin sole fillets**
   All-purpose flour
   About ⅓ cup butter or margarine
   About 2 tablespoons salad oil
- ¼ **cup thinly sliced green onions (including tops)**
- ½ **cup** *each* **dry vermouth and regular-strength chicken broth**
- ⅓ **cup salted or unsalted shelled roasted pistachios, coarsely chopped (about ⅔ cup nuts in the shell)**
   Lemon wedges
   Italian parsley sprigs

Rinse fish and pat dry; dust with flour and shake off excess. Melt 1 tablespoon of the butter in 1 tablespoon of the oil in a wide frying pan over medium-high heat. Add fish, a portion at a time (do not crowd pan). Cook, turning once, until fish is just opaque but still moist in thickest part; cut to test (2 to 4 minutes). As fish is cooked, transfer to a warm platter and keep warm; add more butter and oil to pan as needed.

To pan, add onions, vermouth, and broth; boil over high heat until reduced by half. Reduce heat to low and add ¼ cup butter all at once; stir constantly until butter is completely blended into sauce. Stir in pistachios; then spoon sauce over fish. Garnish with lemon wedges and parsley sprigs. Makes 4 servings.

Per serving: 447 calories, 35 g protein, 10 g carbohydrates, 30 g total fat, 123 mg cholesterol, 501 mg sodium

It's hard to believe that it takes only about 25 minutes to prepare and cook Sole with Pistachio Butter Sauce (recipe on facing page). Accompany it with a tossed salad and hot, crusty rolls.

Broiled Fish Dijon

Preparation time: About 5 minutes
Broiling time: 8 to 10 minutes

Piquant seasonings enliven firm-fleshed fish fillets in this quick and easy entrée. Serve it either hot or cold, with stir-fried green and yellow summer squash.

  4 **firm-textured white-fleshed fish fillets, such as sea bass or rockfish (6 to 8 oz. *each*), each ¾ to 1 inch thick**
  4 **teaspoons lemon juice**
  3 **tablespoons Dijon mustard**
  1 **clove garlic, minced or pressed**
     Paprika
  2 **tablespoons drained capers**

Rinse fish, pat dry, and arrange in a single layer in a rimmed 10- by 15-inch baking pan or broiler pan. Drizzle with lemon juice.

In a small bowl, stir together mustard and garlic; spread over tops of fillets. Broil 4 to 6 inches below heat until fish is just opaque but still moist in thickest part; cut to test (8 to 10 minutes; if necessary, rotate pan to cook fish evenly).

Sprinkle fish with paprika and capers. Serve hot. Or, to serve cold, let cool; then cover and refrigerate for at least 30 minutes or up to 2 hours. Makes 4 servings.

Per serving: 208 calories, 37 g protein, 2 g carbohydrates, 5 g total fat, 81 mg cholesterol, 583 mg sodium

Sea Bass & Shrimp Provencal

Preparation time: About 15 minutes
Cooking time: About 20 minutes

Tender shrimp and white-fleshed sea bass baked in a garlicky tomato-mushroom sauce make an appetizing, flavorful dinner. Accompany with steamed broccoli and thick slices of toast.

  3 **medium-size tomatoes, peeled**
  3 **tablespoons butter or margarine**
  ¼ **pound mushrooms, thinly sliced**
  2 **cloves garlic, minced or pressed**
     Salt and pepper
  2 **pounds sea bass steaks (*each* about 1 inch thick)**
  ½ **pound medium-size raw shrimp (30 to 32 per lb.), shelled and deveined**
     Lemon slices (optional)
     Parsley sprigs (optional)

Seed and coarsely chop 2 of the tomatoes. Cut remaining tomato into 6 wedges; set aside.

Melt butter in a medium-size frying pan over medium-high heat. Add mushrooms and cook, stirring, until limp (about 5 minutes). Stir in chopped tomatoes and garlic; cook, stirring, until hot. Season mixture to taste with salt and pepper; set aside.

Rinse fish, pat dry, and place in a single layer in a shallow baking pan; top with shrimp. Spoon tomato mixture over seafood.

Bake in a 400° oven until shrimp are just opaque in center and fish is just opaque but still moist in thickest part; cut to test (about 15 minutes). Transfer to a warm platter and surround with tomato wedges; garnish with lemon slices and parsley, if desired. Makes 4 to 6 servings.

Per serving: 298 calories, 42 g protein, 5 g carbohydrates, 11 g total fat, 150 mg cholesterol, 256 mg sodium

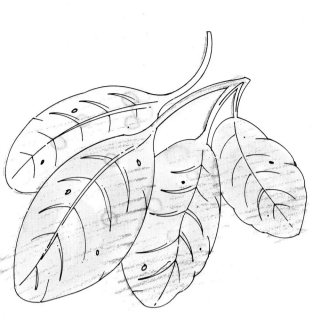

Baked Fish with Tapenade & Tomatoes

Preparation time: About 10 minutes
Baking time: 10 to 15 minutes

To wake up mild fish fillets, top them with pungent tapenade, an olive-garlic paste that's popular in the south of France. Sliced tomatoes bake along with the fish, adding vibrant color and keeping the cooked fillets moist.

- 4 **skinless white-fleshed fish fillets, such as sea bass or cod (about 6 oz. *each*), *each* ½ to ¾ inch thick**
- 5 **tablespoons olive oil or salad oil**
- 2 **medium-size tomatoes, cut into ½-inch-thick slices**
- 1 **can (6 oz.) pitted ripe olives, drained**
- 1 **clove garlic**

Rinse fish, pat dry, and place in a single layer in a shallow baking pan. Brush with 1 tablespoon of the oil; top evenly with tomatoes. Bake in a 400° oven until fish is just opaque but still moist in thickest part; cut to test (10 to 15 minutes).

Meanwhile, in a food processor or blender, whirl olives and garlic until finely minced. Add remaining ¼ cup oil in a thin, steady stream, whirling until mixture forms a paste.

To serve, top fish evenly with olive mixture. Makes 4 servings.

Per serving: 398 calories, 36 g protein, 6 g carbohydrates, 25 g total fat, 54 mg cholesterol, 468 mg sodium

Snapper Florentine

Preparation time: About 15 minutes
Cooking time: 7 to 10 minutes

Snapper fillets get rich quick when you top them with a tart, creamy blend of mayonnaise and sour cream before baking. Serve over briefly cooked fresh spinach.

- ¾ **cup sour cream**
- ⅓ **cup mayonnaise**
- 2 **tablespoons *each* all-purpose flour and lemon juice**
- ¼ **teaspoon dry dill weed**
- 1 **pound Pacific or red snapper fillets (*each* about ½ inch thick)**
  Salt and pepper
- 1½ **to 2 pounds spinach, stems removed, leaves rinsed**
  Paprika

In a bowl, whisk sour cream, mayonnaise, flour, lemon juice, and dill weed until smoothly blended; set aside.

Rinse fish, pat dry, and arrange in a single layer in a 9- by 13-inch baking dish. Season to taste with salt and pepper, then spread evenly with sour cream mixture. Bake in a 400° oven until fish is just opaque but still moist in thickest part; cut to test (7 to 10 minutes).

Meanwhile, place spinach (with water that clings to leaves) in a wide frying pan. Cover and cook over medium-high heat, stirring occasionally, until wilted and bright green in color (2 to 4 minutes); drain well. Arrange spinach on a warm platter; top with fish. Spoon any sauce remaining in baking dish over fish; sprinkle with paprika. Makes 4 servings.

Per serving: 379 calories, 29 g protein, 10 g carbohydrates, 25 g total fat, 72 mg cholesterol, 298 mg sodium

*Hot from a sizzling range-top grill, Salmon Steaks with
Spinach (recipe on facing page) make an irresistible
entrée. Accompany the fish with buttered red potatoes
and marinated cucumbers.*

almon Steaks with Spinach

Pictured on facing page

Preparation time: About 15 minutes
Cooking time: About 25 minutes

Thick, dill-seasoned salmon steaks rest on a bed of spinach in this attractive main course. To complete an appealing party menu, serve with marinated cucumber salad, buttered red potatoes, and chilled white wine.

- ¼ cup butter or margarine
- 1 large onion, chopped
- 1 clove garlic, minced or pressed
- 1½ to 2 pounds spinach, stems removed, leaves rinsed
  Salt and pepper
- 4 salmon steaks (*each* about 1 inch thick)
- 1 teaspoon dry dill weed
  Lemon wedges

Melt 3 tablespoons of the butter in a 5- to 6-quart pan over medium heat. Add onion and garlic and cook, stirring occasionally, until onion is very soft (about 15 minutes). Meanwhile, cut spinach leaves into 1-inch-wide strips.

Stir spinach (with water that clings to leaves) into onion mixture. Cover pan, increase heat to medium-high, and cook until spinach is wilted and bright green in color (2 to 4 minutes). Uncover and cook until liquid has evaporated, stirring occasionally. Remove from heat; season to taste with salt and pepper. Transfer to a warm rimmed platter and keep warm.

While spinach is cooking, rinse salmon and pat dry; then place in a lightly greased baking pan. Broil 4 inches below heat for 5 minutes. Turn salmon over; sprinkle with salt, pepper, and dill weed, then dot with remaining 1 tablespoon butter. Continue to broil until fish is just opaque but still moist in thickest part; cut to test (about 5 more minutes). *To grill salmon:* Place steaks on a lightly greased range-top grill; cook for time specified in broiling instructions above, turning and seasoning with salt, pepper, dill, and butter after 5 minutes.

To serve, place salmon atop spinach and garnish with lemon wedges. Makes 4 servings.

Per serving: 430 calories, 44 g protein, 8 g carbohydrates, 25 g total fat, 140 mg cholesterol, 319 mg sodium

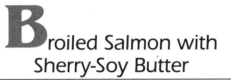

Testing Fish for Doneness

Recognizing when fish is done is essential to cooking it well—if overcooked, it rapidly loses flavor and moisture. Most recipes in this book tell you to cook fish until it's "just opaque but still moist in thickest part." To test, cut to the center of the thickest portion of the whole fish, steak, or fillet—thinner parts may appear to be done while thicker portions are still cool and uncooked inside. As a rule of thumb, allow 8 to 10 minutes of cooking time for each inch of thickness for fish cooked by any method other than microwaving.

Broiled Salmon with Sherry-Soy Butter

Preparation time: About 10 minutes
Cooking time: 9 to 13 minutes

Simple seasonings of soy, sherry, and sesame nicely complement the richness of salmon. You can use fillets, steaks, or baby salmon; choose whatever is available or looks best at the market.

- 1 tablespoon sesame seeds
- 2 tablespoons butter or margarine
- 2 tablespoons *each* thinly sliced green onion (including top) and dry sherry
- 1 tablespoon soy sauce
- 4 boned baby salmon (about ½ lb. *each*), heads removed; or 4 salmon fillets or steaks (about 6 oz. *each*)

Toast sesame seeds in a small frying pan over medium heat until golden (3 to 5 minutes), shaking pan often. Add butter, onion, sherry, and soy sauce; cook, stirring, until butter is melted. Remove from heat.

Rinse fish and pat dry. Place on greased rack of a large broiler pan (spread baby salmon open and place skin sides down). Brush with butter mixture. Broil about 4 inches below heat until just opaque but still moist in thickest part; cut to test (6 to 8 minutes). Serve with any remaining butter mixture. Makes 4 servings.

Per serving: 320 calories, 34 g protein, 2 g carbohydrates, 18 g total fat, 109 mg cholesterol, 392 mg sodium

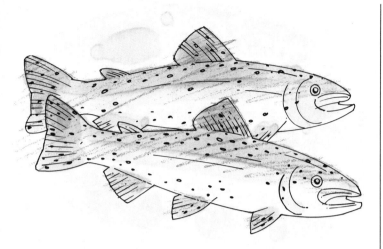

Trout with Carrot Sambal

Preparation time: 15 to 20 minutes
Broiling time: 8 to 10 minutes

Accent buttery broiled trout with a tart, chile-bold carrot and coconut relish—our adaptation of an Asian *sambal*. To balance the spicy flavors, serve sliced tomatoes and brown rice with the fish.

   Carrot Sambal (recipe follows)
4 **trout (about ½ lb.** *each)*
   Salt
2 **tablespoons butter or margarine, melted**
   Lime wedges

Prepare Carrot Sambal; set aside.

If desired, cut off and discard trout heads. Rinse trout and pat dry. Sprinkle lightly with salt, brush with butter, and place on rack of a 12- by 14-inch broiler pan. Broil about 4 inches below heat, turning once, until fish is just opaque but still moist in thickest part; cut to test (8 to 10 minutes). Serve with Carrot Sambal; offer lime wedges to squeeze over fish. Makes 4 servings.

Carrot Sambal. Place ⅓ cup **unsweetened flaked coconut** in a small bowl; add **hot water** to cover. Let stand until coconut is soft (about 10 minutes); drain well. Add 1 cup shredded **carrots;** 2 to 3 teaspoons minced **fresh hot chile;** 2 teaspoons minced **fresh ginger;** ½ teaspoon *each* **ground coriander** and crushed **cumin seeds;** and ¼ to ⅓ cup **lime juice.** Season to taste with **salt.**

Per serving: 278 calories, 24 g protein, 9 g carbohydrates, 17 g total fat, 80 mg cholesterol, 132 mg sodium

Broiled Trout Dijonnaise

Follow directions for **Trout with Carrot Sambal,** but omit Carrot Sambal.

To melted butter, add 1 tablespoon *each* **dry white wine** and **Dijon mustard** and ¼ teaspoon **dry tarragon.** Brush fish inside and out with about half the mixture. Broil as directed, brushing with remaining butter mixture after turning. Omit lime wedges; serve with **lemon wedges.** Makes 4 servings.

Per serving: 220 calories, 23 g protein, 0.6 g carbohydrates, 13 g total fat, 80 mg cholesterol, 229 mg sodium

Baby Salmon with Sautéed Leeks

Preparation time: About 20 minutes
Cooking time: About 20 minutes

Thyme-seasoned sautéed leeks make a simple, delicately flavored stuffing for butterflied baby salmon (or trout). Serve with couscous and a crisp white wine.

   About 1½ pounds leeks, roots and most of dark green tops trimmed
¼ **cup butter or margarine**
½ **teaspoon dry thyme**
2 **tablespoons lemon juice**
   Salt and ground white pepper
6 **boned baby salmon or trout (about ½ lb.** *each*),
   heads removed
   Lemon wedges (optional)

Split leeks lengthwise and rinse well; then thinly slice crosswise (you should have about 3 cups).

Melt 2 tablespoons of the butter in a wide frying pan over medium heat. Add leeks and cook, stirring, until soft (8 to 10 minutes). Remove from heat and stir in thyme and lemon juice; season to taste with salt and white pepper.

Rinse fish and pat dry. Spread open and place, skin sides down, in a single layer in a greased baking pan. Spoon leek mixture down center of each fish. Melt remaining 2 tablespoons butter and drizzle over fish. Bake in a 400° oven until just opaque but still moist in thickest part; cut to test (8 to 10 minutes). Garnish with lemon wedges, if desired. Makes 6 servings.

Per serving: 341 calories, 35 g protein, 7 g carbohydrates, 19 g total fat, 114 mg cholesterol, 164 mg sodium

Steamed Trout with Lettuce & Peas

Preparation time: About 15 minutes
Cooking time: About 15 minutes

Silvery whole trout steamed atop a bed of shredded romaine, fresh mint, and tiny green peas make a light, fresh-tasting entrée that's good-looking, too. There's no prettier way to present the catch of the day!

- 3 **tablespoons chopped fresh mint**
- 1 **tablespoon finely shredded lemon peel**
- 1 **clove garlic, minced or pressed**
- 1 **cup frozen tiny peas, thawed**
- 3 **cups shredded romaine lettuce**
  Salt and pepper
- 4 **trout (about ½ lb.** *each***)**
- 8 **to 12 lemon wedges**
- 1 **tablespoon lemon juice**

Mix mint, lemon peel, garlic, peas, and lettuce; season to taste with salt and pepper. Pat mixture gently into a neat mound on an 8- to 10-inch rimmed plate at least ½ inch smaller in diameter than your steamer. Rinse trout and pat dry. Then neatly arrange fish over lettuce, cavity sides down and heads pointing in same direction; lean fish against each other. Lay lemon wedges on top.

Place a steamer rack over about 1 inch boiling water in a steamer or large pan. Carefully place plate on rack. Cover and steam until fish is just opaque but still moist in thickest part; cut to test (about 15 minutes). If necessary, add boiling water to keep at least ½ inch of water in steamer.

Using thick pot holders, lift plate from steamer. Transfer trout to warm individual plates and spoon lettuce mixture alongside. Sprinkle trout with lemon juice. Makes 4 servings.

Per serving: 214 calories, 27 g protein, 11 g carbohydrates, 8 g total fat, 65 mg cholesterol, 127 mg sodium

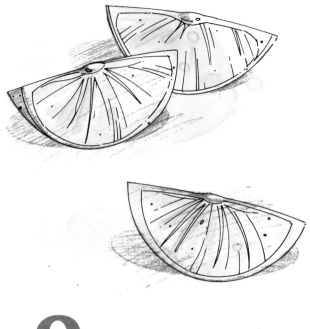

Orange Roughy with Sesame Seeds

Preparation time: About 10 minutes
Baking time: 8 to 10 minutes

Lean, white-fleshed orange roughy is one of the most popular fish available today. Here, the mild fillets are baked in a crunchy sesame seed coating, then served with lemon wedges and soy.

- 1 **egg white**
- ⅓ **cup sesame seeds**
- 1½ **pounds orange roughy fillets** (*each* **about ½ inch thick**)
- 2 **tablespoons salad oil**
  Lemon wedges
  Soy sauce

Beat egg white in a shallow pan until slightly frothy. Place sesame seeds in another shallow pan. Rinse fish fillets and pat dry. Dip each fillet on one side only in egg and drain briefly; then lay egg-moistened side in sesame seeds, coating heavily. Lay fillets, seeded sides up, on wax paper.

Heat a large baking pan in a 400° oven for 5 minutes. Add oil, swirling to coat; then add fillets, seeded sides down, in a single layer. Bake until fish is just opaque but still moist in thickest part; cut to test (8 to 10 minutes). Serve fillets seeded sides up; offer lemon wedges and soy sauce to season fish to taste. Makes 4 servings.

Per serving: 383 calories, 32 g protein, 3 g carbohydrates, 27 g total fat, 40 mg cholesterol, 140 mg sodium

Monkfish Scaloppine with Olives

Preparation time: About 20 minutes
Cooking time: About 15 minutes

Scaloppine is usually made with meat—but delicate-flavored, firm-textured monkfish takes well to this treatment, too. You slice a big fillet, then pound the slices out thin, sauté them briefly, and top with a sauce of sweet peppers and ripe olives.

- 1 large monkfish fillet (1 to 1½ lbs.)
  All-purpose flour
  About 2 tablespoons butter or margarine
  About 2 tablespoons salad oil
- 2 tablespoons olive oil
- 1 small red bell pepper, seeded and diced
- 3 cloves garlic, minced or pressed
- 1 can (6 oz.) pitted ripe olives, drained
- ¼ cup chopped parsley
- ⅔ cup regular-strength chicken broth
- 2 tablespoons lemon juice

Rinse fish and pat dry. If fillet is encased in a tough membrane, cut it off from one side of fillet. Then lay fillet on a board, membrane side down. Starting 3 to 4 inches from tapered end of fillet, cut toward tapered end at about a 45° angle to form a ¼- to ⅜-inch-thick slice. At base of fillet, angle knife to slice flesh free of membrane on bottom. Continue slicing fillet until pieces become too short for large slices. Cut membrane from remaining triangular chunk. Then cut almost through thickest part of chunk; open to flatten.

Place fish slices between sheets of plastic wrap and pound with a flat-surfaced mallet until about ⅛ inch thick. Coat fish with flour; shake off excess. Place fish slices in a single layer on plastic wrap.

Melt 1 tablespoon of the butter in 1 tablespoon of the salad oil in a wide frying pan over medium-high heat. Add fish, a portion at a time (do not crowd pan). Cook, turning once, until fish is just opaque but still moist in center; cut to test (1½ to 2 minutes total). As fish is cooked, transfer to a warm platter and keep warm; add more butter and salad oil to pan as needed.

Scrape browned bits from pan and discard; add olive oil, bell pepper, and garlic to pan. Cook over medium heat, stirring often, until pepper is limp. Add olives, parsley, broth, and lemon juice. Boil over high heat until liquid is reduced by half. Spoon sauce over fish. Makes 4 servings.

Per serving: 356 calories, 22 g protein, 8 g carbohydrates, 26 g total fat, 51 mg cholesterol, 624 mg sodium

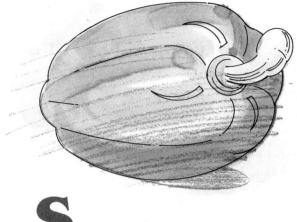

Steamed Clams with Linguisa & Pasta

Pictured on facing page

Preparation time: About 10 minutes
Cooking time: About 25 minutes

Spicy linguisa sausage joins clams steamed in a richly flavored broth dotted with tiny pasta and diced red pepper. For steaming, choose littleneck or Manila clams from the Pacific, littlenecks or cherrystones from the Atlantic.

- ⅓ pound linguisa sausage, cut into ¼-inch-thick slices
- 1 medium-size onion, chopped
- 1 large red bell pepper, seeded and diced
- 3 cups water
- 1½ cups regular-strength chicken broth
- ¾ cup dry white wine
- ¼ cup rice-shaped or other tiny pasta
- ½ teaspoon dry basil
- 32 to 36 clams suitable for steaming, scrubbed
  Minced parsley

In a 5- to 6-quart pan, cook sausage over medium-high heat, stirring, until lightly browned. Add onion and bell pepper; cook, stirring, until onion is soft (about 10 minutes). Add water, broth, wine, pasta, and basil. Bring to a boil; reduce heat, cover, and simmer until pasta is *al dente* (8 to 10 minutes).

Skim and discard fat from broth. Add clams. Cover and bring to a boil; reduce heat and simmer until clams open (5 to 7 minutes). Lift out clams and distribute equally among 4 wide, shallow bowls. Ladle broth over clams. Lightly sprinkle each serving with parsley. Makes 4 servings.

Per serving: 253 calories, 17 g protein, 15 g carbohydrates, 13 g total fat, 52 mg cholesterol, 687 mg sodium

Steamed Clams with Linguisa & Pasta (recipe on facing page) soak up flavors from a savory broth flecked with basil, onion, and red bell pepper. Serve with chunks of crusty sourdough bread.

Seafood Sauces

Simply cooked fish—whether grilled, baked, broiled, or poached—tastes even better when you add a flavorful sauce. The half-dozen choices on this page enhance both fish and shellfish, and almost all are easily prepared in just a few minutes.

Almond Browned Butter

Preparation time: About 5 minutes
Cooking time: 3 to 5 minutes

Melt ¼ cup **butter** or margarine in a small frying pan over medium heat. When butter foams, add ¼ cup **sliced almonds** or slivered blanched almonds and stir just until nuts begin to brown. Remove from heat and stir in 2 tablespoons **lemon juice.** Spoon over cooked fish just before serving. Makes about ½ cup.

Per tablespoon: 71 calories, 0.7 g protein, 0.8 g carbohydrates, 8 g total fat, 16 mg cholesterol, 62 mg sodium

Shallot Butter

Preparation time: About 5 minutes

In a small bowl, stir together ⅓ cup **butter** or margarine (at room temperature), ⅓ cup minced **shallots,** 2 cloves **garlic** (minced or pressed), and 2 tablespoons minced **parsley.** Evenly dot over uncooked fish or shellfish just before baking. Makes about ½ cup.

Per tablespoon: 73 calories, 0.3 g protein, 1 g carbohydrates, 8 g total fat, 20 mg cholesterol, 79 mg sodium

Mignonette Sauce

Preparation time: About 5 minutes

In a small bowl, stir together ¼ cup *each* **white wine vinegar** and **dry white wine,** 1 tablespoon minced **red onion,** and ½ teaspoon **coarsely ground pepper.** Spoon over raw oysters or transfer to small bowls and use as a dip for cooked shellfish. Makes about ½ cup.

Per tablespoon: 7 calories, 0.02 g protein, 0.5 g carbohydrates, 0 g total fat, 0 mg cholesterol, 0.4 mg sodium

Tartar Sauce

Preparation time: 5 to 10 minutes

In a small bowl, stir together ½ cup *each* **mayonnaise** and **sour cream,** 1 teaspoon **lemon juice,** ¼ cup *each* chopped **dill pickle** and sliced **green onion** (including tops), and 1 tablespoon drained **capers,** mashed. For a thinner sauce, add a small amount of **milk,** blending until sauce reaches desired consistency. Serve with cooked fish. Makes about 1⅓ cups.

Per tablespoon: 50 calories, 0.3 g protein, 0.5 g carbohydrates, 5 g total fat, 5 mg cholesterol, 67 mg sodium

Cumin-Garlic-Yogurt Sauce

Preparation time: 5 to 10 minutes
Chilling time: At least 15 minutes

In a small bowl, stir together 1½ cups **plain yogurt,** 2 tablespoons minced **fresh cilantro (coriander),** 1 clove **garlic,** minced or pressed, and 1 teaspoon **cumin seeds.** Cover and refrigerate for at least 15 minutes. Serve with cooked fish. Makes about 1½ cups.

Per tablespoon: 9 calories, 0.8 g protein, 1 g carbohydrates, 0.2 g total fat, 0.9 mg cholesterol, 10 mg sodium

Tomato-Caper Sauce

Preparation time: About 10 minutes
Cooking time: About 20 minutes

Melt ¼ cup **butter** or margarine in a wide frying pan over medium heat. Add l medium-size **onion,** chopped, and l clove **garlic,** minced or pressed. Cook, stirring, until onion is soft (about 10 minutes). Add 2 teaspoons drained **capers** and l can (about 14½ oz.) **pear-shaped tomatoes** (break up with a spoon) and their liquid. Cook, stirring occasionally, until reduced and thickened (about 10 minutes). Stir in 1 tablespoon **lemon juice** and 2 tablespoons minced **parsley.** Serve with cooked fish. Makes about 1½ cups.

Per ¼ cup: 91 calories, 0.8 g protein, 4 g carbohydrates, 8 g total fat, 22 mg cholesterol, 223 mg sodium

Sautéed Shrimp in Mint Beurre Blanc

Preparation time: About 20 minutes
Cooking time: About 10 minutes

Cool, fresh mint brightens the rich butter sauce that bathes these quickly cooked shrimp. Alongside, serve a sliced tomato salad and tiny potatoes steamed in their jackets.

- ½ teaspoon grated lemon peel
- 1 cup firmly packed fresh mint leaves
- 6 to 8 tablespoons butter or margarine
- 1 to 1½ pounds medium-size raw shrimp (30 to 32 per lb.), shelled and deveined
- 1 cup dry white wine
- Lemon slices
- Mint sprigs

In a food processor or blender, whirl lemon peel, mint leaves, and ¼ cup of the butter until well blended; set aside.

Melt 2 tablespoons of the butter in a wide frying pan over medium-high heat. Add shrimp and cook, stirring, until just opaque in center; cut to test (about 5 minutes). With a slotted spoon, transfer shrimp to a warm plate; keep warm.

Add wine to pan and boil over high heat, stirring, until liquid is reduced to ⅓ cup (about 5 minutes). Add mint butter all at once and stir until butter is smoothly blended into sauce. For a thicker sauce, stir in remaining 1 to 2 tablespoons plain butter.

Pour sauce into a warm serving dish; then add shrimp. Garnish with lemon slices and mint sprigs. Makes 4 servings.

Per serving: 280 calories, 24 g protein, 2 g carbohydrates, 19 g total fat, 221 mg cholesterol, 348 mg sodium

How Much to Buy

Though appetites vary, you'll still find it helpful to use the following suggested amounts per person when shopping for fish or shellfish: • Fish, fillets or steaks, ⅓ to ½ pound; whole or cleaned fish, ½ to 1 pound. • Clams, shucked, about ¼ pound; in the shell, about 1½ pounds. • Mussels in the shell, about 1 pound. • Lobster or crab, whole or live, 1 to 2 pounds; cooked crabmeat, about ¼ pound. • Oysters, shucked, 4 or 5 ounces; in the shell, 6 to 9 oysters. • Scallops, ¼ to ½ pound. • Shrimp, shelled, about ¼ pound; unshelled, ¼ to ½ pound.

Sautéed Hoisin Shrimp

Preparation time: About 20 minutes
Cooking time: About 5 minutes

To balance these gloriously spicy stir-fried shrimp, serve a side dish of steamed snow peas tossed with crisp sliced water chestnuts.

- 3 tablespoons hoisin sauce
- 2 tablespoons *each* unseasoned rice vinegar and water
- 2 teaspoons sugar
- ½ teaspoon *each* ground ginger and cornstarch
- ⅛ teaspoon crushed red pepper flakes
- 2 tablespoons salad oil
- 1 pound medium-size raw shrimp (30 to 32 per lb.), shelled and deveined
- 1 clove garlic, minced or pressed
- 6 green onions (including tops), cut diagonally into 1-inch lengths

In a bowl, mix hoisin sauce, vinegar, water, sugar, ginger, cornstarch, and red pepper flakes; set aside.

Heat oil in a wide frying pan or wok over medium-high heat. Add shrimp and garlic and cook, stirring occasionally, for about 2 minutes. Add onions and hoisin mixture and continue to cook, stirring, until sauce is thickened and shrimp are just opaque in center; cut to test (about 3 more minutes). Makes 4 servings.

Per serving: 192 calories, 20 g protein, 9 g carbohydrates, 9 g total fat, 140 mg cholesterol, 520 mg sodium

*Fit for a feast, skewered Broiled Prawns Wrapped in
Bacon (recipe on facing page) spearhead an easy,
delicious summertime menu. As accents, offer fresh fruit
and a rice pilaf.*

Broiled Prawns Wrapped in Bacon

Pictured on facing page

Preparation time: About 30 minutes
Broiling time: 6 to 10 minutes

Jumbo shrimp—also called prawns—make a handsome and flavorful entrée when wrapped in bacon, skewered, and broiled.

  8 slices bacon
 16 jumbo raw shrimp (16 to 20 per lb.)

Soak eight 10-inch-long bamboo skewers in hot water to cover for about 30 minutes.

Meanwhile, in a wide frying pan, cook bacon over medium heat until some of the fat has cooked out and bacon begins to brown (3 to 4 minutes); bacon should not be crisp. Drain, then cut each slice in half lengthwise.

Shell shrimp (leave tails on) and devein. Wrap a bacon half-slice around each shrimp. Thread shrimp on pairs of skewers as shown in photo on facing page. Then place on rack of a broiler pan and broil about 4 inches below heat, turning once, until bacon is golden brown and shrimp are just opaque in center; cut to test (6 to 10 minutes). Makes 4 servings.

Per serving: 170 calories, 23 g protein, 0.9 g carbohydrates, 8 g total fat, 151 mg cholesterol, 338 mg sodium

Stir-fried Shrimp with Green Onions

Preparation time: About 15 minutes
Cooking time: About 5 minutes

For a Chinese-style feast, offer this exquisite stir-fry with steamed rice and ginger-seasoned cooked carrots. (Be sure to have all the ingredients ready before you start to cook, since stir-frying goes very quickly.)

  1 pound large raw shrimp (25 to 30 per lb.), shelled and deveined
  1 tablespoon rice wine or dry sherry
  1 tablespoon cornstarch
  2 tablespoons salad oil
  4 green onions (including tops), thinly sliced
     Soy sauce (optional)

In a small bowl, mix shrimp, wine, and cornstarch.

Heat oil in a wok or wide frying pan over high heat. Add shrimp mixture and cook, stirring, until shrimp turn bright pink (2 to 3 minutes). Add onions and continue to cook, stirring, until shrimp are just opaque in center; cut to test (about 2 more minutes). Offer soy sauce to add to taste, if desired. Makes 3 servings.

Per serving: 228 calories, 25 g protein, 5 g carbohydrates, 11 g total fat, 186 mg cholesterol, 183 mg sodium

Scallops & Shrimp in Béarnaise Cream

Preparation time: About 20 minutes
Cooking time: About 15 minutes

The moist, tender textures and mild flavors of scallops and shrimp blend in this rich, tarragon-seasoned dinner dish. To complement the seafood, you might offer steamed broccoli or asparagus.

- 2 tablespoons butter or margarine
- 1 pound sea scallops, rinsed and patted dry (cut large ones in half)
- ½ pound large raw shrimp (25 to 30 per lb.), shelled and deveined
- ⅓ cup finely chopped shallots
- ¾ cup tarragon wine vinegar or white wine vinegar
- ½ cup regular-strength chicken broth
- ¼ teaspoon dry tarragon
- 1 tablespoon Dijon mustard
- ½ cup whipping cream
  Salt and ground white pepper

Melt butter in a wide frying pan over medium-high heat. Add scallops and shrimp, a portion at a time (do not crowd pan). Cook, stirring, until seafood is just opaque in center; cut to test (3 to 5 minutes). As seafood is cooked, remove from pan with a slotted spoon and transfer to a bowl.

Add shallots, vinegar, broth, and tarragon to pan. Boil over high heat until liquid is reduced to ½ cup. Pour any accumulated juices from seafood into pan along with mustard and cream. Return to a boil; boil until sauce is reduced to about ¾ cup. Stir in seafood. Season to taste with salt and white pepper. Makes 4 servings.

Per serving: 314 calories, 30 g protein, 10 g carbohydrates, 17 g total fat, 157 mg cholesterol, 559 mg sodium

Scallops & Tomato au Gratin

Preparation time: About 15 minutes
Cooking time: About 20 minutes

Cloaked in a luscious, creamy tomato-mushroom sauce and crowned with Gruyère cheese, these delicate scallops are worthy of a special-occasion menu. Serve with rice and a crisp spinach salad.

- 2 tablespoons butter or margarine
- 1 tablespoon salad oil
- 1½ pounds sea scallops, rinsed and patted dry (cut large ones in half)
- ¼ cup thinly sliced shallots
- 6 mushrooms, sliced
- 1 small pear-shaped tomato, seeded and chopped
- 1 teaspoon minced fresh tarragon or ¼ teaspoon dry tarragon
- ¼ teaspoon salt
- ⅓ cup dry white wine
- ½ cup whipping cream
- ½ cup shredded Gruyère or Swiss cheese

Melt butter in oil in a wide frying pan over medium-high heat. Add scallops, a portion at a time (do not crowd pan). Cook, stirring, until scallops are just opaque in center; cut to test (3 to 5 minutes). As scallops are cooked, remove from pan with a slotted spoon and transfer to a bowl.

Add shallots and mushrooms to pan; cook over high heat, stirring often, just until mushrooms are lightly browned and almost all liquid has evaporated. Stir in tomato, tarragon, salt, and wine. Boil, stirring occasionally, until almost all liquid has evaporated. Add cream; boil, stirring often, until liquid is reduced by about half and large, shiny bubbles appear. Pour any accumulated juices from scallops into pan; bring to a boil and cook until sauce has thickened. Remove from heat and lightly mix in scallops.

Spoon mixture into four 7-inch scallop shells or shallow individual baking dishes. Place on a rimmed baking sheet. Sprinkle with cheese. Broil about 4 inches below heat until cheese is melted and scallop mixture is lightly browned (2 to 3 minutes). Makes 4 servings.

Per serving: 396 calories, 35 g protein, 9 g carbohydrates, 24 g total fat, 120 mg cholesterol, 531 mg sodium

Scallops in Garlic Butter

Preparation time: About 15 minutes
Cooking time: About 15 minutes

If you love scallops, you'll want to try this simple dish—just a pound (or more) of the tender, juicy shellfish in a savory garlic-butter bath. Be sure to provide crusty bread for dunking!

> 3 tablespoons sliced almonds
> ¼ cup butter or margarine
> 5 large cloves garlic, minced or pressed
> 2 tablespoons chopped parsley
> 1 teaspoon grated lemon peel
> 1 to 1½ pounds sea scallops, rinsed and patted dry (cut large ones in half)

Spread almonds on a baking sheet and toast in a 350° oven until golden (about 6 minutes); set aside.

Melt butter in a wide frying pan over medium heat. Add garlic, parsley, and lemon peel; cook, stirring, for about 1 minute. Add scallops, a portion at a time (do not crowd pan). Cook, stirring, until scallops are just opaque in center; cut to test (3 to 5 minutes). As scallops are cooked, transfer to a warm platter; keep warm. When all scallops are done, top with almonds and serve immediately. Makes 4 servings.

Per serving: 261 calories, 25 g protein, 6 g carbohydrates, 15 g total fat, 78 mg cholesterol, 348 mg sodium

Scallop & Vegetable Pesto Sauté

Preparation time: About 15 minutes
Cooking time: About 15 minutes

Aromatic pesto sauce gives this colorful seafood sauté its unforgettable flavor. Use purchased pesto, or make your own sauce from the recipe on page 69.

> 3 tablespoons butter or margarine
> 1 carrot, cut into ¼-inch-thick slices
> 1 small onion, cut into 1-inch squares
> 1 small zucchini, cut into ¼-inch-thick slices
> 8 to 10 small mushrooms, cut in half
> 1 small green bell pepper, seeded and cut into 1-inch squares
> 2 tablespoons pesto sauce, homemade (page 69) or purchased
> ¾ pound sea scallops, rinsed, patted dry, and cut into ¼-inch-thick slices
> Salt
> Grated Parmesan cheese

Melt 2 tablespoons of the butter in a wide frying pan over medium-high heat. Add carrot and onion and cook, stirring, for 5 minutes. Add zucchini, mushrooms, and bell pepper; cook, stirring, until vegetables are tender-crisp to bite (about 5 more minutes). Remove vegetables from pan; set aside.

Melt remaining 1 tablespoon butter in pan, then stir in pesto sauce. Add scallops and cook, stirring, until just opaque in center; cut to test (about 3 minutes). Return vegetables to pan and cook, stirring, just until heated through. Remove from heat; season to taste with salt. Sprinkle with cheese before serving. Makes 2 servings.

Per serving: 421 calories, 32 g protein, 15 g carbohydrates, 26 g total fat, 105 mg cholesterol, 556 mg sodium

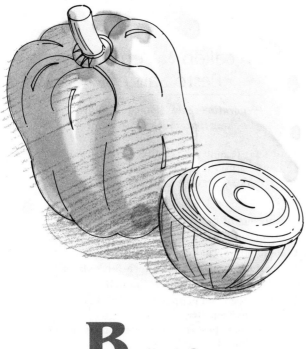

Broiled Oysters, Bacon & Cheese

Preparation time: About 25 minutes
Broiling time: 7 to 8 minutes

Tender oysters nestle under a savory blanket of bell pepper and onion strips, melted cheese, and crisp bacon. Round out a superb supper with hot buttered toast and iced tea or beer.

- 6 slices bacon
- 1 medium-size green bell pepper, seeded and cut into julienne strips
- 1 small onion, thinly slivered
- 2 jars (8 to 10 oz. *each)* small Pacific oysters, drained and patted dry
- ¾ cup shredded Cheddar cheese
  Hot buttered French bread toast (optional)

In a wide frying pan, cook bacon over medium heat until crisp (about 8 minutes). Lift out, drain, crumble, and set aside. Discard all but 1½ tablespoons of the drippings.

Add bell pepper and onion to pan. Cook, stirring occasionally, until onion is soft (about 10 minutes). Meanwhile, arrange oysters in a single layer in a 9- by 13-inch baking pan. Broil 3 inches below heat just until edges of oysters begin to curl (about 3 minutes); turn and broil until edges curl again (about 3 more minutes). Spoon onion mixture over oysters and sprinkle with cheese and bacon. Broil just until cheese is melted (1 to 2 more minutes). Serve with toast, if desired. Makes 4 servings.

Per serving: 281 calories, 18 g protein, 8 g carbohydrates, 19 g total fat, 112 mg cholesterol, 467 mg sodium

Mussels Marinière

Pictured on facing page

Preparation time: 15 to 20 minutes
Cooking time: About 7 minutes

Here's a particularly appealing example of French seafood cookery. Mussels steamed in a subtle wine broth develop tempting flavor—in under 10 minutes. Offer chunks of crusty bread to soak up the flavorful cooking juices.

- 3 to 4 pounds mussels, scrubbed
- 3 tablespoons butter or margarine
- 4 green onions (including tops), thinly sliced
- 1 clove garlic, minced or pressed
- 1 cup dry white wine
- ½ cup lightly packed minced parsley
- ⅛ teaspoon pepper

Discard any mussels that do not close when tapped. Tear beard (clump of fibers along side of shell) off each mussel with a quick tug. Set mussels aside.

Melt butter in a 4- to 6-quart pan over medium heat. Add onions and garlic and cook, stirring occasionally, until soft (about 2 minutes). Add wine, parsley, and pepper; bring to a boil over high heat. Add mussels; reduce heat, cover, and simmer until mussels open (about 5 minutes). Discard any unopened shells.

With a slotted spoon, transfer mussels to individual serving bowls; evenly pour cooking liquid over each portion. Makes 4 servings.

Per serving: 171 calories, 12 g protein, 6 g carbohydrates, 11 g total fat, 51 mg cholesterol, 378 mg sodium

For a meal that looks spectacular but requires little effort, serve up Mussels Marinière (recipe on facing page) steamed in a wine-infused broth. Provide crusty bread to dip in the delectable juices.

Butter-basted Crab

Preparation time: 5 to 10 minutes
Cooking time: About 25 minutes

Hot cracked crab, simple and glorious! To prepare this feast, heat crab in a nippy lemon-butter sauce.

- ¼ cup butter or margarine
- ¼ teaspoon grated lemon peel
- 3 tablespoons lemon juice
- 1 tablespoon thinly sliced green onion (including top)
- 1 teaspoon *each* finely chopped parsley and soy sauce
  Liquid hot pepper seasoning
- 1 cooked Dungeness crab in the shell (1½ to 2 lbs.), cleaned and cracked
  Lemon wedges

Melt butter in a small pan over medium heat; add lemon peel, lemon juice, onion, parsley, and soy sauce. Season to taste with hot pepper seasoning, then simmer for 3 to 5 minutes. Rinse crab pieces, pat dry, and arrange in an even layer in a 7- by 11-inch baking dish. Brush butter mixture over crab, cover, and bake in a 300° oven until heated through (about 20 minutes), basting often with pan juices. Garnish with lemon wedges; provide nutcrackers and small forks for removing meat from shells. Makes 2 servings.

Per serving: 327 calories, 23 g protein, 2 g carbohydrates, 25 g total fat, 176 mg cholesterol, 728 mg sodium

Cracked Crab with Red Pepper Aïoli

Preparation time: About 30 minutes
Cooking time: About 15 minutes

There's nothing wrong with enjoying chilled cracked crab completely plain—but when you're in the mood for a more festive presentation, dip each bite of seafood into a tangy, garlicky red pepper mayonnaise. (Dunk artichokes or other vegetables in the aïoli, too.)

- 2 red bell peppers
- 1 tablespoon olive oil
- ½ teaspoon dry thyme
- 1 or 2 cloves garlic, slivered
- ¼ teaspoon salt
- 1 tablespoon white wine vinegar
- 1 egg
- ½ cup *each* salad oil and olive oil
- 2 or 3 cooked Dungeness crabs in the shell (1½ to 2 lbs. *each*), cleaned and cracked

Brush bell peppers with the 1 tablespoon olive oil and sprinkle with thyme. Place on rack of a broiler pan; broil about 4 inches below heat, turning often, until charred (about 10 minutes). Enclose peppers in a plastic bag and let stand for 15 minutes; then pull off and discard skins, stems, and seeds. Cut peppers into quarters.

To prepare aïoli, whirl peppers, garlic, salt, vinegar, and egg in a blender or food processor until smooth. With motor running, add salad oil and the ½ cup olive oil in a thin, steady stream; continue to whirl until aïoli is smooth. If made ahead, cover and refrigerate for up to 1 week.

Rinse crab pieces, pat dry, and pile onto a platter. Provide nutcrackers and small forks for removing meat from shells; dip shelled meat into aïoli to eat. Makes 4 to 6 servings.

Per serving of crab: 82 calories, 17 g protein, 0.7 g carbohydrates, 0.9 g total fat, 56 mg cholesterol, 281 mg sodium

Per tablespoon of aïoli: 67 calories, 0.2 g protein, 0.3 g carbohydrates, 7 g total fat, 7 mg cholesterol, 19 mg sodium

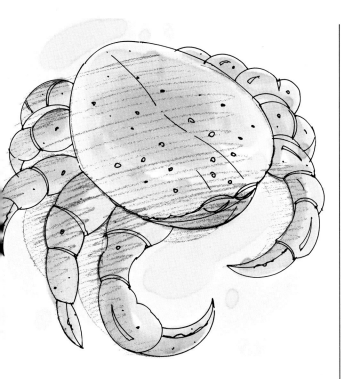

Steamed Soft-shell Crabs with Ginger Sauce

Preparation time: About 5 minutes
Cooking time: About 8 minutes

Delectable and wholly edible, soft-shell crabs are available fresh during summer and frozen the rest of the year. Have fresh crabs cleaned at the fish market (frozen shellfish are sold already cleaned). Because the crabs are small, allow about three per serving; accompany with potato chips and beer.

- 6 cleaned soft-shell blue crabs (about 2 oz. *each*), thawed if frozen
- ⅓ cup unseasoned rice vinegar
- 1 to 2 tablespoons sliced green onion (including top)
- 1½ tablespoons minced fresh ginger
- 1 teaspoon sugar

Drain crabs; then arrange, back sides up, in a single layer on rack. Cover and steam over high heat until crabs are just opaque in center; cut to test (about 8 minutes).

Meanwhile, stir together vinegar, onion, ginger, and sugar in a small bowl.

Transfer crabs to warm plates; offer ginger flavored sauce to spoon over each portion. Makes 2 servings.

Per serving: 156 calories, 27 g protein, 5 g carbohydrates, 2 g total fat, cholesterol and sodium data not available

Crab Lace Patties on Lettuce

Preparation time: About 15 minutes
Cooking time: About 6 minutes

In a medley of delicious contrasts, these hot, crisp crab cakes combine with cool, delicate avocado and lettuce.

- ¾ pound cooked crabmeat
- ¾ cup grated Parmesan cheese
- 2 tablespoons minced parsley
- ½ teaspoon dry oregano
- 2 cloves garlic, minced or pressed
- ¼ cup fine dry bread crumbs
- 2 green onions (including tops), thinly sliced
- 1 egg, beaten
- ¼ cup whipping cream
  About 1 tablespoon olive oil or salad oil
- 1 large firm-ripe avocado
- 8 to 12 large butter lettuce leaves, rinsed and crisped

Break crab into flakes. Place in a bowl; add cheese, parsley, oregano, garlic, crumbs, onions, egg, and cream. Mix lightly.

Heat 2 teaspoons of the oil in a wide frying pan over medium heat. Mound 3 tablespoons of the crab mixture in pan, spreading to make a 3-inch cake. Repeat until pan is filled, but don't crowd patties in pan. Cook patties until lightly browned on bottoms (about 2 minutes); then turn and cook until other side is very lightly browned (about 1 minute). Lift out and arrange on a warm plate; keep warm. Repeat until all patties are cooked, adding more oil as needed.

To serve, pit, peel, and slice avocado. On 4 dinner plates, arrange lettuce, avocado slices, and crab patties. Makes 4 servings.

Per serving: 381 calories, 28 g protein, 12 g carbohydrates, 25 g total fat, 167 mg cholesterol, 592 mg sodium

*Mellowed by gentle cooking, whole garlic cloves infuse
simmered drumsticks and red-skinned potatoes with
their distinctive flavor. Garlic Chicken & Potatoes
(recipe on page 121) is based on a French classic.*

Poultry

When you're cooking poultry, "quick and easy" doesn't always mean "plain and simple." Consider a few of the recipes in this chapter: crisp, wine-sauced chicken quarters with sweet red grapes; tender turkey scaloppine crowned with Parmesan cheese and savory tomato sauce; roast game hens gilded with a buttery mustard glaze or wreathed with herbs and vegetables. The recipes in the following pages prove that it's possible to turn out tempting, even elegant poultry entrées without spending hours in the kitchen.

Thawing Chicken in the Microwave

Unwrap a frozen 3- to 3½-pound cut-up chicken, then place on a microwave-safe plate; cover loosely with heavy-duty plastic wrap. Microwave on MEDIUM (50%) for 10 minutes, turning chicken over and giving plate a quarter turn after 5 minutes. Let stand for 10 minutes. Repeat, microwaving and standing; as soon as possible, separate pieces and arrange in a single layer, with meatiest portions toward edge of plate. Wings should be thawed after second 10-minute period. Microwave remaining pieces on MEDIUM (50%) for 5 more minutes; let stand for 5 minutes. If needed, microwave on MEDIUM (50%) for 2 more minutes. Thawed chicken should be flexible, but still very cold.

Honey-baked Chicken

Preparation time: About 10 minutes
Baking time: 15 to 20 minutes

Nutty-tasting sesame seeds add crunch to these glazed baked chicken breasts; the pan juices make a tart-sweet sauce to spoon over the meat (and a side dish of rice, if you like).

- 2 tablespoons sesame seeds
- 3 tablespoons honey
- ¼ cup Dijon mustard
- ¼ cup dry sherry or dry white wine
- 1 tablespoon lemon juice
- 3 whole chicken breasts (about 1 lb. *each*), skinned, boned, and split

Toast sesame seeds in a small frying pan over medium heat until golden (3 to 5 minutes), shaking pan frequently. Pour into a bowl; stir in honey, mustard, sherry, and lemon juice. Rinse chicken and pat dry; arrange pieces slightly apart in a 9- by 13-inch baking dish. Pour sesame sauce evenly over chicken. Bake in a 400° oven, basting several times with pan juices, until meat in thickest part is no longer pink; cut to test (15 to 20 minutes). Transfer chicken to warm plates; pour pan juices into a bowl and pass at the table. Makes 6 servings.

Per serving: 229 calories, 35 g protein, 12 g carbohydrates, 4 g total fat, 86 mg cholesterol, 398 mg sodium

Chicken Breasts La Jolla

Preparation time: About 10 minutes
Cooking time: 25 to 30 minutes

Buttery-smooth avocados and a luxurious, creamy sauce distinguish this dish. For an attractive presentation, arrange the avocado slices and chicken pieces alternately in the baking dish.

- 1 large firm-ripe avocado, pitted, peeled, and thinly sliced
- ¼ cup lemon juice
- 2 whole chicken breasts (about 1 lb. *each*), skinned, boned, and split
  Salt and pepper
- 2 tablespoons butter or margarine
- 2 cloves garlic, minced or pressed
- 1 cup whipping cream
- 3 tablespoons dry vermouth
  Paprika
- ¼ cup finely chopped fresh cilantro (coriander)

Place avocado slices in a small, shallow bowl and coat with 3 tablespoons of the lemon juice. Rinse chicken, pat dry, and sprinkle with salt and pepper; set aside.

Melt butter in a wide frying pan over medium heat; add garlic and cook, stirring, until golden (about 2 minutes). Add chicken to pan, increase heat to medium-high, and cook, turning once, until lightly browned on both sides (7 to 8 minutes). Lift out chicken, reserving drippings in pan, and transfer to a shallow 1½- to 2-quart baking dish.

Drain lemon juice from avocado into pan; then add remaining 1 tablespoon lemon juice, cream, and vermouth. Boil over high heat, stirring often, until reduced to about ⅔ cup (about 5 minutes). Arrange avocado slices between chicken pieces; pour sauce evenly over all. Sprinkle with paprika and cilantro. Bake in a 350° oven until sauce is bubbly (10 to 12 minutes). Makes 4 servings.

Per serving: 499 calories, 37 g protein, 9 g carbohydrates, 36 g total fat, 167 mg cholesterol, 186 mg sodium

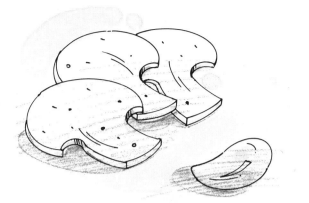

Herbed Chicken with Artichokes

Preparation time: About 10 minutes
Baking time: 20 to 25 minutes

A topping of cool sour cream helps smooth the piquant flavors of this hearty chicken casserole. You'll need only simple accompaniments—perhaps just a green salad and a loaf of crusty bread.

- 3 **whole chicken breasts (about 1 lb.** *each***), skinned, boned, and split**
- 1 **jar (6 oz.) marinated artichoke hearts, drained**
- ¼ **cup butter or margarine**
- ¼ **pound mushrooms, thinly sliced**
- 1 **clove garlic, minced or pressed**
- 1 **can (8 oz.) tomato sauce**
- ½ **teaspoon** *each* **dry basil, dry oregano, and ground turmeric**
  Paprika
  Sour cream

Rinse chicken, pat dry, and arrange in a 9- by 13-inch baking dish; tuck artichokes between chicken pieces. Melt butter in a wide frying pan; drizzle half the butter over chicken, reserving remainder in pan. Bake chicken in a 375° oven for 10 minutes.

Meanwhile, add mushrooms to butter remaining in frying pan and cook over medium-high heat, stirring often, until soft. Add garlic and cook, stirring often, for about 1 minute. Stir in tomato sauce, basil, oregano, and turmeric. Bring to a boil; set aside.

After chicken has baked for 10 minutes, pour mushroom mixture over it; sprinkle with paprika. Return to oven and continue to bake until meat in thickest part is no longer pink; cut to test (10 to 15 more minutes). Offer sour cream to add to individual portions. Makes 6 servings.

Per serving: 275 calories, 36 g protein, 6 g carbohydrates, 12 g total fat, 106 mg cholesterol, 550 mg sodium

Kung Pao Chicken

Preparation time: 15 to 20 minutes
Marinating time: 15 minutes
Cooking time: 7 to 10 minutes

Hot red chiles, garlic, and fresh ginger give this Chinese classic its spicy bite. Serve over rice; for dessert, offer chilled pineapple spears or a fruit compote.

- 1 **tablespoon** *each* **dry sherry and cornstarch**
- ⅛ **teaspoon ground white pepper**
- 1½ **pounds chicken breasts, skinned, boned, and cut into bite-size pieces**
  About ¼ cup salad oil
  Cooking Sauce (recipe follows)
- 4 **to 6 small dried hot red chiles**
- ½ **cup salted roasted peanuts**
- 1 **teaspoon** *each* **minced garlic and grated fresh ginger**
- 2 **green onions (including tops), cut into 1½-inch lengths**

In a bowl, stir together sherry, cornstarch, and white pepper. Add chicken and stir to coat, then stir in 1 tablespoon of the oil and let marinate for 15 minutes. Prepare Cooking Sauce and set aside.

Heat 1 tablespoon of the oil in a wok or wide frying pan over medium heat. Add chiles and peanuts and cook, stirring, until chiles just begin to char. (If chiles become completely black, discard them. Remove peanuts from pan and set aside; repeat with new oil and chiles.) Remove peanuts and chiles from pan; discard chiles. Set peanuts aside.

Add 2 more tablespoons oil to pan and increase heat to high. When oil begins to heat, add garlic and ginger; stir once. Then add chicken mixture, a portion at a time (do not crowd pan); cook, stirring, until chicken is lightly browned (about 3 minutes), adding more oil as needed. Return all chicken to pan, then add peanuts and onions. Stir Cooking Sauce and pour into pan; stir until sauce boils and thickens. Makes 4 servings.

Cooking Sauce. Mix 2 tablespoons **soy sauce,** 1 tablespoon *each* **white wine vinegar** and **dry sherry,** 3 tablespoons **regular-strength chicken broth** or water, and 2 teaspoons *each* **sugar** and **cornstarch.**

Per serving: 505 calories, 34 g protein, 12 g carbohydrates, 35 g total fat, 87 mg cholesterol, 726 mg sodium

Chutney Chicken Breasts

Preparation time: 10 to 15 minutes
Baking time: 15 to 18 minutes

Chutney, rum, and slivered almonds transform plain baked chicken into company fare. Complete the menu with wild or brown rice and steamed green beans.

- **2 tablespoons rum**
- **3 tablespoons butter or margarine, melted**
  About ⅓ cup seasoned fine dry bread crumbs
- **3 whole chicken breasts (about 1 lb.** *each*)**,
  skinned, boned, and split**
- **1 jar (about 9 oz.) Major Grey's chutney,
  chopped**
- **2 tablespoons slivered blanched almonds**
  Hot cooked wild or brown rice

Combine rum and butter in a shallow pan. Spread crumbs in another shallow pan.

Rinse chicken and pat dry. Then cup each piece, skinned side down, in the palm of your hand. Fill cavity with about 1 tablespoon of the chutney and 1 teaspoon of the almonds. Fold and roll chicken around filling to enclose. Dip each piece in butter mixture, then in crumbs, coating well on all sides. Place chicken rolls, seam sides down, in a 9- by 13-inch baking pan. Drizzle with any remaining butter mixture.

Bake in a 425° oven until meat in thickest part is no longer pink; cut to test (15 to 18 minutes). Spoon pan drippings over chicken. Serve with rice and remaining chutney. Makes 6 servings.

Per serving: 294 calories, 36 g protein, 16 g carbohydrates, 9 g total fat, 101 mg cholesterol, 364 mg sodium

Thai Chicken & Basil Stir-fry

Pictured on facing page

Preparation time: 20 to 25 minutes
Cooking time: About 20 minutes

While the shiitake mushrooms soak, prepare the remaining ingredients for this exotic Thai stir-fry. You'll find dried shiitakes, as well as the fish sauce and coconut milk you need to make the cooking sauce, in Asian grocery stores and well-stocked supermarkets.

- **6 dried shiitake mushrooms (***each* **2 to 3 inches
  in diameter)**
  Coconut Milk Cooking Sauce (recipe follows)
- **2 to 4 tablespoons salad oil**
- **1 medium-size yellow onion, thinly sliced
  and separated into rings**
- **3 cloves garlic, minced or pressed**
- **2 tablespoons minced fresh ginger**
- **2 whole chicken breasts (about 1 lb.** *each*)**,
  skinned, boned, and cut into ½-inch-wide strips**
- **5 green onions (including tops), cut into
  1-inch pieces**
- **1½ cups lightly packed slivered fresh basil leaves**
  Hot cooked rice

Soak mushrooms in warm water to cover until soft (10 to 15 minutes); drain well. Cut off and discard stems. Slice caps into ¼-inch slivers; set aside. Prepare Coconut Milk Cooking Sauce; set aside.

Heat 2 tablespoons of the oil in a wok or wide frying pan over high heat. Add yellow onion, garlic, and ginger; cook, stirring, until onion is lightly browned. With a slotted spoon, transfer onion mixture to a bowl; set aside. Add chicken to pan, a portion at a time (do not crowd pan); cook, stirring, until lightly browned (about 3 minutes), adding more oil as needed. As chicken is cooked, lift out and add to onion mixture.

Pour cooking sauce into pan; boil, stirring constantly, until reduced by about a third. Return onion mixture and chicken to pan. Add mushrooms, green onions, and basil; stir just until heated through. Serve over rice. Makes 4 servings.

Coconut Milk Cooking Sauce. Mix ¾ cup **canned or thawed frozen coconut milk,** 3 tablespoons **soy sauce,** 3 tablespoons **unseasoned rice vinegar** or white wine vinegar, 1½ tablespoons **fish sauce** (*nam pla*) or soy sauce, and ½ to 1 teaspoon **crushed red pepper flakes**.

Per serving: 410 calories, 39 g protein, 15 g carbohydrates, 22 g total fat, 86 mg cholesterol, 879 mg sodium

*Savor flavors of Southeast Asia—coconut milk,
fresh basil, and fiery bursts of crushed red pepper—
in exotic Thai Chicken & Basil Stir-fry (recipe
on facing page).*

Cook-ahead Poultry

When time is short, having cooked chicken or turkey in the refrigerator is a lifesaver—it lets you put together casseroles, salads, sandwiches, or other family favorites in a hurry.

Roasting a whole chicken or a good-sized piece of turkey (such as a breast half or thigh) is well worth your time, since you'll usually end up with enough meat for at least two meals. On this page, we give directions both for roasting poultry and for steeping chicken or turkey breast; the latter method produces exceptionally moist, smooth-textured cooked meat.

Roasting Chicken or Turkey

Select a **broiler-fryer chicken** (3 to 4 lbs.), roasting chicken (5 to 6 lbs.), whole turkey (8 to 15 lbs.), turkey breast half (bone in or boneless, 2 to 4 lbs.), or turkey thigh (1 to 1½ lbs.).

If roasting a whole bird, remove neck and giblets from body cavity; reserve for other uses. Rinse bird inside and out; pat dry. If desired, place **lemon wedges** and **parsley sprigs** or other fresh herbs in cavity.

Place whole bird, breast up (or turkey pieces, skin side up), on a rack in a shallow roasting pan. Brush lightly with melted **butter** or margarine or spray with vegetable oil cooking spray. For a whole bird, insert a meat thermometer in thickest part of thigh (not touching bone); for turkey

breast, insert thermometer in thickest part (not touching bone).

Approximate roasting times and temperatures are as follows:

Broiler-fryer chicken: 17 to 20 minutes per pound; 375° oven; thermometer reading, 185°F

Roasting chicken: 20 to 25 minutes per pound; 350° oven; thermometer reading, 185°F

Turkey: 15 minutes per pound; 325° oven; thermometer reading, 185°F

Turkey breast: 20 minutes per pound; 350° oven; thermometer reading, 170°F

Turkey thigh: 1 hour per pound; 350° oven; thermometer reading, 185°F

Steeped Chicken Breasts

Split 2 whole **chicken breasts** (about 1 lb. *each*); place in a wide 4- to 5-quart pan. Pour in enough **water** to cover chicken by 1 to 2 inches. Lift out chicken. Add 2 or 3 thin **lemon slices**; cover pan and bring water to a rolling boil over high heat. Remove pan from heat and quickly immerse chicken.

Cover pan tightly and let stand for 20 minutes; do *not* uncover until time is up. Chicken is done when meat in thickest part is no longer pink; cut to test. If meat is not done after 20 minutes, return to pan, cover, and let stand until done.

Drain chicken, plunge into ice water to cool quickly, and drain again; pat dry. Skin and bone chicken. If made ahead, cover and refrigerate for up to 2 days.

Steeped Turkey Breast

Place a 2½- to 3-pound **turkey breast half** in a 6- to 8-quart pan. Pour in enough **water** to cover turkey by 1 to 2 inches. Lift out turkey. Add 3 or 4 **parsley sprigs**; cover pan and bring water to a rolling boil over high heat. Add turkey, cover, and immediately turn heat to very low. Cook for 20 minutes. Remove from heat (do *not* uncover); let stand for 1 to 1½ hours.

Remove turkey from pan. Turkey is done when meat in thickest part is no longer pink; cut to test. If turkey is not done, cover it loosely; then cover pan, bring water to a simmer, and remove from heat. Add turkey, cover, and let stand until done. Drain, plunge into ice water to cool quickly, and drain again; pat dry.

Skin and bone turkey. If made ahead, cover and refrigerate for up to 2 days.

Hazelnut Chicken

Preparation time: About 15 minutes
Cooking time: About 15 minutes

A crisp coat of toasted, finely ground hazelnuts covers these moist boneless chicken breasts; a creamy mustard-wine sauce is drizzled on top. Serve with colorful vegetables, such as steamed snow peas and baby carrots.

- ½ **cup hazelnuts**
- 2 **tablespoons fine dry bread crumbs**
- 1 **egg white**
- 2 **tablespoons Dijon mustard**
- 2 **whole chicken breasts (about 1 lb. *each*), skinned, boned, and split**
  Ground white pepper
  All-purpose flour
- 1 **tablespoon butter or margarine**
- 1 **tablespoon salad oil**
- 2 **tablespoons dry white wine**
- ½ **cup whipping cream**
  Watercress sprigs

Spread hazelnuts in a shallow baking pan and toast in a 350° oven until skins begin to split (8 to 10 minutes). Pour nuts onto a clean towel; rub nuts with towel to remove most of skins. Let cool slightly, then whirl in a blender or food processor until finely ground. Pour into a shallow dish, mix in crumbs, and set aside. In another shallow bowl, beat egg white with 1 tablespoon of the mustard; set aside.

Rinse chicken, pat dry, sprinkle lightly with white pepper, and dust with flour. Dip chicken in egg white mixture to coat lightly; then coat with hazelnut mixture. Melt butter in oil in a wide frying pan over medium heat. Add chicken and cook, turning once, until browned on both sides and no longer pink in thickest part; cut to test (10 to 12 minutes). Remove chicken from pan and arrange in a warm serving dish; keep warm.

Add wine, cream, and remaining 1 tablespoon mustard to drippings in pan. Boil over high heat, stirring constantly, until slightly thickened. Drizzle over chicken. Garnish with watercress. Makes 4 servings.

Per serving: 431 calories, 38 g protein, 8 g carbohydrates, 27 g total fat, 127 mg cholesterol, 398 mg sodium

Buying & Storing Poultry

Fresh poultry should never be left at room temperature for long. If you buy your chicken and turkey at a supermarket, make it one of the last items you pick up; then get it home and into the refrigerator as quickly as possible. Cook fresh poultry within 3 days of purchase. If you can't use it that soon, enclose it securely in heavy-duty foil, freezer paper, or plastic bags, then freeze for up to 6 months.

Chicken & Apple Sauté

Preparation time: About 15 minutes
Cooking time: 25 to 30 minutes

On a crisp fall evening, make this sherry-accented sauté the star of your dinner menu. For the supporting cast, you might choose Bacon Polenta (page 173) and a spinach salad.

- 2 **whole chicken breasts (about 1 lb. *each*), boned and split**
- ¼ **cup butter or margarine**
- 2 **large tart apples, peeled, cored, and cut into ¼-inch-thick slices**
- 1 **large onion, chopped**
- ⅔ **cup dry sherry or apple juice**
- ⅓ **cup whipping cream**

Rinse chicken, pat dry, and set aside. Melt 2 tablespoons of the butter in a wide frying pan over medium heat. Add apples and cook, stirring often, just until tender when pierced (2 to 4 minutes). Lift out and keep warm.

Increase heat to medium-high and melt remaining 2 tablespoons butter in pan. Add chicken and cook, turning once, until lightly browned on both sides (7 to 8 minutes). Lift out and keep warm.

Add onion to pan and cook, stirring, until golden (about 7 minutes). Add sherry; boil for 1 minute. Return chicken to pan, skin sides up. Reduce heat, cover, and simmer until meat in thickest part is no longer pink; cut to test (about 5 minutes). Transfer to a warm platter; top with apples and keep warm. Add cream to pan and boil, stirring, until sauce is slightly thickened (2 to 3 minutes). Pour over chicken. Makes 4 servings.

Per serving: 396 calories, 35 g protein, 19 g carbohydrates, 20 g total fat, 139 mg cholesterol, 224 mg sodium

*Generously coated with both black and pink
peppercorns, pounded Chicken Breasts au Poivre (recipe
on facing page) are an elegant dinner dish. Serve
spring-fresh asparagus alongside.*

Chicken Breasts au Poivre

Pictured on facing page

Preparation time: About 10 minutes
Cooking time: About 10 minutes

Pink and black peppercorns add two-tone excitement to sautéed chicken breasts. The familiar black peppercorns deliver the more potent flavor. The pink ones, from an ornamental tree, have a milder heat and a sweet-hot, flowery impact; they're sold in specialty shops, either canned in brine or freeze-dried. (Some people are allergic to pink peppercorns, so if you've never tried them before, start out cautiously.)

2 **whole chicken breasts (about 1 lb. *each*), skinned, boned, and split**
1 **teaspoon crushed black peppercorns**
4 **teaspoons crushed pink peppercorns**
2 **to 3 tablespoons butter or margarine**
½ **cup Madeira or dry sherry**
½ **cup whipping cream**
1 **teaspoon minced fresh rosemary or ¼ teaspoon dry rosemary**
   Rosemary sprigs (optional)

Rinse chicken and pat dry, then place each piece between sheets of plastic wrap and pound with a flat-surfaced mallet until about ¼ inch thick. Sprinkle each side of each piece with ⅛ teaspoon of the black peppercorns and ½ teaspoon of the pink peppercorns; lightly pound peppercorns into chicken.

Melt 2 tablespoons of the butter in a wide frying pan over high heat. Add chicken pieces, a portion at a time (do not crowd pan). Cook, turning once, until meat in thickest part is no longer pink; cut to test (about 1 minute). As chicken is cooked, transfer to a warm platter and keep warm; add more butter to pan as needed.

Pour Madeira into pan, stirring to scrape browned bits free. Add cream and minced rosemary; boil, stirring often, until reduced by half. Pour over chicken. Garnish with rosemary sprigs, if desired. Makes 4 servings.

Per serving: 334 calories, 35 g protein, 6 g carbohydrates, 18 g total fat, 138 mg cholesterol, 183 mg sodium

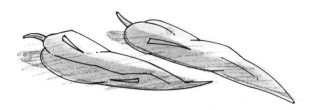

Chicken & Green Chile Enchiladas

Preparation time: About 30 minutes
Baking time: 12 to 15 minutes

While these spicy chicken-cheese enchiladas are baking, prepare a simple lettuce and avocado salad. To round out a festive Mexican-style menu, serve sliced mangoes or wedges of chilled watermelon for dessert.

8 **to 10 small flour tortillas (*each* about 6 inches in diameter)**
1 **tablespoon salad oil**
1 **medium-size onion, thinly sliced**
½ **teaspoon ground cumin**
¼ **teaspoon dry oregano**
1 **can (4 oz.) diced green chiles**
½ **cup whipping cream**
3 **cups diced cooked chicken**
1 **small tomato, seeded and chopped**
2 **cups (8 oz.) shredded jack cheese**
1 **cup (4 oz.) shredded Cheddar cheese**
   Sour cream (optional)
   Sliced ripe olives (optional)

Stack tortillas, wrap in foil, and place in a 350° oven until heated through (about 15 minutes).

Meanwhile, heat oil in a wide frying pan over medium heat. Add onion, cumin, and oregano; cook, stirring often, until onion is soft (about 10 minutes). Stir in chiles and cream. Boil over high heat, stirring often, until thickened (about 2 minutes). Add chicken and tomato; remove from heat and stir in 1 cup of the jack cheese.

Spoon an equal amount of chicken filling on each tortilla; roll up tortillas and place, seam sides down, in a single layer in a lightly greased 8- by 12-inch baking dish. Sprinkle with Cheddar cheese and remaining 1 cup jack cheese. Bake in a 425° oven until cheese is melted and enchiladas are heated through (12 to 15 minutes). Garnish with sour cream and olives, if desired. Makes 4 servings.

Per serving: 892 calories, 56 g protein, 36 g carbohydrates, 59 g total fat, 206 mg cholesterol, 1,103 mg sodium

Roast an Extra Chicken

If you're planning a roast chicken dinner, keep in mind that you can roast two birds as easily as one—then use the meat from the second bird for sandwiches, main-dish salads, or casseroles. One 3- to 3¼-pound frying chicken yields about 3 cups of diced cooked meat.

Orange-Herb Chicken

Preparation time: About 10 minutes
Baking time: About 35 minutes

A baste of soy sauce, orange juice, and herbs gives these baked chicken pieces their appealing flavor. Offer a bulgur pilaf alongside to share the assertive sauce.

> Orange-Herb Baste (recipe follows)
> 1 chicken (3 to 3¼ lbs.), cut up
> Vegetable oil cooking spray
> ¼ cup regular-strength chicken broth

Prepare Orange-Herb Baste; set aside. Rinse chicken and pat dry.

Spray a shallow 12- by 15-inch baking pan with cooking spray. Set chicken breasts aside; place remaining chicken pieces, skin sides down, in pan and top evenly with about a third of the baste. Bake in a 400° oven for 15 minutes. Turn chicken over, add breasts to pan, and spoon remaining baste over chicken.

Return to oven and continue to bake until meat in thickest part of breasts is no longer pink; cut to test (about 20 more minutes). Transfer chicken to a warm platter and keep warm.

Pour broth into baking pan, stirring to scrape browned bits free; then pour into a 1½- to 2-quart pan. Bring to a boil over high heat, stirring; spoon over chicken. Makes 4 servings.

Orange-Herb Baste. Mix 1 can (6 oz.) **frozen orange juice concentrate,** thawed; ⅓ cup **soy sauce;** 1½ teaspoons minced **fresh ginger** or ½ teaspoon ground ginger; 1 clove **garlic,** minced or pressed; and 1 teaspoon *each* chopped **fresh thyme, sage, marjoram, rosemary, and oregano** (or ½ teaspoon *each* of the dry herbs).

Per serving: 346 calories, 40 g protein, 23 carbohydrates, 10 g total fat, 113 mg cholesterol, 1,531 mg sodium

Baked Chicken Quarters with Port & Grapes

Preparation time: About 10 minutes
Baking time: About 35 minutes

Many of us associate elegant cuisine with time-consuming preparation—so it's hard to believe that this exquisite dish comes to the table in such short order. Before you start preparing the chicken, pop small whole sweet potatoes into the oven to serve alongside.

> 1 chicken (3 to 3¼ lbs.), cut into quarters
> 1 tablespoon butter or margarine, melted
> Salt and ground white pepper
> ¾ cup regular-strength chicken broth
> ½ cup tawny port
> 1 tablespoon cornstarch, blended with 1 tablespoon water
> 1 tablespoon firmly packed brown sugar
> ⅛ teaspoon dry thyme
> 1½ cups seedless red grapes

Rinse chicken and pat dry. Brush skin sides with butter; sprinkle with salt and white pepper. Place chicken quarters, well apart and skin sides down, in a shallow baking pan. Bake in a 400° oven for 20 minutes. Turn over and continue to bake until skin is crisp and browned and meat near thighbone is no longer pink; cut to test (about 15 more minutes). Transfer chicken to a warm deep platter and keep warm.

Pour broth into baking pan, stirring to scrape browned bits free; then pour into a 2-quart pan. Add port, cornstarch mixture, sugar, and thyme. Boil over high heat, stirring constantly, until sauce is thickened and clear. Add grapes; stir just until heated through.

Pour half the port sauce over and around chicken. Pass remaining sauce at the table. Makes 4 servings.

Per serving: 329 calories, 38 g protein, 15 g carbohydrates, 13 g total fat, 121 mg cholesterol, 328 mg sodium

Garlic Chicken & Potatoes

Pictured on page 110

Preparation time: About 15 minutes
Cooking time: 35 to 40 minutes

Don't let the amount of garlic keep you from trying this hearty combination of chicken and potatoes; with long, gentle simmering, the pungent cloves take on a surprisingly mild, sweet flavor.

- 4 **whole chicken legs (1½ to 2 lbs. *total*)**
- 3 **tablespoons olive oil or salad oil**
- 8 **small red thin-skinned potatoes (*each* 1½ to 2 inches in diameter), scrubbed**
- 1½ **teaspoons minced fresh rosemary or 1 teaspoon dry rosemary**
- ¼ **cup water**
- 24 **large cloves garlic, peeled and slightly crushed**
  Salt and pepper
  Rosemary sprigs (optional)

Rinse chicken and pat dry. Heat oil in a wide frying pan over medium-high heat. Add chicken and potatoes; cook, turning potatoes occasionally and chicken once, until chicken pieces are browned on both sides (10 to 12 minutes).

Reduce heat to low and add minced rosemary and water to pan. Cover and cook for 15 minutes. Turn chicken again and add garlic. Cover and continue to cook, turning potatoes and garlic occasionally, until potatoes are tender throughout when pierced and meat near thighbone is no longer pink; cut to test (about 10 more minutes). Transfer chicken, potatoes, and garlic to a warm platter.

Stir pan drippings, scraping browned bits free; pour over chicken and vegetables. Season to taste with salt and pepper. Garnish with rosemary sprigs, if desired. Makes 4 servings.

Per serving: 463 calories, 30 g protein, 23 g carbohydrates, 28 g total fat, 121 mg cholesterol, 124 mg sodium

Chicken Legs in Cassis

Preparation time: About 5 minutes
Cooking time: 40 to 45 minutes

In Europe, fruit is a favorite accent for meats and poultry. Here, the sweet-tart flavor of black currants—in vinegar, liqueur, and the actual dried fruit—lends distinction to tender chicken legs. Serve with oven-crisp French fries and a salad of watercress and lettuce.

- 4 **whole chicken legs (1½ to 2 lbs. *total*)**
  Salt, ground white pepper, and ground nutmeg
- 2 **tablespoons butter or margarine**
- 1 **tablespoon salad oil**
- 1 **clove garlic, minced or pressed**
- 2 **tablespoons cassis vinegar or raspberry vinegar**
- 2 **teaspoons tomato paste**
- ¼ **cup dried currants**
- ¾ **cup regular-strength chicken broth**
- ¼ **cup *each* dry white wine and crème de cassis (black currant liqueur)**
- 1 **tablespoon all-purpose flour**

Rinse chicken, pat dry, and sprinkle with salt, white pepper, and nutmeg. Melt 1 tablespoon of the butter in oil in a wide frying pan over medium-high heat. Add chicken and cook, turning once, until browned on both sides (10 to 12 minutes). Stir in garlic, vinegar, and tomato paste; sprinkle with currants. Pour in broth, wine, and crème de cassis. Bring to a boil. Reduce heat, cover, and simmer until meat near thighbone is no longer pink; cut to test (about 25 minutes).

Smoothly mix flour with remaining 1 tablespoon butter; set aside. Lift chicken from pan, reserving drippings; transfer chicken to an ovenproof platter or shallow casserole and keep warm in a low oven while completing sauce. Boil liquid in frying pan over high heat, stirring often, until reduced by about a third. Blend in butter-flour mixture a little at a time, stirring constantly with a whisk, until sauce is thickened and shiny. Pour over chicken. Makes 4 servings.

Per serving: 413 calories, 28 g protein, 14 g carbohydrates, 27 g total fat, 136 mg cholesterol, 383 mg sodium

Chicken Thighs Provençal

Preparation time: About 10 minutes
Cooking time: About 30 minutes

Though the ingredients come from the south of France, the quick tempo of this recipe is definitely American. You chop chicken thighs into shorter pieces to speed their cooking time, then simmer them in an anise-flavored tomato sauce.

- 6 **chicken thighs (2 to 2¼ lbs. *total*)**
- 2 **tablespoons olive oil**
  Salt and pepper
- 2 **tablespoons Pernod, anisette, or brandy**
- 1 **small onion, finely chopped**
- 2 **cloves garlic, minced or pressed**
- 1 **teaspoon herbes de Provence or Italian herb seasoning; or ¼ teaspoon *each* dry basil, dry oregano, dry thyme, and dry marjoram**
- 1 **tablespoon all-purpose flour**
- ½ **cup dry white wine**
- 1 **can (about 14½ oz.) diced tomatoes in purée**
- ¼ **cup Niçoise or small ripe olives**

Rinse chicken and pat dry. Then, with a cleaver or heavy knife, cut each thigh in half through bone. Heat oil in a wide frying pan over medium-high heat. Add chicken pieces and cook, turning once, until browned on both sides and no longer pink near bone; cut to test (15 to 20 minutes). Season to taste with salt and pepper.

Pour Pernod into pan and set aflame (not beneath an exhaust fan or near flammable items); shake pan until flames die. Lift out chicken; set aside. Discard all but 1 tablespoon of the drippings.

Add onion, garlic, and herbs to pan and cook over medium-high heat, stirring often, until onion is lightly browned. Sprinkle in flour and cook, stirring, until bubbly. Blend in wine and bring to a boil. Add tomatoes and their liquid and bring to a simmer. Stir in olives. Return chicken to pan and cook, stirring gently, just until heated through. Makes 4 servings.

Per serving: 460 calories, 33 g protein, 13 g carbohydrates, 30 g total fat, 119 mg cholesterol, 361 mg sodium

Blue Cheese–stuffed Chicken with Walnuts

Pictured on facing page

Preparation time: About 15 minutes
Cooking time: About 25 minutes

As these tender chicken paupiettes simmer, nuggets of blue cheese inside them melt, enriching the creamy wine sauce. Butter-toasted walnuts add a crisp finishing touch. To complete an easy, elegant meal, offer a green salad and golden French fries or a sliced baguette.

- 6 **boneless chicken thighs (about 1¼ lbs. *total*), skinned**
- 6 **sticks blue-veined cheese (about 3 oz. *total*), *each* ½ by 2 inches**
  All-purpose flour
- 1 **tablespoon butter or margarine**
- 1 **tablespoon salad oil**
- ½ **cup coarsely chopped walnuts**
- ½ **cup dry white wine or regular-strength chicken broth**
- ½ **cup whipping cream**
  Watercress sprigs

Rinse chicken and pat dry, then place pieces between sheets of plastic wrap and pound with a flat-surfaced mallet until about ¼ inch thick. Place pieces skinned sides down; put a stick of cheese at one end of each. Fold in sides and roll up compactly; fasten securely with skewers or wooden picks. Dust with flour.

Melt butter in oil in a wide frying pan over medium heat. Add walnuts and cook, stirring occasionally, until lightly browned (2 to 3 minutes). With a slotted spoon, remove nuts from pan and set aside.

Add chicken to pan; cook, turning as needed, until lightly browned on all sides (about 5 minutes). Pour in wine. Reduce heat, cover, and simmer until meat is no longer pink in center; cut to test (12 to 15 minutes). Transfer chicken to a warm platter; discard wooden picks and keep chicken warm.

Stir cream into pan juices. Boil over high heat, stirring often, until reduced by about half. Pour sauce over chicken; sprinkle with walnuts and garnish with watercress. Makes 3 servings.

Per serving: 592 calories, 37 g protein, 8 g carbohydrates, 47 g total fat, 187 mg cholesterol, 569 mg sodium

*Nestled on a bed of watercress, Blue Cheese–stuffed
Chicken with Walnuts (recipe on facing page) offers both
a creamy stuffing and a crunchy garnish. Serve with
crisp French-fried shoestring potatoes.*

Broiled Chicken & Cheese Mexicana

Preparation time: About 20 minutes
Broiling time: 10 to 12 minutes

This saladlike Mexican main dish features cheese-gilded chicken that's festively flavored with lime, garlic, and red pepper. Complete a summer menu with ice-cold beer and hot, buttery corn on the cob.

- 6 boneless chicken thighs (about 1¼ lbs. *total*), skinned
- 2 tablespoons lime or lemon juice
- 1 tablespoon red wine vinegar
- 2 tablespoons olive oil or salad oil
- 1 clove garlic, minced or pressed
- ⅛ teaspoon *each* salt, ground cumin, and crushed red pepper flakes
- 3 cups lightly packed shredded iceberg lettuce
- 1 medium-size firm-ripe avocado
- ½ cup shredded jack cheese
- ½ cup shredded sharp Cheddar cheese
- 1 medium-size tomato, cut into wedges
  Lime wedges (optional)
  Fresh cilantro (coriander) sprigs (optional)

Rinse chicken and pat dry, then place pieces between sheets of plastic wrap and pound with a flat-surfaced mallet until about ¼ inch thick. In a small bowl, mix lime juice, vinegar, oil, garlic, salt, cumin, and red pepper flakes; reserve 2 tablespoons of the mixture, then brush chicken all over with some of the remaining mixture.

Place chicken on rack of a broiler pan. Broil about 4 inches below heat, turning once and brushing with remaining lime juice mixture, until meat in thickest part is no longer pink; cut to test (8 to 10 minutes).

Meanwhile, spread lettuce on a platter. Pit, peel, and slice avocado; drizzle avocado and lettuce with reserved 2 tablespoons lime juice mixture. Sprinkle chicken with jack and Cheddar cheeses; return to oven and continue to broil until cheese is melted (about 2 more minutes). Arrange chicken, avocado, and tomato on lettuce. Garnish with lime wedges and cilantro, if desired. Makes 3 servings.

Per serving: 519 calories, 39 g protein, 10 g carbohydrates, 37 g total fat, 149 mg cholesterol, 445 mg sodium

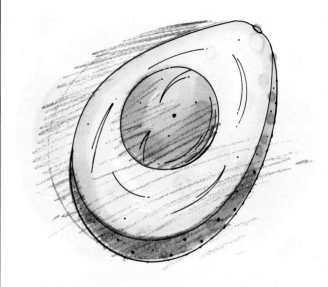

Kauai Chicken

Preparation time: About 5 minutes
Baking time: 30 to 35 minutes

Dark, spicy-sweet hoisin sauce traditionally accompanies Peking duck; here, it enhances a speedily prepared chicken dish from Hawaii.

- 8 small chicken thighs (2 to 2½ lbs. *total*)
- ¼ cup *each* granulated sugar and firmly packed brown sugar
- ⅓ cup soy sauce
- 2 tablespoons hoisin sauce
- 1 clove garlic, minced or pressed

Rinse chicken pieces, pat dry, and arrange, skin sides down, slightly apart in a shallow rimmed baking pan or casserole. Stir together granulated sugar, brown sugar, soy sauce, hoisin sauce, and garlic. Spoon about half the mixture over chicken.

Bake in a 400° oven for 20 minutes. Turn chicken over and top with remaining sauce. Return to oven and continue to bake until meat near bone is no longer pink; cut to test (10 to 15 more minutes). Makes 4 servings.

Per serving: 450 calories, 35 g protein, 30 g carbohydrates, 21 g total fat, 123 mg cholesterol, 1,728 mg sodium

Santa Fe Chicken Drumsticks with Rice

Preparation time: About 10 minutes
Cooking time: 30 to 35 minutes

Flavored with bits of onion and smoky bacon, a bed of fluffy rice absorbs the chili-seasoned juices from these tender baked drumsticks.

- 8 **small chicken drumsticks (1½ to 2 lbs.** *total***)**
- 2 **tablespoons butter or margarine**
- 1 **tablespoon salad oil**
- ⅓ **cup all-purpose flour**
- 1 **teaspoon chili powder**
- ½ **teaspoon paprika**
- ¼ **teaspoon pepper**
  Onion Rice (recipe follows)
  Chopped parsley

Rinse chicken, pat dry, and set aside. Combine butter and oil in a shallow rimmed baking pan. Set in a 400° oven until butter is melted. Meanwhile, combine flour, chili powder, paprika, and pepper in a small bag. Add chicken to bag, about half at a time; shake to coat lightly with seasoned flour. Arrange chicken in a single layer in baking pan; turn to coat with butter mixture.

Bake in a 400° oven until drumsticks are well browned and meat near bone is no longer pink; cut to test (30 to 35 minutes). Meanwhile, prepare Onion Rice. To serve, arrange rice on a warm platter; top with chicken and garnish with parsley. Makes 4 servings.

Onion Rice. In a medium-size frying pan, cook 2 slices **bacon,** diced, over medium heat until fat is melted. Add ⅓ cup chopped **onion** and ⅔ cup **long-grain white rice;** cook, stirring, until rice is lightly browned (about 5 minutes). Add ⅔ cup *each* **water** and **regular-strength chicken broth.** Bring to a boil; reduce heat, cover, and simmer until rice is tender to bite and all liquid has been absorbed (about 20 minutes).

Per serving: 510 calories, 30 g protein, 34 g carbohydrates, 27 g total fat, 109 mg cholesterol, 394 mg sodium

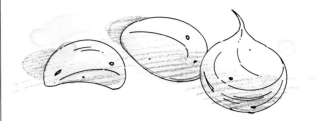

Mustard Chicken Chunks with Vermicelli

Preparation time: About 15 minutes
Cooking time: About 20 minutes

Fans of dark-meat chicken will enjoy this dish. You simmer morsels of chicken thigh in a Dijon mustard–wine sauce dotted with crunchy mustard seeds, then spoon the combination over hot vermicelli or another favorite pasta.

- 1 **tablespoon butter or margarine**
- 1 **tablespoon olive oil or salad oil**
- 1¼ **to 1½ pounds boneless chicken thighs, skinned and cut into bite-size chunks**
- 1 **small clove garlic, minced or pressed**
- 1 **teaspoon mustard seeds, coarsely crushed**
- ¼ **teaspoon dry tarragon**
- ⅓ **cup dry white wine**
- 6 **ounces dry vermicelli or other pasta strands**
- 2 **teaspoons Dijon mustard**
- ¼ **cup thinly sliced green onions (including tops)**
- ½ **cup sour cream**

Melt butter in oil in a wide frying pan over medium-high heat. Add chicken; cook, stirring often, until browned on all sides (about 5 minutes). Stir in garlic, mustard seeds, tarragon, and wine. Reduce heat, cover, and simmer until meat is no longer pink in center; cut to test (8 to 10 minutes). Meanwhile, in a 4- to 5-quart pan, cook vermicelli in 2 quarts boiling water until *al dente* (10 to 12 minutes); or cook according to package directions. Drain, pour onto a warm platter, and keep warm.

Add Dijon mustard and 3 tablespoons of the onions to chicken. Cook over medium-high heat, stirring often, until almost all liquid has evaporated. Remove from heat and stir in sour cream until smoothly combined. Serve over vermicelli; sprinkle with remaining 1 tablespoon onions. Makes 4 servings.

Per serving: 419 calories, 29 g protein, 34 g carbohydrates, 18 g total fat, 114 mg cholesterol, 221 mg sodium

In Turkey Scaloppine alla Pizzaiola (recipe on facing page), poultry stands in deliciously for the more traditional veal. Complement the savory tomato sauce with a side dish of stir-fried zucchini.

Turkey Scaloppine alla Pizzaiola

Pictured on facing page

Preparation time: About 20 minutes
Cooking time: About 20 minutes

If you enjoy veal scaloppine, you'll appreciate this zesty entrée. It goes together almost as quickly as you can say "pizzaiola"—the Neapolitan-style sauce that tops the sautéed turkey slices. (For another version of turkey scaloppine, see page 128.)

>   Tomato-Caper Sauce (recipe follows)
> 1¼ pounds boneless turkey breast, cut into ½-inch-thick slices
>   All-purpose flour
> 1 egg beaten with 1 tablespoon water
> 2 tablespoons butter or margarine
> 1 tablespoon olive oil
> ¼ cup grated Parmesan cheese
>   Chopped parsley

Prepare Tomato-Caper Sauce and keep warm over lowest heat (or set aside, then reheat).

Rinse turkey and pat dry; then place slices between sheets of plastic wrap and pound with a flat-surfaced mallet until about ¼ inch thick. Dust with flour; dip into egg mixture to coat lightly.

Melt 1 tablespoon of the butter in oil in a wide frying pan over medium-high heat. Add turkey, a portion at a time (do not crowd pan); cook, turning once, until golden brown on both sides, adding remaining 1 tablespoon butter as needed. As turkey is cooked, transfer to a warm shallow platter, overlapping pieces slightly; keep warm.

To serve, sprinkle turkey with cheese, then top with hot Tomato-Caper Sauce and garnish with parsley. Makes 4 servings.

Tomato-Caper Sauce. Heat 1 tablespoon **olive oil** in a wide frying pan over medium-high heat. Add 3 small **pear-shaped tomatoes,** seeded and finely chopped; ½ teaspoon **Italian herb seasoning** or ⅛ teaspoon *each* dry basil, dry oregano, dry thyme, and dry marjoram; 1 clove **garlic,** minced or pressed; 1 tablespoon **tomato paste;** ½ cup **dry white wine;** and 2 teaspoons drained **capers.** Boil, stirring often, until tomatoes are soft (6 to 8 minutes).

Per serving: 346 calories, 38 g protein, 7 g carbohydrates, 18 g total fat, 161 mg cholesterol, 341 mg sodium

Raspberry-glazed Turkey Tenderloins

Preparation time: About 15 minutes
Broiling time: 8 to 10 minutes

A raspberry-mustard glaze keeps lean, light turkey tenderloins (sometimes called fillets) moist during broiling—and doubles as a distinctive sauce. Serve with herb-sprinkled pasta and Greens Plus (page 32).

> 4 turkey breast tenderloins (about 2¼ lbs. *total*)
> ½ cup seedless raspberry jam
> 6 tablespoons raspberry vinegar
> ¼ cup Dijon mustard
> 1 teaspoon grated orange peel
> ½ teaspoon dry thyme

Rinse turkey and pat dry; set aside. In a 2- to 3-quart pan, whisk together jam, vinegar, mustard, orange peel, and thyme. Bring to a boil over high heat and boil, stirring, until reduced by about a fourth (2 to 3 minutes). Reserve about ½ cup of the glaze and keep warm; coat turkey with some of the remaining glaze.

Set turkey on rack of a broiler pan. Broil about 4 inches below heat, turning and basting once with remaining glaze, until meat is no longer pink in center; cut to test (8 to 10 minutes). Slice crosswise and arrange on warm plates. Offer with reserved ½ cup glaze. Makes 4 to 6 servings.

Per serving: 337 calories, 48 g protein, 25 g carbohydrates, 4 g total fat, 127 mg cholesterol, 501 mg sodium

Stir-fried Poultry

In today's markets, you'll find a wide selection of skinless, boneless cuts of chicken and turkey that are ideal for stir-fries. Allow about 1 pound boneless poultry for 4 servings. To prepare for cooking, pound with a flat-surfaced mallet until about ¼ inch thick; cut larger pieces into thin strips or 1-inch squares.

Turkey Scaloppine

Preparation time: About 15 minutes
Cooking time: About 15 minutes

Sliced, pounded turkey breast, sautéed and served with a mushroom-wine sauce and juicy lemon wedges, makes a simple yet sophisticated meal.

- 1 **pound boneless turkey breast, cut into ¼-inch-thick slices**
  All-purpose flour
- ½ **cup (¼ lb.) butter or margarine**
- ½ **pound medium-size mushrooms, sliced**
- ½ **cup Marsala**
  Lemon wedges (optional)
  Parsley sprigs (optional)

Rinse turkey and pat dry, then place slices between sheets of plastic wrap and pound with a flat-surfaced mallet until about ⅛ inch thick. Coat with flour; shake off excess.

Melt 2 tablespoons of the butter in a wide frying pan over medium-high heat. Add turkey, a portion at a time (do not crowd pan); cook, turning once, until lightly browned on both sides (about 2 minutes), adding more butter as needed. As turkey is cooked, transfer to a warm platter; keep warm.

Add mushrooms to drippings in pan and cook, stirring, until browned (5 to 7 minutes). Add Marsala, stirring to scrape browned bits free. Lift out mushrooms and spoon over turkey. Boil pan juices over high heat, stirring, until large, shiny bubbles form (about 1 minute). Add remaining butter; stir until smoothly blended into sauce. Pour sauce over turkey and garnish with lemon wedges and parsley, if desired. Makes 4 servings.

Per serving: 376 calories, 28 g protein, 9 g carbohydrates, 25 g total fat, 133 mg cholesterol, 315 mg sodium

Swiss Turkey & Mushrooms

Preparation time: About 20 minutes
Cooking time: About 20 minutes

The original version of this recipe features quickly cooked slivered veal in a brandied cream sauce—but the dish is equally tempting when made with turkey breast. Serve with butter-browned potato chunks or fresh egg noodles.

- 1¼ **pounds boneless turkey breast, cut into ½-inch-thick slices**
  Salt, ground white pepper, and freshly ground nutmeg
  All-purpose flour
- 3 **tablespoons butter or margarine**
- 1 **tablespoon salad oil**
- ¼ **pound small mushrooms, quartered**
- ¼ **cup chopped shallots**
- ¼ **cup dry white wine**
- ¾ **cup whipping cream**
- ¼ **cup brandy**
  Chopped parsley

Rinse turkey and pat dry, then place pieces between sheets of plastic wrap and pound with a flat-surfaced mallet until about ¼ inch thick. Sprinkle both sides of each turkey slice with salt, white pepper, and nutmeg; dust with flour. Cut into thin bite-size strips.

Melt 2 tablespoons of the butter in oil in a wide frying pan over medium-high heat. Cook turkey, about half at a time, until golden brown on all sides. Lift out and set aside on a rimmed plate.

Melt remaining 1 tablespoon butter in pan. Stir in mushrooms and shallots; cook, stirring often, until mushrooms are lightly browned (5 to 7 minutes). Add wine and cream. Boil, stirring often, until liquid is reduced by about half. Return turkey and any accumulated juices to pan. Stir just until heated through, then remove pan from heat.

In a small, long-handled pan, heat brandy until just barely warm. Pour over turkey mixture. Set aflame (not beneath an exhaust fan or near flammable items); shake pan until flames die. Stir turkey mixture over medium-high heat to blend in brandy. Sprinkle with parsley. Makes 4 servings.

Per serving: 429 calories, 36 g protein, 7 g carbohydrates, 28 g total fat, 161 mg cholesterol, 201 mg sodium

Turkey-Bacon Logs

Preparation time: About 15 minutes
Cooking time: 15 to 20 minutes

Traditional holiday partners—turkey and cranberries—team up in an easy entrée to enjoy all year round. Crisp bacon wraps around logs of well-seasoned ground turkey; canned cranberry sauce, dressed up with spices and sweet raisins, is served alongside.

- 1 egg
- ¼ cup fine dry bread crumbs
- ¼ teaspoon *each* salt and ground white pepper
- 1 pound ground turkey
- ¼ cup *each* minced parsley and sliced green onions (including tops)
- 8 slices bacon
   Cranberry Sauce (recipe follows)

In a bowl, beat egg; stir in crumbs, salt, and white pepper. Let stand for 1 minute. Add turkey, parsley, and onions; mix lightly until well combined. Divide mixture into 8 equal portions and shape each into a 3½-inch-long log. Wrap a bacon slice spiral-fashion around each log, securing ends of each slice with a wooden pick.

Place turkey logs on a greased rack in a baking pan. Bake in a 450° oven until meat is no longer pink in center; cut to test (15 to 20 minutes). Meanwhile, prepare Cranberry Sauce; place in a serving bowl to pass at the table. Remove picks from logs before serving. Makes 4 servings.

Cranberry Sauce. In a 1-quart pan, stir together 1 small can (about 8 oz.) **whole-berry cranberry sauce,** 3 tablespoons *each* **sugar** and **water,** ½ cup **golden raisins,** ¼ teaspoon *each* **ground cinnamon** and **grated lemon peel,** l tablespoon **lemon juice,** and ⅛ teaspoon **ground cloves.** Cook over medium heat, stirring occasionally, until heated through (about 10 minutes).

Per serving: 458 calories, 27 g protein, 52 g carbohydrates, 16 g total fat, 147 mg cholesterol, 527 mg sodium

Minced Turkey in Lettuce

Preparation time: About 20 minutes
Cooking time: 6 to 8 minutes

A savory blend of turkey, mushrooms, water chestnuts, and bright green peas makes a delectable filling for crisp lettuce cups. (Another time, you might wrap the meat mixture in warm flour tortillas.) To complete the meal, try seedless grapes or sliced oranges.

   Cooking Sauce (recipe follows)
- ¼ cup salad oil
- 2 large cloves garlic, minced or pressed
- 1 teaspoon grated fresh ginger
- ¼ to ½ teaspoon crushed red pepper flakes
- 1 pound ground turkey; or 1½ pounds chicken breasts, skinned, boned, and minced
- 1 can (about 8 oz.) bamboo shoots, drained and minced
- 1 can (about 8 oz.) water chestnuts, drained and minced
- ¼ pound mushrooms, minced
- 4 green onions (including tops), minced
- ½ cup frozen peas
   Hoisin sauce (optional)
   Butter lettuce or romaine leaves, rinsed and crisped
- 2 green onions (green part only), cut into 1½-inch lengths

Prepare Cooking Sauce and set aside. Heat 2 tablespoons of the oil in a wok or wide frying pan over high heat. Add garlic, ginger, and red pepper flakes and stir once. Add turkey and cook, stirring to break up large chunks, until no longer pink (about 3 minutes); remove from pan and set aside.

Heat remaining 2 tablespoons oil in pan. Add bamboo shoots, water chestnuts, mushrooms, and minced onions; cook, stirring, for 2 minutes. Return turkey to pan, then add peas. Stir Cooking Sauce, pour into pan, and stir until sauce boils and thickens. Serve immediately.

To eat, spread a little hoisin sauce (if used) on a lettuce leaf. Place a piece of green onion on top and spoon in some of the turkey mixture, then wrap up and eat out of hand. Makes 4 to 6 servings.

Cooking Sauce. Mix 2 teaspoons **cornstarch,** 1 tablespoon **dry sherry,** 2 tablespoons *each* **soy sauce** and **water,** and ½ teaspoon **sugar.**

Per serving: 291 calories, 19 g protein, 13 g carbohydrates, 18 g total fat, 66 mg cholesterol, 521 mg sodium

Braised Game Hens in Chianti

Preparation time: About 5 minutes
Cooking time: About 40 minutes

Smoky pancetta accents Cornish hen halves simmered in robust red wine. Offer golden polenta on the side to share the marvelous sauce.

- **2 Cornish game hens (1¼ to 1½ lbs. *each*), thawed if frozen and split lengthwise**
  Ground white pepper
- **2 tablespoons butter or margarine**
- **1 tablespoon olive oil**
- **2 slices pancetta or bacon (about 2 oz. *total*), coarsely chopped**
- **1 clove garlic, minced or pressed**
- **½ teaspoon dry marjoram**
- **1 tablespoon tomato paste**
- **1¼ cups Chianti or other dry red wine**
- **1 tablespoon all-purpose flour**
  Chopped parsley

Rinse hen halves, pat dry, and sprinkle with white pepper. Set aside.

Melt 1 tablespoon of the butter in oil in a wide, deep frying pan over medium heat. Add pancetta and cook, stirring often, until lightly browned. With a slotted spoon, remove pancetta from pan; drain and set aside.

Add hen halves to drippings in pan and cook over medium-high heat, turning as needed, until browned on all sides. Spoon off and discard drippings. Stir in garlic, marjoram, and tomato paste; add wine. Bring to a boil. Reduce heat, cover, and simmer until meat near thighbone is no longer pink; cut to test (about 25 minutes). Meanwhile, blend remaining 1 tablespoon butter with flour; set aside.

Lift hen halves from pan and transfer to a shallow ovenproof casserole; sprinkle with pancetta and keep warm in a 300° oven. To prepare sauce, bring pan juices to a boil over high heat, stirring. Blend in butter mixture a little at a time, stirring constantly with a whisk; cook until sauce is thickened and shiny. Pour sauce over hen halves; sprinkle with parsley. Makes 4 servings.

Per serving: 450 calories, 39 g protein, 4 g carbohydrates, 30 g total fat, 140 mg cholesterol, 271 mg sodium

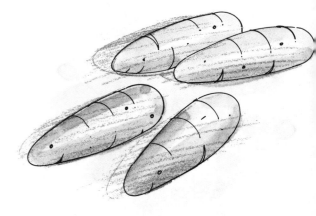

Baked Game Hens with Vegetables

Pictured on facing page

Preparation time: 10 to 15 minutes
Baking time: About 35 minutes

Sweet baby carrots, shallots, and sliced red potatoes bake alongside these succulent game hens, sharing simple seasonings of lemon juice, olive oil, rosemary, and garlic.

- **2 Cornish game hens (1¼ to 1½ lbs. *each*), thawed if frozen and split lengthwise**
- **3 tablespoons lemon juice**
- **3 tablespoons olive oil or salad oil**
- **2 teaspoons dry rosemary**
- **1 clove garlic, minced or pressed**
- **4 shallots**
- **16 to 20 baby carrots, unpeeled**
- **6 to 8 small red thin-skinned potatoes (*each* 1½ to 2 inches in diameter), scrubbed and cut into ¼-inch-thick slices**
  Lemon wedges
  Italian parsley sprigs

Rinse hen halves and pat dry; then place, skin sides up, down center of a shallow 10- by 15-inch baking pan. Mix lemon juice, oil, rosemary, and garlic; pour over hens. Cut unpeeled shallots in half lengthwise. Arrange shallots (cut sides down), carrots, and potatoes evenly around hens.

Bake in a 450° oven until vegetables are tender when pierced and meat near thighbone is no longer pink; cut to test (about 35 minutes). Transfer hen halves and vegetables to a warm platter; garnish with lemon wedges and parsley sprigs. Makes 4 servings.

Per serving: 553 calories, 41 g protein, 31 g carbohydrates, 29 g total fat, 121 mg cholesterol, 164 mg sodium

Golden game hen halves, tiny potatoes, carrots, and shallots all cook together for a one-pan meal: Baked Game Hens with Vegetables (recipe on facing page). You might also serve steamed whole green beans.

Game Hens with Mustard Crust

Preparation time: About 10 minutes
Baking time: About 35 minutes

Brushed with butter, mustard, and herbs, these small birds make a showy presentation. You might serve them with a bright purée of sweet potatoes or winter squash.

- ¼ cup butter or margarine
- ¼ cup coarse-grained or Dijon mustard
- 1½ teaspoons minced fresh rosemary or 1 teaspoon dry rosemary
- 2 cloves garlic, minced or pressed
- 4 Cornish game hens (1¼ to 1½ lbs. *each*), thawed if frozen and split lengthwise
  Rosemary sprigs (optional)

Melt butter in a small pan; mix in mustard, minced rosemary, and garlic. Set aside.

Rinse hen halves, pat dry, and coat all over with mustard mixture. Set slightly apart, skin sides up, in a 9- by 13-inch baking pan.

Bake hen halves in a 450° oven until meat near thighbone is no longer pink; cut to test (about 35 minutes). Transfer to a warm platter and garnish with rosemary sprigs, if desired. Makes 4 servings.

Per serving: 721 calories, 68 g protein, 3 g carbohydrates, 47 g total fat, 251 mg cholesterol, 772 mg sodium

Italian Baked Game Hens & Potatoes

Preparation time: About 10 minutes
Baking time: About 35 minutes

Golden potato wedges complement hen halves seasoned with thyme and oregano—or with dry mustard and fines herbes, if you prefer. Garnish the serving platter with juicy cherry tomatoes.

- 2 Cornish game hens (1¼ to 1½ lbs. *each*), thawed if frozen and split lengthwise
- ½ cup (¼ lb.) butter or margarine
- ¼ teaspoon *each* paprika, dry oregano, and dry thyme
- 2 large russet potatoes, scrubbed
  Cherry tomatoes

Rinse hens; pat dry. Combine butter, paprika, oregano, and thyme in a small pan; stir over medium heat until butter is melted. Brush about 1 tablespoon of the herb butter over cut surfaces of hen halves; then place halves, skin sides up, slightly apart in a 9- by 13-inch baking pan.

Cut potatoes in half lengthwise; then cut each half lengthwise into 4 wedges. Brush cut surfaces of potatoes with remaining herb butter. Place potatoes, skin sides down, in a 9-inch-square baking pan.

Place pans side by side in a 450° oven. Bake until potatoes are tender when pierced and meat near thighbone is no longer pink; cut to test (about 35 minutes). Transfer hen halves to a warm platter; surround with potatoes and garnish with cherry tomatoes. Makes 4 servings.

Per serving: 610 calories, 38 g protein, 21 g carbohydrates, 41 g total fat, 178 mg cholesterol, 351 mg sodium

French Baked Game Hens & Potatoes

Follow directions for **Italian Baked Game Hens & Potatoes,** but omit paprika, oregano, and thyme. Add 1 tablespoon finely minced **onion** to melted butter and cook, stirring, until onion is soft (about 10 minutes). Stir in a dash of **liquid hot pepper seasoning** and ¼ teaspoon *each* **dry mustard, fines herbes,** and **garlic powder.** Makes 4 servings.

Per serving: 610 calories, 38 g protein, 21 g carbohydrates, 41 g total fat, 178 mg cholesterol, 353 mg sodium

Timesaver: The Microwave Oven

Microwaving is a boon to the busy cook. Even if you don't want to prepare a whole meal in your microwave, you can save a lot of time by using it for small tasks. Here are some ways the microwave can help speed up your meal preparation.

Reheating bread & rolls

Breads, doughnuts, and sweet rolls reheat easily and quickly in the microwave—so quickly, in fact, that you must be vigilant. It takes just 10 to 15 seconds on **HIGH (100%)** to reheat each roll or bread slice.

To reheat a roll or bread slice, wrap it in a paper towel or paper napkin (to keep the bottom from becoming soggy); then heat only until the outside feels warm to the touch. If heated too long, the bread will turn tough and hard as it cools. The sugary fillings and icings of sweet rolls attract more microwaves than the pastry itself, so to avoid burning yourself, let the rolls stand for a few minutes before serving.

Melting butter

Unwrap a ½-cup (¼-lb.) stick of butter or margarine and place it in a 10-ounce microwave-safe dish or custard cup. Microwave, uncovered, on **HIGH (100%)** for 1 minute.

Softening butter

Unwrap a ½-cup (¼-lb.) stick of butter or margarine and place it on a microwave-safe saucer. Microwave, uncovered, on **MEDIUM (50%)** for 10 to 15 seconds. Let stand for 5 minutes to complete softening.

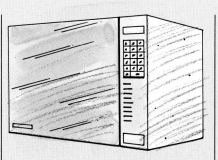

Softening cream cheese

Unwrap a package of cream cheese and place it on a small microwave-safe plate; cover loosely with heavy-duty plastic wrap. Microwave a 3-ounce package of cream cheese on **MEDIUM (50%)** for 30 seconds to 1 minute. Microwave an 8-ounce package for 1½ to 2 minutes.

Softening cheese

For easier slicing of refrigerated cheese, wrap it in heavy-duty plastic wrap and place directly on floor of microwave. (Or put cheese on a microwave-safe plate and cover loosely with plastic wrap.) Microwave on **MEDIUM (50%)** for 30 seconds to 1 minute (depending on size) or until cheese is slightly soft to the touch.

Softening ice cream

Place an unopened half gallon package of hard ice cream on oven floor. Microwave on **MEDIUM (50%)** for 45 seconds to 1 minute; let stand for a minute or two before serving.

Warming tortillas

To warm an unopened package of tortillas, cut a slit in package and place it on oven floor. Microwave on **HIGH (100%)** for 1 minute. Or wrap a number of tortillas in paper towels; microwave on **HIGH (100%)** for 6 to 7 seconds per tortilla.

Softening frozen juice concentrates

Remove one end of a 6- or 12-oz. can of frozen juice. Place, upright, directly on oven floor. Microwave on **HIGH (100%)** for 1 minute. Let concentrate stand for a minute or two before preparing juice.

Making broth

Place a bouillon cube (chicken, beef, or vegetable) or a teaspoon of stock base in a 1-cup glass measure filled with water. Microwave, uncovered, on **HIGH (100%)** for 1½ to 2 minutes. Stir until bouillon is dissolved.

Toasting nuts

To toast ½ cup pine nuts or whole or slivered blanched almonds, arrange nuts in a single layer in a 9- or 10-inch microwave-safe baking dish. Microwave, uncovered, on **HIGH (100%)** for 6 to 8 minutes, stirring every 2 minutes. Nuts should be just golden; they'll continue to cook while standing.

Melting chocolate

Unwrap 1 square (1 oz.) unsweetened or semisweet chocolate and place in a small microwave-safe bowl or dish. Cover and microwave on **MEDIUM (50%)** for 2 minutes or until soft but not completely melted (chocolate will scorch if overheated). Stir until fully melted.

For a mouth-watering experience, wrap up stir-fried steak, chiles, and red pepper in a steamy-warm flour tortilla. Top off Fajitas Stir-fry (recipe on page 136) with avocado, sour cream, and a squeeze of fresh lime.

Meats

By choosing the right cuts and cooking methods, you can enjoy rich, robust beef, lamb, pork, and veal in short order. This chapter spotlights barbecuing, broiling, pan-frying, and stir-frying—all speedy techniques designed to put dinner on the table fast. Choose grilled pounded chops or tender steaks; go elegant with brandy-sauced sautéed veal or opt for a casual stir-fry of pork and green onions. And for that simmered-all-day flavor in just 30 minutes, try our hearty chili.

Fajitas Stir-fry

Pictured on page 134

Preparation time: *About 20 minutes*
Cooking time: *About 15 minutes*

This speedy version of fajitas features warm flour tortillas filled with a stir-fry of lean steak strips, onion, bell pepper, and hot chiles. Serve with sour cream and diced avocado, or choose other favorite fajita trimmings.

- 8 flour tortillas (*each* 7 to 8 inches in diameter)
- ¼ cup salad oil
- 1 pound lean beef steak, such as sirloin or top round (about 1 inch thick), cut into ⅛-inch-thick strips
- 2 cloves garlic, minced or pressed
- 1 large onion, thinly sliced and separated into rings
- 2 or 3 fresh jalapeño chiles, stemmed, seeded, and minced
- 1 large red bell pepper, seeded and cut into thin strips
- 2 teaspoons ground cumin
- 3 tablespoons lime juice
- 1 teaspoon cornstarch
- 2 medium-size pear-shaped tomatoes, seeded and diced
  Salt and pepper
- 1 large firm-ripe avocado
  Lime wedges
  Sour cream

Stack tortillas, wrap in foil, and place in a 350° oven until heated through (about 15 minutes).

Meanwhile, heat 1 tablespoon of the oil in a wok or wide frying pan over high heat. Add a third of the beef and cook, stirring, until lightly browned (about 2 minutes). With a slotted spoon, transfer beef to a bowl. Repeat to brown remaining beef, using 2 more tablespoons of the oil.

Add remaining 1 tablespoon oil to pan; then add garlic, onion, chiles, and bell pepper. Cook, stirring, until onion is tender-crisp to bite (about 2 minutes). In a small bowl, mix cumin, lime juice, and cornstarch; add to pan. Stir in tomatoes, then add beef and accumulated juices; bring to a boil, stirring. Season mixture to taste with salt and pepper, then transfer to a warm serving dish and keep warm.

Pit, peel, and dice avocado. Spoon beef mixture into warm tortillas; offer avocado, lime wedges, and sour cream to add to taste. Makes 4 servings.

Per serving: 647 calories, 34 g protein, 63 g carbohydrates, 29 g total fat, 69 mg cholesterol, 502 mg sodium

Pepper Beef Stir-fry

Preparation time: *About 15 minutes*
Marinating time: *15 minutes*
Cooking time: *About 10 minutes*

Two kinds of pepper—one adding heat, the other bright color—give this dish its lively personality. Serve over thin rice noodles.

- 1 pound sirloin steak (about 1 inch thick), cut into ⅛-inch-thick strips
- 2 teaspoons cracked pepper
- 1 clove garlic, minced or pressed
- 2 tablespoons Worcestershire
- ¼ cup salad oil
- 1 large onion, thinly sliced
- 1 *each* large red and green bell pepper, seeded and cut into thin strips
  Salt

In a bowl, mix beef, cracked pepper, garlic, and Worcestershire; set aside for 15 minutes.

Heat 1 tablespoon of the oil in a wok or wide frying pan over high heat. Add a third of the beef and cook, stirring, until lightly browned (about 2 minutes). With a slotted spoon, transfer beef to a bowl; keep warm. Repeat to brown remaining beef, using 2 more tablespoons of the oil.

Add remaining 1 tablespoon oil to pan, then add onion and bell peppers; cook, stirring, just until vegetables are tender-crisp to bite (about 2 minutes). Stir in beef and accumulated juices. Season to taste with salt. Makes 4 servings.

Per serving: 404 calories, 23 g protein, 8 g carbohydrates, 31 g total fat, 76 mg cholesterol, 146 mg sodium

Grilled Beef Steaks

Preparation time: About 5 minutes
Grilling time: 10 to 30 minutes

When you're in the mood for a splurge, try this beef-eater's delight. Grill your favorite thick steaks over hot coals, then top the meat with dollops of a savory seasoned butter.

Horseradish Butter (recipe follows) or
Cilantro-Chili Butter (page 149)
4 tender steaks, such as boneless top sirloin or T-bone (6 to 8 oz. *each*); or 1½ to 2 pounds top round (about 2 inches thick)
Salt and pepper

Prepare flavored butter of your choice. Set aside.

Place meat on a lightly greased grill 4 to 6 inches above a solid bed of hot coals. Cook, turning once, until meat is well browned on outside and done to your liking; cut to test (for rare, allow 10 to 12 minutes for individual steaks, 24 to 30 minutes for thick steak).

Season steak to taste with salt and pepper. If using top round, cut into thin, slanting slices; place on a warm platter. Offer flavored butter to spoon over individual portions. Makes 4 servings.

Horseradish Butter. In a small bowl, mix ¼ cup **butter** or margarine (at room temperature), 1 teaspoon **prepared horseradish,** and 1 tablespoon **Dijon mustard** until well combined. Transfer to a small serving crock. Makes about ¼ cup.

Per serving of steak: 345 calories, 37 g protein, 0 g carbohydrates, 21 g total fat, 120 mg cholesterol, 84 mg sodium

Per tablespoon of Horseradish Butter: 107 calories, 0.1 g protein, 0.6 g carbohydrates, 12 g total fat, 31 mg cholesterol, 231 mg sodium

Quick-cooking Meat Cuts

If you're short on time, choose quick-cooking meat cuts—for example, those taken from the least-exercised parts of an animal (such as the middle of the back, called the loin). The loin portion of a steer yields porterhouse and T-bone steaks; the same portion of a lamb, pig, or calf produces lamb chops, pork chops, or veal loin chops. Less tender cuts, such as those from the round, flank, and chuck, can also be quick-cooked, but they'll need to be tenderized first. One popular tenderizing technique calls for soaking the meat in a wine, vinegar, or citrus juice marinade; you can also break down the meat's muscle fibers by pounding the pieces out thin with a heavy, flat mallet.

Broiled Steak with Swiss Mustard Sauce

Preparation time: About 5 minutes
Broiling time: 10 to 15 minutes

Thick Porterhouse steak needs only the simplest of sauces—such as this blend of butter, Dijon mustard, and dry vermouth. As you slice the steak, its juices add even more flavor to the sauce.

1 Porterhouse steak (about 1½ inches thick)
3 tablespoons butter or margarine
1 tablespoon Dijon mustard
2 tablespoons dry vermouth or dry white wine
¼ teaspoon Worcestershire

Slash fat around edge of steak at 2- to 3-inch intervals, cutting just to lean meat. Place steak on lightly greased rack of a broiler pan. Broil 3 to 4 inches below heat, turning once, until done to your liking; cut to test (10 to 15 minutes for rare to medium-rare).

Meanwhile, melt butter in a small pan over medium-high heat. Blend in mustard, vermouth, and Worcestershire. Transfer steak to a warm platter; pour sauce around or over meat. Slice steak, swirling slices in sauce before transferring them to individual plates. Makes 3 servings.

Per serving: 593 calories, 39 g protein, 2 g carbohydrates, 47 g total fat, 162 mg cholesterol, 368 mg sodium

Broiled Flank Steak

Preparation time: About 5 minutes
Marinating time: 30 minutes
Broiling time: 8 to 10 minutes

Soaked in an oil-vinegar marinade before broiling, lean flank steak turns out deliciously succulent. You might serve the thinly sliced beef with Broccoli Polonaise (page 161).

- 1 **clove garlic, minced or pressed**
- ⅓ **cup salad oil**
- 3 **tablespoons red wine vinegar**
- 2 **teaspoons *each* Worcestershire, soy sauce, and dry mustard**
- ¼ **teaspoon pepper**
  Few drops of liquid hot pepper seasoning
- 1 **to 1½ pounds flank steak, trimmed of fat**

In a shallow dish, mix garlic, oil, vinegar, Worcestershire, soy sauce, mustard, pepper, and hot pepper seasoning. Place steak in dish; turn to coat with marinade. Let stand for 30 minutes, turning over several times.

Remove steak from marinade; drain briefly, reserving marinade. Place steak on lightly greased rack of a broiler pan. Pour marinade into a small pan and bring to a boil over high heat. Broil steak about 4 inches below heat, turning once and basting several times with marinade, until done to your liking; cut to test (8 to 10 minutes for rare).

To serve, cut steak across the grain into thin, slanting slices. Makes 4 to 6 servings.

Per serving: 323 calories, 22 g protein, 1 g carbohydrates, 25 g total fat, 56 mg cholesterol, 228 mg sodium

Pan-browned Spice Steak

Pictured on facing page

Preparation time: 5 to 10 minutes
Cooking time: About 30 minutes

A pungent coating of crushed juniper berries, black pepper, and allspice turns simple steak into a connoisseur's choice. Diced sweet potatoes, baked in melted butter, offer a mellow counterpoint to the spicy beef.

- ¼ **cup butter or margarine**
- 4 **medium-size sweet potatoes or yams (about 2 lbs. *total*), peeled and diced**
- 1 **tablespoon *each* juniper berries, whole black peppercorns, and whole allspice**
- 1¼ **to 1½ pounds flank steak or skirt steak, trimmed of fat and cut into 4 pieces**
- 1 **tablespoon salad oil**
- 2 **tablespoons gin or water**
  Watercress or parsley sprigs
  Pickled onions
  Salt

Place butter in a shallow 10- by 15-inch baking pan and heat in a 450° oven until melted. Add potatoes; stir to coat with butter. Return to oven and bake, turning potatoes several times with a wide spatula, until potatoes are lightly browned and soft when pressed with a fork (about 30 minutes).

Meanwhile, in a blender or food processor, whirl juniper berries, peppercorns, and allspice until coarsely ground. Press mixture into all sides of each piece of steak.

About 10 minutes before potatoes are done, heat oil in a wide frying pan over medium-high heat. Add steaks and cook, turning once, until well browned on both sides and rare in center; cut to test (3 to 5 minutes). Lift steaks from pan and keep warm. (To cook steaks further, place in oven with potatoes until meat is done to your liking.)

Add gin to pan, stirring to scrape browned bits free. Add potatoes; mix lightly to coat. Garnish steak and potatoes with watercress and pickled onions. Season to taste with salt. Makes 4 servings.

Per serving: 570 calories, 35 g protein, 42 g carbohydrates, 27 g total fat, 109 mg cholesterol, 255 mg sodium

This meat-and-potatoes platter features boldly seasoned
Pan-browned Spice Steak (recipe on facing page).
With it, serve buttery hash-browned sweet potatoes,
which bake in the oven while you fry the steaks.

Oven-roasted Prime Rib Bones

Pictured on page 166

Preparation time: 10 to 15 minutes
Roasting time: 20 to 25 minutes

Have plenty of napkins handy when you serve up this finger-food spree! To accompany the meaty beef bones, try Peas in Pods (page 167) and Baked Potato Sticks (page 168).

- 3½ to 4 pounds standing rib bones
- ⅓ cup Dijon mustard
- 2 tablespoons red wine vinegar
- ¼ cup salad oil
- 1 clove garlic, minced or pressed
- ½ teaspoon *each* dry thyme and Worcestershire
- ¼ teaspoon pepper
  Watercress (optional)
  Pickled sweet cherry peppers (optional)

Trim excess fat from ribs, then place ribs in a shallow roasting pan or broiler pan. In a small bowl, whisk together mustard and vinegar. Beating constantly, slowly pour in oil. Then add garlic, thyme, Worcestershire, and pepper; beat until well blended. Generously brush about two-thirds of the mustard mixture over all sides of meat, then pierce meat all over with tines of a fork.

Roast in a 425° oven, turning ribs over several times and basting with remaining mustard mixture, until done to your liking; cut to test (20 to 25 minutes for medium-rare). To serve, cut into individual ribs; arrange on a warm platter and garnish with watercress and cherry peppers, if desired. Makes 4 servings.

Per serving: 623 calories, 30 g protein, 3 g carbohydrates, 53 g total fat, 112 mg cholesterol, 685 mg sodium

Beef with Mushrooms & Madeira Sauce

Preparation time: About 10 minutes
Cooking time: About 15 minutes

For especially elegant eating, prepare this entrée with beef fillet steaks; for more casual meals, substitute patties of lean ground beef. Accent either version with a salad of avocado and watercress.

- 1½ pounds lean ground beef; or 4 small beef fillet steaks (*each* 1 to 1½ inches thick)
- 1 tablespoon butter or margarine
- 1 tablespoon salad oil
- 4 diagonal slices French bread (*each* about ¾ inch thick)
  Butter or margarine
- ½ pound mushrooms, thinly sliced
- ½ cup Madeira; or ½ cup regular-strength beef broth and 1½ teaspoons lemon juice
- ½ cup whipping cream

If using ground beef, shape meat into 4 oval patties, each about 1 inch thick.

Melt the 1 tablespoon butter in oil in a wide frying pan over medium-high heat. Add meat and cook, turning once, until well browned on both sides and done to your liking; cut to test (6 to 10 minutes for rare). Meanwhile, toast bread and spread with butter; place a slice of toast on each of 4 dinner plates.

Top each piece of toast with a beef patty or steak and keep warm. Add mushrooms to pan and cook over high heat, stirring, until lightly browned; spoon over meat. Add Madeira and cream to pan and boil, stirring often, until sauce is reduced by about half; pour sauce over meat and mushrooms. Makes 4 servings.

Per serving: 708 calories, 35 g protein, 24 g carbohydrates, 52 g total fat, 170 mg cholesterol, 336 mg sodium

Skewered Beef with Apple & Lettuce

Preparation time: About 10 minutes
Marinating time: 5 to 10 minutes
Broiling time: About 8 minutes

Broiled chunks of soy-marinated beef offer both rich flavor and interesting eating—they're topped with apple slices, wrapped in crisp lettuce, and eaten out of hand.

- 1 piece fresh ginger (about 1 inch square), peeled and minced
- ¼ cup soy sauce
- 2 tablespoons *each* firmly packed brown sugar and dry white wine
- 1 tablespoon sesame seeds
- 1½ teaspoons Oriental sesame oil
- 1 tablespoon hot chili oil or ½ teaspoon ground red pepper (cayenne)
- 2 pounds boneless beef chuck or top round, trimmed of fat and cut into 1½-inch chunks
- 1 large apple
  Butter lettuce leaves, rinsed and crisped

In a bowl, mix ginger, soy sauce, sugar, wine, sesame seeds, sesame oil, and chili oil. Stir in beef and let stand for 5 to 10 minutes.

Lift beef from marinade and drain briefly; reserve marinade. Thread beef equally onto 4 metal skewers; place skewers on greased rack of a broiler pan. Pour marinade into a small pan and bring to a boil over high heat.

Broil beef 4 to 6 inches below heat, turning as needed and brushing often with marinade, until browned on outside but still pink in center; cut to test (about 8 minutes). Meanwhile, core and slice apple and line a platter with lettuce leaves.

To serve, push beef off skewers onto lettuce. Wrap beef and apple slices in lettuce and eat out of hand. Makes 4 servings.

Per serving: 396 calories, 44 g protein, 11 g carbohydrates, 18 g total fat, 148 mg cholesterol, 711 mg sodium

Zucchini-crusted Ground Beef Bake

Preparation time: About 15 minutes
Cooking time: About 30 minutes

Let your food processor help you prepare this unusual casserole—it can quickly shred the zucchini and cheese that make a savory vegetable "crust" for a lightly spiced filling of beef and mushrooms. For a satisfying summer supper, serve with corn on the cob and minted iced tea.

- 1½ pounds medium-size zucchini, shredded (about 4 cups)
- 2 eggs
- 1 cup (4 oz.) shredded mozzarella cheese
- 1 cup (4 oz.) shredded sharp Cheddar cheese
- 1 pound lean ground beef
- 1 clove garlic, minced or pressed
- 1 medium-size onion, chopped
- ½ teaspoon salt
- 1 can (8 oz.) tomato sauce
- 2 teaspoons dry oregano
- 1 green or red bell pepper, seeded and cut into thin strips
- ¼ pound mushrooms, sliced
- ⅓ cup grated Parmesan cheese

With your hands, press out any moisture from zucchini. Beat eggs in a large bowl. Lightly mix in zucchini and ½ cup each of the mozzarella and Cheddar cheeses. Spread evenly in a lightly greased shallow 10- by 15-inch baking pan. Bake in a 450° oven for 10 minutes.

Meanwhile, crumble beef into a wide frying pan; stir in garlic and onion. Cook over medium-high heat, stirring often, until onion is soft (about 10 minutes); discard drippings. Stir in salt, tomato sauce, and oregano. Spoon mixture evenly over zucchini crust. Arrange bell pepper and mushrooms evenly over sauce. Sprinkle with remaining ½ cup each mozzarella and Cheddar cheeses; top with Parmesan cheese.

Return to oven and continue to bake until topping is bubbly and lightly browned (about 20 more minutes). To serve, cut into squares. Makes 6 servings.

Per serving: 366 calories, 28 g protein, 10 g carbohydrates, 24 g total fat, 155 mg cholesterol, 749 mg sodium

*To cool the spicy fire of Borrego Beef & Chorizo Chili
(recipe on facing page), spoon the savory stew over
shredded lettuce or crisp tortilla chips. Offer cold
Mexican beer to sip alongside.*

Mexican Beef Bake

Preparation time: About 15 minutes
Cooking time: About 20 minutes

Try tacos in a new form—as individual beef-and-tortilla casseroles. You line ramekins with browned corn tortilla wedges, then spoon in a chili-seasoned meat sauce and top with jack cheese. Round out the meal with sliced oranges, additional warm tortillas, and a dry red wine.

- 1   **pound lean ground beef**
- 1   **large onion, chopped**
- 1   **clove garlic, minced or pressed**
- ½   **cup catsup**
- 1   **tablespoon chili powder**
-    **Salt and pepper**
-    **About 2 tablespoons butter or margarine**
- 1   **egg**
- 4   **corn tortillas (***each* **about 6 inches in diameter)**
- 1½ **cups (6 oz.) shredded jack cheese**
- 1   **large firm-ripe avocado**
-    **Sour cream**

Crumble beef into a wide frying pan; cook over medium-high heat, stirring often, until browned. Add onion and garlic and cook until onion is soft (about 10 minutes); discard drippings, then stir in catsup and chili powder. Season to taste with salt and pepper. Reduce heat and simmer, uncovered, for 5 minutes.

Meanwhile, melt about 1½ teaspoons of the butter in a 7-inch frying pan over medium heat. In a rimmed plate or pie pan, beat egg just until blended. Dip one tortilla in egg and drain briefly; then cook in butter, turning as needed, until lightly browned on both sides. Repeat to brown remaining tortillas, adding more butter as needed. Cut each tortilla into 4 wedges.

In each of four 1-cup ramekins, arrange 4 tortilla wedges, pointed ends up. Spoon meat mixture over tortillas, then evenly sprinkle with cheese. Broil 3 to 4 inches below heat until cheese is melted.

Pit, peel, and slice avocado; top each serving with avocado slices and a dollop of sour cream. Makes 4 servings.

Per serving: 658 calories, 36 g protein, 30 g carbohydrates, 45 g total fat, 175 mg cholesterol, 799 mg sodium

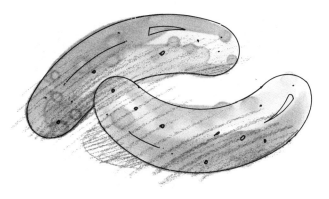

Borrego Beef & Chorizo Chili

Pictured on facing page

Preparation time: About 15 minutes
Cooking time: About 30 minutes

Created in the California desert town of Borrego Springs, this rich, red chili freezes well for a second meal. Serve it over cool, crisp shredded lettuce or crunchy corn chips.

- 1½ **pounds lean ground beef**
- ½   **pound chorizo sausages, casings removed, meat cut into ½-inch-thick slices**
- 1   **medium-size onion, sliced**
- 2   **cloves garlic, minced or pressed**
- 3   **to 4 tablespoons chili powder**
- 1   **teaspoon** *each* **dry oregano and ground cumin**
- 1   **can (about 14½ oz.) diced tomatoes in purée**
- 1   **can (about 15 oz.) kidney beans**
- 1   **can (8 oz.) tomato sauce**
- 4   **to 6 cups lightly packed shredded iceberg lettuce; or 4 to 6 cups corn chips**
-    **About ⅔ cup shredded jack cheese**
-    **About ⅔ cup shredded sharp Cheddar cheese**

Crumble beef into a 4- to 5-quart pan; add chorizo. Cook over medium-high heat, stirring occasionally, until beef is browned. Discard all but about 2 tablespoons of the drippings. Add onion and garlic; cook, stirring, until onion is soft (5 to 10 minutes). Blend in chili powder, oregano, and cumin; cook, stirring, for 1 more minute.

Stir in tomatoes and their liquid, undrained kidney beans, and tomato sauce. Bring to a boil; then reduce heat, cover, and simmer for 15 minutes, stirring occasionally. Line individual bowls with lettuce and top with chili. Sprinkle with jack and Cheddar cheeses. Makes 4 to 6 servings.

Per serving: 676 calories, 45 g protein, 31 g carbohydrates, 42 g total fat, 143 mg cholesterol, 1,185 mg sodium

San Francisco Burgers

Preparation time: About 10 minutes
Cooking time: About 11 minutes

When you're hankering for hamburgers, try a special recipe inspired by San Francisco's Chinatown. French fries are the traditional accompaniment; sprinkle them with crushed red pepper flakes for an unusual twist.

1½	**pounds lean ground beef**
	Salad oil
	Oyster sauce
4	**thick slices sourdough or French bread**
	Dijon mustard
4	**large butter lettuce leaves, rinsed and crisped**

Shape beef into 4 patties, each about ¾ inch thick. Lightly coat a wide frying pan with oil; set over medium-high heat. When pan is hot, add patties and cook, turning once, until done to your liking; cut to test (about 10 minutes for medium-rare). Remove patties from pan and discard drippings.

Spread one side of each patty with about 1½ teaspoons of the oyster sauce; return patties to pan, sauce sides down, and cook just until glazed (about 30 seconds). Spread top of each patty with 1½ teaspoons oyster sauce; turn over and cook for 30 more seconds.

Lightly toast bread and place on 4 plates. Spread each slice with 1 teaspoon of the mustard and 2 teaspoons of the oyster sauce. Top with a lettuce leaf and a beef patty. Offer additional mustard and oyster sauce to add to taste. Makes 4 servings.

Per serving: 482 calories, 36 g protein, 27 g carbohydrates, 25 g total fat, 104 mg cholesterol, 1,056 mg sodium

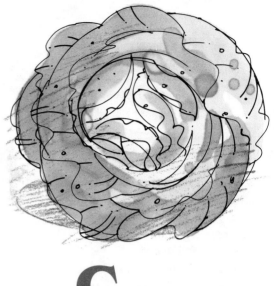

Curry Beef Wrapped in Lettuce

Preparation time: About 10 minutes
Cooking time: About 15 minutes

This Thai-style entrée is tops for casual dining. Just enclose hot, curry-seasoned beef and mushrooms in lettuce leaves to make neat, edible bundles; serve rice or thin noodles alongside, either to eat separately or to include in the lettuce wrappers.

1	**tablespoon salad oil**
1	**medium-size onion, chopped**
2	**tablespoons curry powder**
2	**tablespoons *each* tomato paste and sugar**
¾	**pound lean ground beef**
2	**ounces mushrooms, chopped**
2	**tablespoons distilled white vinegar**
	Salt
1	**medium-size head butter lettuce, separated into leaves, rinsed, and crisped**

Heat oil in a wide frying pan over medium-high heat. Add onion and cook, stirring, until edges begin to brown (about 5 minutes). Mix in curry powder and cook, stirring, for about 1 minute. Then add tomato paste and sugar; stir until mixture is bubbly (about 1 minute). Crumble in meat; add mushrooms and vinegar. Cook, stirring, until almost all liquid has evaporated and meat is no longer pink (about 8 minutes); mixture should still be moist enough to cling together. Season to taste with salt.

Spoon meat mixture into a warm serving bowl; arrange lettuce in a basket or on a plate. Spoon hot meat mixture into lettuce; roll lettuce around meat and eat out of hand. Makes 4 servings.

Per serving: 313 calories, 17 g protein, 13 g carbohydrates, 22 g total fat, 64 mg cholesterol, 128 mg sodium

Veal & Asparagus Platter

Preparation time: About 15 minutes
Cooking time: 35 to 40 minutes

Sautéed veal strips and tender asparagus spears are topped with a creamy, brandy-spiked mushroom sauce in this elegant springtime entrée. Accompany the meat and vegetables with fluffy rice or boiled tiny potatoes.

    1½ pounds lean boneless veal, cut into
        ½-inch-thick slices
        Salt and pepper
        All-purpose flour
        About ¼ cup butter or margarine
        About 2 tablespoons salad oil
    2   pounds asparagus, tough ends removed
    ½   pound mushrooms, sliced
    2   tablespoons brandy (optional)
    ½   teaspoon *each* dry tarragon and dry mustard
    ⅔   cup half-and-half
    1   tablespoon lemon juice

Trim and discard any fat and membrane from veal. Sprinkle veal lightly with salt and pepper and dust with flour; shake off excess. Melt 1 tablespoon of the butter in 1 tablespoon of the oil in a wide frying pan over medium heat. Add about a third of the veal and cook, turning as needed, until well browned on both sides and no longer pink in center; cut to test (about 10 minutes). Transfer to a warm platter; keep warm. Repeat to cook remaining veal, adding more butter and oil as needed.

Meanwhile, in a wide frying pan, bring 1½ inches water to a boil over high heat. Add asparagus, reduce heat, cover, and boil gently just until tender when pierced (5 to 7 minutes). Drain well; arrange on platter with veal.

In frying pan used for veal, melt 2 more tablespoons butter over medium heat; add mushrooms and cook until lightly browned. Stir in 1 tablespoon flour; cook, stirring, for 1 minute. In a small, long-handled pan, heat brandy (if used) just until barely warm. Set aflame (not beneath an exhaust fan or near flammable items), pour into frying pan, and shake pan until flames die. Add tarragon, mustard, and half-and-half. Cook, stirring, until bubbly and thickened. Remove from heat, stir in lemon juice, and pour over veal and asparagus. Makes 6 servings.

Per serving: 305 calories, 27 g protein, 8 g carbohydrates, 19 g total fat, 126 mg cholesterol, 187 mg sodium

Plan Ahead for Leftovers

When time permits, cook a larger cut of meat—one that will yield more than enough for one meal. Roast beef, lamb, or veal can be sliced and quickly reheated; or use the meat in hot or cold sandwiches, stir-fries, or other dishes.

Italian Veal with Peppers

Preparation time: About 15 minutes
Cooking time: About 20 minutes

Red and green bell peppers make this quick supper dish especially pretty.

    1   pound lean boneless veal, cut into
        ³/₁₆-inch-thick slices
        All-purpose flour
        About 3 tablespoons butter or margarine
        About 3 tablespoons salad oil
    1   *each* large red and green bell pepper, seeded
        and cut into ½-inch-wide strips
    1   teaspoon dry oregano
    1   clove garlic, minced or pressed
    ⅔   cup dry white wine
        Salt and pepper

Trim and discard any fat and membrane from veal; cut meat into pieces about 3 inches square. Dredge veal squares in flour to coat lightly; shake off excess. Set aside. Melt 1 tablespoon of the butter in 1 tablespoon of the oil in a wide frying pan over medium heat; add bell peppers, oregano, and garlic and cook, stirring, until peppers are soft (about 10 minutes). With a slotted spoon, transfer pepper mixture to a warm serving dish; keep warm.

Increase heat to medium-high; add 1 more tablespoon each butter and oil to pan. When butter mixture is hot, add about a third of the veal and cook, turning as needed, just until lightly browned on both sides (1½ to 2 minutes). Arrange cooked veal in dish with peppers. Repeat to cook remaining veal, adding more butter and oil as needed.

Add wine to pan; bring to a boil. Boil, stirring to scrape browned bits free, until sauce is reduced by about half. Season sauce to taste with salt and pepper; pour over veal. Makes 4 servings.

Per serving: 328 calories, 24 g protein, 8 g carbohydrates, 22 g total fat, 119 mg cholesterol, 186 mg sodium

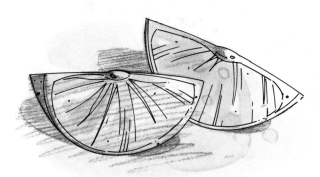

Pounded Veal Chops with Lemon & Thyme

Pictured on facing page

Preparation time: About 15 minutes
Grilling time: 4 to 5 minutes

Rubbed with a fragrant blend of herbs and lemon, pounded thin, and then grilled over a hot fire, these chops are a delightful choice for a warm-weather supper. To keep the menu simple, use the barbecue to prepare Grilled Vegetables (page 162) as well.

> 4 **veal rib or loin chops (about 1¼ lbs. *total*), each ¾ to 1 inch thick**
> 3 **tablespoons minced fresh thyme or 1½ tablespoons dry thyme**
> 2 **teaspoons grated lemon peel**
> ½ **cup minced parsley**
> 2 **tablespoons olive oil or salad oil**
> **Thyme sprigs (optional)**
> **Lemon wedges**

Slash connective tissue around edge of each chop at 1-inch intervals, cutting just to meat. Stir together minced thyme, lemon peel, parsley, and oil; rub each side of each chop with about 1½ teaspoons of the thyme mixture. Then place chops between sheets of plastic wrap and pound with a flat-surfaced mallet until meat is about ¼ inch thick.

Place chops on a greased grill about 6 inches above a solid bed of hot coals. Cook, turning once, until meat is done to your liking; cut to test (4 to 5 minutes for medium). Transfer to a warm platter and garnish with thyme sprigs, if desired. Offer lemon wedges to squeeze over individual portions. Makes 4 servings.

Per serving: 255 calories, 28 g protein, 2 g carbohydrates, 15 g total fat, 122 mg cholesterol, 107 mg sodium

Veal Chops Milanese

Preparation time: About 15 minutes
Cooking time: 8 to 12 minutes

Crisp outside and juicy inside, these well-seasoned sautéed veal chops are just right for a simple Italian meal. Serve with crusty bread and robust red wine.

> 6 **boneless veal chops (about 1½ lbs. *total*), each ¾ to 1 inch thick**
> 3 **eggs**
> **About 1 cup seasoned fine dry bread crumbs**
> **About ⅓ cup all-purpose flour**
> **Salt and pepper**
> **About ¼ cup butter or margarine**
> **About ¼ cup salad oil**
> **Lemon wedges**

Slash connective tissue around edge of each chop at 1-inch intervals, cutting just to meat. Then place chops between sheets of plastic wrap and pound with a flat-surfaced mallet until about ¼ inch thick. Set aside.

In a shallow pan, beat eggs to blend; spread crumbs in another shallow pan. Dredge chops in flour; shake off excess. Season to taste with salt and pepper. Dip each chop in eggs, drain briefly, and roll in crumbs to coat well, pressing crumbs into meat so they adhere. Set chops aside.

Melt 1 tablespoon of the butter in 1 tablespoon of the oil in a wide frying pan over medium-high heat. Add chops, a few at a time (do not crowd pan). Cook, turning once, until golden brown on both sides and just slightly pink in center; cut to test (about 4 minutes). Add more butter and oil to pan as needed. To serve, offer lemon wedges to squeeze over individual portions. Makes 6 servings.

Per serving: 467 calories, 28 g protein, 19 g carbohydrates, 30 g total fat, 218 mg cholesterol, 736 mg sodium

*Grilled to tantalizing succulence and surrounded by
fresh herbs, Pounded Veal Chops with Lemon & Thyme
(recipe on facing page) are easy on the cook
for a summer supper.*

Veal with Olives & Dried Tomatoes

Pictured on page 3

Preparation time: About 20 minutes
Cooking time: 15 to 20 minutes

A vivid blend of dried tomatoes and salty, oil-cured olives crowns this sophisticated scaloppine. Serve it over buttered spinach fettuccine.

 8 slices boneless leg of veal (about 1¼ lbs. *total*), *each* about ¼ inch thick
   Olives & Dried Tomatoes (recipe follows)
 1 egg
 ½ cup milk
 ¾ cup fine dry bread crumbs
 1 tablespoon chopped parsley
 ¾ teaspoon pepper
 2 tablespoons butter or margarine
   Salt
   Lemon wedges

Trim and discard any tough membrane from veal slices. Then place slices between sheets of plastic wrap and pound with a flat-surfaced mallet until about ⅛ inch thick. Prepare Olives & Dried Tomatoes and set aside.

In a shallow pan, beat egg with milk. In another shallow pan, mix crumbs, parsley, and pepper. Dip each veal slice in egg mixture to coat, drain briefly, and coat with crumbs. Place slices in a single layer on plastic wrap.

Drain and reserve oil from Olives & Dried Tomatoes. Heat half the oil with 1 tablespoon of the butter in a wide frying pan over medium-high heat. Add veal, a portion at a time (do not crowd pan); cook, turning once, until well browned on both sides (4 to 5 minutes), adding remaining oil and remaining 1 tablespoon butter as needed. As veal is cooked, transfer to a warm platter, overlapping slices slightly; keep warm.

To serve, top veal with Olives & Dried Tomatoes. Season to taste with salt and garnish with lemon wedges. Makes 4 servings.

Olives & Dried Tomatoes. In a medium-size frying pan, combine 2 tablespoons *each* **salad oil** and **olive oil**, ¼ cup chopped **dried tomatoes packed in oil**, and ¼ cup chopped **oil-cured ripe olives**. Stir over low heat until oil takes on flavors of olives and tomatoes (8 to 10 minutes). Use warm or at room temperature.

Per serving: 560 calories, 35 g protein, 18 g carbohydrates, 38 g total fat, 185 mg cholesterol, 737 mg sodium

Pork Tenderloins with Stilton & Port

Preparation time: About 10 minutes
Cooking time: About 20 minutes

Two classic partners—Stilton cheese and port—join in the sauce for these elegant roasted pork tenderloins; minced jalapeño chiles add a bold, fiery accent. Sautéed Peppers & Pears (page 168) enhance the dish especially well.

 1 tablespoon salad oil
 2 or 3 pork tenderloins (1½ lbs. *total*), trimmed of fat
 1 cup port
 ½ cup regular-strength chicken broth
 ½ cup whipping cream
 4 ounces Stilton cheese, crumbled
 1 or 2 small fresh jalapeño chiles, stemmed, seeded, and diced (optional)

Heat oil in a wide frying pan over medium-high heat. Add pork and cook, turning as needed, until browned on all sides (about 4 minutes). Transfer meat to a baking pan and bake in a 400° oven until a meat thermometer inserted in thickest part registers 160°F (about 15 minutes).

Meanwhile, discard drippings from frying pan and add port and broth. Boil over high heat until reduced to about ¾ cup (about 3 minutes). Stir in cream and continue to boil, stirring, until large, shiny bubbles form (about 5 more minutes). Add cheese and stir until melted; stir in chiles, if desired. Remove from heat.

To serve, thinly slice pork across the grain; fan slices out on warm plates and spoon sauce over meat. Makes 4 to 6 servings.

Per serving: 367 calories, 37 g protein, 7 g carbohydrates, 21 g total fat, 144 mg cholesterol, 500 mg sodium

Pork Medallions with Prunes

Preparation time: About 20 minutes
Cooking time: About 20 minutes

Dress up each plump, prune-garnished pork medallion with sprigs of peppery watercress; offer hot buttered noodles alongside.

- 1 **pork tenderloin (about ¾ lb.), trimmed of fat and cut across the grain into 1-inch-thick slices**
- ¾ **cup Madeira**
- ½ **cup regular-strength beef broth**
- 1 **tablespoon red wine vinegar**
- 2 **teaspoons cornstarch**
- 3 **whole cloves**
- 2 **tablespoons butter or margarine**
- 12 **moist-pack pitted prunes**
- ⅓ **cup chopped shallots**
  Watercress sprigs
  Salt

Place pork slices between sheets of plastic wrap and pound with a flat-surfaced mallet until about ⅜ inch thick. In a small bowl, stir together Madeira, broth, vinegar, cornstarch, and cloves; set aside.

Melt butter in a wide frying pan over medium-high heat. Add pork, a portion at a time (do not crowd pan). Cook, turning once, until well browned on both sides and no longer pink in center; cut to test (4 to 5 minutes). As pork is cooked, transfer to a warm plate and keep warm.

After all pork is done, add prunes to pan, turning them in drippings to warm; then lift from pan with a slotted spoon and place on plate with pork. Add shallots to pan and cook, stirring, until limp. Add Madeira mixture and any accumulated pork juices; bring to a boil, stirring.

To serve, arrange pork and prunes on 3 warm dinner plates; spoon sauce over meat and fruit. Garnish with watercress and season to taste with salt. Makes 3 servings.

Per serving: 327 calories, 26 g protein, 33 g carbohydrates, 11 g total fat, 94 mg cholesterol, 280 mg sodium

Seasoned Butters

To add a fillip of flavor to grilled or broiled meats, poultry, seafood, and vegetables, top them with an enticing seasoned butter. In addition to the three choices here, you'll want to sample Dill Butter (page 88), Horseradish Butter (page 137), and Parsley Butter (page 156). All keep well in the refrigerator for up to 2 weeks.

Cilantro-Chili Butter

Preparation time: 5 to 10 minutes

In a small bowl, mix ¼ cup **butter** or margarine (at room temperature), 1 teaspoon **chili powder,** and 1 tablespoon minced **fresh cilantro (coriander)** until well combined. Transfer to a small serving crock. Makes about ¼ cup.

Per tablespoon: 104 calories, 0.2 g protein, 0.3 g carbohydrates, 12 g total fat, 31 mg cholesterol, 123 mg sodium

Fresh Herb Butter

Preparation time: 5 to 10 minutes

In a small bowl, mix ½ cup (¼ lb.) **butter** or margarine (at room temperature); ½ cup lightly packed **fresh basil,** chives, mint, parsley, or watercress (minced); and 1 teaspoon **lemon juice** until well combined. Transfer to a small serving crock. Makes about ½ cup.

Per tablespoon: 103 calories, 0.2 g protein, 0.4 g carbohydrates, 12 g total fat, 31 mg cholesterol, 119 mg sodium

Lemon Butter

Preparation time: 5 to 10 minutes

In a small bowl, mix ½ cup (¼ lb.) **butter** or margarine (at room temperature), 1 teaspoon **grated lemon peel,** 3 tablespoons chopped **parsley,** ½ teaspoon **dry tarragon,** and 1½ tablespoons **lemon juice** until well combined. Transfer to a small serving crock. Makes about ½ cup.

Per tablespoon: 103 calories, 0.2 g protein, 0.4 g carbohydrates, 12 g total fat, 31 mg cholesterol, 118 mg sodium

Stir-fried ribbons of bell peppers, a light wine sauce, and the robust pungency of garlic distinguish Sautéed Pork with Red Peppers (recipe on facing page). Crusty French bread contributes quiet balance to this festive entrée.

Sautéed Pork with Red Peppers

Pictured on facing page

Preparation time: About 15 minutes
Cooking time: About 35 minutes

Pork, like veal (see page 145), is superbly enhanced by a light, garlicky sauce and plenty of bright bell pepper strips. Add still more color to the menu with a side dish of butter-steamed zucchini.

- 2 **pounds boneless center-cut pork loin, trimmed of fat and cut into ½-inch-thick slices**
- 4 **cloves garlic, minced or pressed**
  Pepper
- 2 **tablespoons butter or margarine**
- 4 **medium-size red bell peppers, seeded and cut into thin strips**
  About 2 tablespoons salad oil
- ¾ **cup** *each* **dry white wine and regular-strength chicken broth**
  Lemon wedges
  Italian parsley sprigs

Sprinkle pork with garlic and season to taste with pepper. Set aside.

Melt butter in a wide frying pan over medium-high heat. Add bell peppers and cook, stirring often, until soft (about 10 minutes). Transfer to a warm platter and keep warm.

Add 1 tablespoon of the oil to pan. Then add pork, a portion at a time (do not crowd pan); cook, turning once, until browned on both sides (4 to 5 minutes), adding more oil as needed. As pork is cooked, transfer to platter with peppers.

Add wine and broth to pan; stir to scrape browned bits free. Bring to a boil; boil, stirring often, until sauce is reduced to ½ cup (8 to 10 minutes). Pour over pork and peppers. Garnish with lemon wedges and parsley sprigs. Makes 6 servings.

Per serving: 345 calories, 35 g protein, 6 g carbohydrates, 20 g total fat, 106 mg cholesterol, 267 mg sodium

Stir-fried Pork with Green Onions

Preparation time: About 10 minutes
Cooking time: 4 to 6 minutes

This Asian-seasoned medley of pork and onions proves what busy cooks have long known—for quick cooking and fresh flavor, stir-frying is hard to beat.

- ½ **pound boneless pork, such as loin or shoulder**
- 1 **tablespoon cornstarch**
- 1 **tablespoon rice wine or dry sherry**
- 2 **tablespoons salad oil**
- ½ **pound green onions (including tops), cut into slivers**
- 3 **cloves garlic, minced or pressed**
  Salt and pepper

Cut pork across the grain into thin slices; then cut each slice into matchstick-size strips. In a bowl, combine cornstarch and wine; add pork and stir to coat well.

Heat oil in a wok or wide frying pan over high heat. Add pork mixture and cook, stirring, until lightly browned (2 to 3 minutes). Add onions and garlic and continue to cook, stirring, until heated through (2 to 3 more minutes). Season to taste with salt and pepper. Makes 2 servings.

Per serving: 486 calories, 23 g protein, 12 g carbohydrates, 38 g total fat, 79 mg cholesterol, 70 mg sodium

Baked Pork Chops Dijon

Preparation time: 5 to 10 minutes
Baking time: 18 to 20 minutes

A tangy mustard baste keeps these pork chops moist and tender as they bake. You might round out the menu with Spiced Spinach & Potatoes (page 169) and a Merlot wine.

- 6 **loin pork chops (about 2½ lbs. *total*),**
  each about ¾ inch thick
- 6 **tablespoons olive oil or salad oil**
- ¼ **cup red wine vinegar**
- 2 **tablespoons Dijon mustard**
- 1 **tablespoon minced chives**
- 1 **teaspoon dry tarragon**
  Freshly ground pepper

Arrange chops in a foil-lined rimmed baking pan. In a small bowl, whisk together oil, vinegar, mustard, chives, and tarragon; season to taste with pepper. Spread 1 tablespoon of the mustard baste over each chop.

Bake on upper rack of a 475° oven for 10 minutes. Turn chops over and spread each one with 1 more tablespoon of the baste. Continue to bake until meat in thickest part is no longer pink; cut to test (8 to 10 more minutes). Makes 6 servings.

Per serving: 401 calories, 28 g protein, 1 g carbohydrates, 31 g total fat, 101 mg cholesterol, 146 mg sodium

Smoked Pork Chops with Curried New Potatoes & Green Beans

Preparation time: About 15 minutes
Cooking time: About 30 minutes

Here's a perfect choice for busy days when guests are due for dinner. Savory smoked pork chops, curry-seasoned red potatoes, and fresh green beans add up to a complete meal you can prepare in less than an hour.

- 10 **to 12 small red thin-skinned potatoes**
  (*each* 1½ to 2 inches in diameter), scrubbed
- 1 **pound green beans, ends removed**
- 6 **tablespoons butter or margarine**
- 6 **smoked pork chops (*each* about ¾ inch thick)**
- 2 **tablespoons mustard seeds**
- 2 **teaspoons curry powder**

Place unpeeled potatoes in a 5-quart pan; add water to cover. Bring to a boil over high heat, then cover and boil for 15 minutes. Add beans and continue to boil until potatoes are tender throughout when pierced and beans are just tender-crisp to bite (about 6 more minutes). Drain vegetables well.

While potatoes are cooking, melt about 2 teaspoons of the butter in a wide frying pan over medium heat. Add chops, 3 at a time; cook, turning once, until lightly browned on both sides (about 10 minutes). Arrange chops on a warm platter; keep warm.

Melt remaining butter in pan; stir in mustard seeds and curry powder. Cut potatoes in half; add to pan, cut sides down, and cook until lightly browned (about 5 minutes). Lift out and arrange on platter with chops. Add beans to pan, turn to coat in butter mixture, and heat through; arrange on platter. Drizzle vegetables with remaining butter mixture. Makes 6 servings.

Per serving: 523 calories, 33 g protein, 30 g carbohydrates, 30 g total fat, 124 mg cholesterol, 2,280 mg sodium

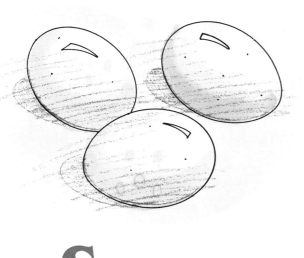

Sausage & Fig Grill

Preparation time: About 10 minutes
Grilling time: About 15 minutes

In this all-grill menu, spicy sausages cook alongside herbed bread and skewers of cheese and fresh figs. To cool the palate, offer mint-garnished white wine spritzers for sipping. (You can use either black or green figs; you'll find them in markets in early summer and again in autumn.)

4 **to 8 mild or hot Italian sausages (¾ to 1½ lbs. *total*)**
¼ **cup butter or margarine, melted**
1½ **teaspoons minced fresh rosemary or 1 teaspoon dry rosemary**
8 **thin slices French bread**
12 **small or 6 large fresh figs, stems trimmed**
6 **ounces Jarlsberg cheese, cut into 1-inch chunks**

Place sausages on a grill about 6 inches above a solid bed of hot coals. Cook, turning often, until meat is no longer pink in center; cut to test (about 15 minutes).

Meanwhile, stir together butter and rosemary. Brush bread with some of the mixture, place on a cooler area of grill, and cook, turning once, until toasted on both sides (about 5 minutes). Set aside.

If using large figs, cut them in half. Alternate figs and cheese on each of 4 metal skewers. Place on grill and cook, turning once and basting with remaining butter mixture, until figs are warm and cheese is soft (2 to 4 minutes).

To serve, transfer skewers to a warm platter and accompany with toast and sausages. Makes 4 servings.

Per serving: 853 calories, 38 g protein, 58 g carbohydrates, 52 g total fat, 145 mg cholesterol, 1,653 mg sodium

Joe's Sausage & Greens with Eggs

Preparation time: About 20 minutes
Cooking time: About 15 minutes

Any San Franciscan knows that Joe's Special is a dish made with eggs, spinach, and ground beef. This version varies the choice of greens and meat, replacing the usual selections with red Swiss chard and Italian sausage, but it's still a delicious partner for crusty San Francisco sourdough bread.

1 **pound mild or hot Italian sausages, casings removed**
1 **large onion, finely chopped**
2 **cloves garlic, minced or pressed**
½ **pound mushrooms, thinly sliced**
¼ **teaspoon *each* ground nutmeg, pepper, and dry oregano**
¾ **pound red Swiss chard, cut into thin shreds (about 6 cups; keep stems and leaves separate)**
4 **eggs**
 Salt
1 **cup (4 oz.) shredded jack cheese**

Crumble sausages into a wide frying pan; cook over high heat, stirring, until meat is well browned. Discard all but 2 tablespoons of the drippings; then add onion, garlic, mushrooms, nutmeg, pepper, and oregano. Cook, stirring often, until onion is soft and all liquid has evaporated (about 10 minutes). Stir in chard, a portion at a time, starting with stems, and cook until chard is just wilted (3 to 4 minutes).

In a bowl, beat eggs until blended. Add eggs to chard mixture; stir over low heat just until eggs are softly set. Season to taste with salt, then sprinkle with cheese. Makes 4 servings.

Per serving: 542 calories, 33 g protein, 11 g carbohydrates, 41 g total fat, 307 mg cholesterol, 1,197 mg sodium

Quick Lamb Curry

Preparation time: About 15 minutes
Cooking time: 30 to 35 minutes

For curry in a hurry, brown a pound of lean ground lamb; then add chopped vegetables, spices, and broth and let the mixture simmer. While the curry is cooking, you'll have time to steam some rice and prepare your choice of condiments.

- 1 **pound lean ground lamb**
- 2 **cloves garlic, minced or pressed**
- 1 **large onion, chopped**
- 1 **tablespoon curry powder**
- ½ **teaspoon** *each* **ground ginger and ground cumin**
- 1 **medium-size carrot, thinly sliced**
- 1 **small red apple, cored and chopped**
- 1 **small green bell pepper, seeded and chopped**
- 1 **can (14½ oz.) regular-strength beef broth**
  Salt and ground red pepper (cayenne)
  Condiments: Sliced bananas, Major Grey's chutney, plain yogurt, chopped salted roasted peanuts, and/or crumbled bacon

Crumble lamb into a wide frying pan; cook over medium heat, stirring, until browned. Discard all but 2 tablespoons of the drippings. Add garlic, onion, curry powder, ginger, and cumin; reduce heat to low and cook, stirring often, until onion is very soft. Add carrot, apple, bell pepper, and broth. Bring to a boil; then reduce heat and simmer, uncovered, until vegetables are tender to bite and sauce is slightly thickened (about 20 minutes). Season to taste with salt and red pepper.

While curry is cooking, prepare 3 or 4 condiments of your choice and place each in a separate bowl; pass at the table to sprinkle over individual portions. Makes 4 servings.

Per serving: 347 calories, 24 g protein, 12 g carbohydrates, 23 g total fat, 89 mg cholesterol, 455 mg sodium

Lemon-Mint Lamb Meatballs

Pictured on facing page

Preparation time: About 20 minutes
Cooking time: 15 to 20 minutes

Family dinner or company entrée? Tender lamb meatballs in a tart lemon-mint sauce easily play either role. Serve over rice; accompany with Cream-glazed Anise Carrots (page 161), if you like.

- 2 **pounds lean ground lamb**
- 2 **eggs**
- ¼ **cup all-purpose flour**
- 1 **tablespoon dry mint**
- ½ **teaspoon** *each* **salt and pepper**
- 2 **tablespoons salad oil**
- ⅓ **cup finely chopped parsley**
- 1¾ **cups thinly sliced green onions (including tops)**
  Hot cooked rice
- 1 **can (14½ oz.) regular-strength chicken broth**
- ⅓ **cup lemon juice**
- 1 **tablespoon** *each* **cornstarch and water**
  Lemon zest
  Mint sprigs

In a large bowl, combine lamb, eggs, flour, dry mint, salt, and pepper; mix well, then shape into 1½-inch balls. Set slightly apart on an ungreased large rimmed baking sheet. Bake in a 500° oven until well browned (about 10 minutes).

Meanwhile, heat oil in a wide frying pan over medium heat; add parsley and 1½ cups of the onions and cook, stirring often, until onions are soft. Remove pan from heat.

With a slotted spoon, arrange meatballs over a bed of hot cooked rice in a serving dish; keep warm. Discard drippings from baking pan. Pour a small amount of the broth into pan and stir to scrape browned bits free; then pour broth mixture into frying pan and add remaining broth and lemon juice. Place pan over medium-high heat. In a small bowl, stir together cornstarch and water; stir into broth mixture and cook, stirring, until sauce is thickened. Pour sauce over meatballs and garnish with remaining ¼ cup onions, lemon zest, and mint sprigs. Makes 8 servings.

Per serving: 323 calories, 24 g protein, 6 g carbohydrates, 22 g total fat, 136 mg cholesterol, 449 mg sodium

*Greek cooks often enhance meat with the flavors of
lemon and mint, as in refreshingly different Lemon-Mint
Lamb Meatballs (recipe on facing page). Serve
with Cream-glazed Anise Carrots (recipe on page 161).*

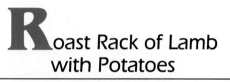

Roast Rack of Lamb with Potatoes

Preparation time: About 10 minutes
Roasting time: About 35 minutes

Elegant entrées don't get much easier than this. Just rub a rack of lamb with parsley-garlic butter, then roast meat and red potatoes in a hot oven.

> **Parsley Butter (recipe follows)**
> 1 **rack of lamb (2 to 2½ lbs.)**
> 4 to 6 **red thin-skinned potatoes (***each*
> **2 to 2½ inches in diameter), scrubbed**

Prepare Parsley Butter and rub about 1½ tablespoons over all sides of lamb. Place lamb, fat side up, in a shallow roasting pan; insert a meat thermometer in thickest part (not touching bone). Pierce unpeeled potatoes in several places; arrange in pan beside lamb. Roast in a 425° oven until meat thermometer registers 145°F for medium-rare and potatoes feel soft when squeezed (about 35 minutes). If lamb is done before potatoes, remove it from pan and keep warm.

To serve, cut lamb between ribs into individual chops; offer remaining Parsley Butter to top lamb and potatoes. Makes 2 servings.

Parsley Butter. Mix ¼ cup **butter** or margarine (at room temperature), 3 tablespoons minced **parsley,** and 1 small clove **garlic** (minced or pressed). Season to taste with **salt** and **pepper.**

Per serving: 1,930 calories, 65 g protein, 33 g carbohydrates, 169 g total fat, 385 mg cholesterol, 488 mg sodium

Broiled Lamb Chops with Papaya Chutney

Pictured on page 171

Preparation time: About 15 minutes
Cooking time: About 20 minutes

Lamb and fruit are popular partners in many cuisines; here, juicy rib chops are topped with a quick homemade papaya chutney. (The chutney is good made with nectarines or peaches, too.)

> **Seasoned Yogurt (recipe follows)**
> ¼ cup *each* **sugar and cider vinegar**
> 1 **small onion, minced**
> ½ **cup raisins**
> 1 **teaspoon** *each* **ground cinnamon**
> **and ground ginger**
> 1 **large papaya or 3 medium-size nectarines or**
> **peaches (about 1 lb.** *total***), peeled, seeded or**
> **pitted, and cut into ¼-inch-thick slices**
> 8 to 10 **single-rib lamb chops (1½ to 2 lbs.** *total***),**
> **trimmed of fat**
> **Salt and pepper**
> 1 **large cucumber, seeded and cut into strips**
> **(optional)**

Prepare Seasoned Yogurt; set aside.

Combine sugar, vinegar, onion, raisins, cinnamon, and ginger in a wide frying pan. Cook over medium-high heat, stirring often, until onion is soft and raisins are plump (about 10 minutes). Add papaya and stir gently until heated through (about 3 minutes). Keep warm.

Place lamb chops on rack of a broiler pan and broil about 4 inches below heat, turning once, until well browned on both sides but still pink in center; cut to test (6 to 8 minutes). Season to taste with salt and pepper. Spoon papaya chutney mixture over lamb chops or serve in a separate bowl. Offer Seasoned Yogurt and, if desired, cucumber strips alongside. Makes 4 servings.

Seasoned Yogurt. Mix 2 cups **plain yogurt,** ¼ teaspoon **chili powder,** ½ teaspoon **ground cumin,** 1 teaspoon **sugar,** and 1 tablespoon **mustard seeds.** Makes about 2 cups.

Per serving of lamb and chutney: 297 calories, 19 g protein, 38 g carbohydrates, 8 g total fat, 58 mg cholesterol, 60 mg sodium

Per tablespoon of Seasoned Yogurt: 11 calories, 0.6 g protein, 0.9 g carbohydrates, 0.6 g total fat, 2 mg cholesterol, 7 mg sodium

Pounded Lamb Chops with Rosemary

Preparation time: About 15 minutes
Grilling time: About 4 minutes

Brush a robust blend of garlic, herbs, and olive oil over lamb rib chops—then pound the meat out thin, both to work in the seasonings and to reduce the grilling time.

  4 **lamb rib or loin chops (about 1¼ lbs. *total*),** *each ¾ to 1 inch thick*
  4 **cloves garlic, minced or pressed**
  2 **tablespoons minced fresh rosemary or 1 tablespoon dry rosemary**
  ½ **cup minced parsley**
  2 **tablespoons olive oil or salad oil Rosemary sprigs (optional)**

Slash fat around edge of each lamb chop at 1-inch intervals, cutting just to meat. Stir together garlic, minced rosemary, parsley, and oil. Rub each side of each chop with about 1 tablespoon of the rosemary mixture, then place chops between sheets of plastic wrap and pound with a flat-surfaced mallet until meat is about ¼ inch thick.

Place chops on a greased grill about 6 inches above a solid bed of hot coals. Cook, turning once, until done to your liking; cut to test (about 4 minutes for medium-rare). Garnish with rosemary sprigs, if desired. Makes 4 servings.

Per serving: 288 calories, 31 g protein, 2 g carbohydrates, 17 g total fat, 96 mg cholesterol, 89 mg sodium

Lamb Shish Kebabs

Preparation time: About 20 minutes
Marinating time: 15 to 20 minutes
Broiling time: 10 to 15 minutes

Just about everyone likes shish kebabs! This version features cubes of lean lamb flavored in a lemony marinade, then skewered with fresh vegetables and broiled until richly browned.

  1 **to 1½ pounds lean boneless lamb (shoulder or leg), cut into 1½-inch cubes Lemon Marinade (recipe follows)**
  1 **medium-size red or green bell pepper**
  1 **medium-size white onion**
  8 **medium-size mushrooms**

Trim and discard excess fat from lamb; place lamb in a bowl. Prepare Lemon Marinade and pour over lamb; let marinate for 15 to 20 minutes. Seed bell pepper and cut into 1½-inch squares; cut onion into 8 wedges and separate each into layers.

Remove lamb from marinade and drain briefly; reserve marinade. Divide lamb into 4 equal portions; thread lamb and vegetables alternately on four 10- to 12-inch metal skewers, starting and ending each skewer with a mushroom. Place skewers on greased rack of a broiler pan. Pour marinade into a small pan and bring to a boil over high heat.

Broil lamb 3 to 4 inches below heat, turning as needed and basting frequently with marinade, until browned on all sides but still pink in center; cut to test (10 to 15 minutes). Makes 4 servings.

Lemon Marinade. Mix 2 tablespoons chopped **parsley**, ⅓ cup **salad oil**, 1 tablespoon **soy sauce**, ½ teaspoon *each* **dry mustard** and **Worcestershire**, ¼ cup **lemon juice**, and 1 clove **garlic** (minced or pressed).

Per serving: 305 calories, 31 g protein, 5 g carbohydrates, 17 g total fat, 96 mg cholesterol, 219 mg sodium

Glorious green spears banded with a citrus beurre blanc, Asparagus with Orange-Butter Sauce (recipe on page 160) is a side dish that's sure to attract attention.

Side Dishes

Mealtime excitement may focus on the main dish, but it doesn't have to stop there. When you complement your entrée with any of our tempting vegetable and grain choices, you have the makings of a memorable dinner. Start by choosing the very freshest produce from market or garden—then enhance it with a special sauce, a flavored butter, or just a careful combination of herbs. If you're looking for a heartier accompaniment, offer golden polenta, an elegant rice-and-pasta pilaf, or one of our sturdy potato specialties.

Asparagus with Orange-Butter Sauce

Pictured on page 158

Preparation time: About 10 minutes
Cooking time: About 15 minutes

Crisp asparagus topped with a citrusy butter sauce is a stunning complement to Pounded Lamb Chops with Rosemary (page 157), Game Hens with Mustard Crust (page 132), or any other elegant entrée.

- **2 pounds asparagus, tough ends removed**
- **½ cup (¼ lb.) butter or margarine**
- **⅓ cup minced shallots**
- **1¼ teaspoons Dijon mustard**
- **1⅓ cups fresh orange juice**
- **Salt and pepper**
- **Orange slices; or strips of orange peel tied in knots (optional)**

In a wide frying pan, bring 1½ inches water to a boil over high heat. Add asparagus; reduce heat, cover, and boil gently just until tender when pierced (5 to 7 minutes). Drain, place on a warm platter, and keep warm.

Melt 1 tablespoon of the butter in a 1- to 2-quart pan over medium heat. Add shallots and cook, stirring, for 1 minute. Add mustard and orange juice, increase heat to high, and bring to a boil; boil until reduced to ⅔ cup (about 5 minutes). Reduce heat to low, add remaining 7 tablespoons butter all at once, and cook, stirring constantly, until butter is smoothly blended into sauce. Season to taste with salt and pepper. Spoon sauce over asparagus; garnish with orange slices or orange peel, if desired. Makes 4 to 6 servings.

Per serving: 223 calories, 4 g protein, 12 g carbohydrates, 19 g total fat, 50 mg cholesterol, 229 mg sodium

Green Beans with Bacon & Tomato Dressing

Preparation time: About 10 minutes
Cooking time: About 15 minutes

Serve this sweet-sour specialty hot or cold, You might try it at your next patio picnic; it's good alongside grilled steaks, hamburgers, or crisp fried chicken.

- **4 slices bacon**
- **1 pound green beans, ends removed**
- **6 tablespoons catsup**
- **¼ cup white wine vinegar**

In a wide frying pan, cook bacon over medium heat until crisp (about 8 minutes). Lift out, drain, crumble, and set aside. Reserve drippings in pan.

In a 3-quart pan, bring 1 inch water to a boil over high heat. Add beans; then reduce heat, cover, and boil gently just until tender-crisp to bite (4 to 7 minutes). Drain. Use hot; or, to serve cold, immerse in ice water, then drain.

Add catsup and vinegar to drippings in frying pan and stir over medium heat just until blended. Use hot; or let cool and use cold.

To serve, spoon dressing onto 4 salad plates, then divide beans among plates. Sprinkle with bacon. Makes 4 servings.

Per serving: 190 calories, 5 g protein, 15 g carbohydrates, 13 g total fat, 15 mg cholesterol, 429 mg sodium

Broccoli Polonaise

Preparation time: About 10 minutes
Cooking time: 7 to 12 minutes

Purists like their broccoli with nothing more than a squeeze of lemon—but most of us don't object to slightly more elaborate embellishments! Here, the tender green spears are sprinkled with a tasty blend of buttered crumbs, chopped egg, and herbs.

- 1 to 1½ pounds broccoli
- 5 tablespoons butter or margarine
- ½ cup fine dry bread crumbs
- 1 hard-cooked egg, chopped
- 1 tablespoon *each* thinly sliced green onion (including top) and minced parsley

Trim and discard tough stalk bases from broccoli; peel stalks, then cut broccoli lengthwise into uniform spears.

In a wide frying pan, bring 1 inch water to a boil over high heat. Add broccoli; then reduce heat, cover, and boil gently just until stalks are tender when pierced (7 to 12 minutes). Drain. While broccoli is cooking, melt butter in a small pan over medium heat. Add crumbs and stir until browned. Remove from heat; stir in egg, onion, and parsley. Sprinkle crumb mixture over hot broccoli. Makes 4 to 6 servings.

Per serving: 176 calories, 5 g protein, 11 g carbohydrates, 13 g total fat, 74 mg cholesterol, 222 mg sodium

Cream-glazed Anise Carrots

Pictured on page 155

Preparation time: About 10 minutes
Cooking time: 7 to 12 minutes

Here's an unusual treatment for sweet sliced carrots: the bright orange coins are cloaked in reduced cream and accented with aromatic anise seeds.

- 2 tablespoons butter or margarine
- 3 cups thinly sliced carrots
  About 3 tablespoons water
- ¼ teaspoon anise seeds, crushed
- 3 tablespoons whipping cream
  Salt and pepper

Melt butter in a wide frying pan over high heat. Add carrots, 3 tablespoons of the water, and anise seeds; cover and cook, stirring often and adding more water as needed, just until carrots are tender-crisp to bite (5 to 10 minutes). Add cream and cook, uncovered, stirring constantly, until almost all liquid has evaporated. Season to taste with salt and pepper. Makes 4 servings.

Per serving: 119 calories, 1 g protein, 9 g carbohydrates, 9 g total fat, 28 mg cholesterol, 91 mg sodium

Risotto-style Corn

Preparation time: About 10 minutes
Cooking time: 20 to 25 minutes

Fresh corn kernels become delectably creamy when simmered and stirred constantly, risotto style. Serve the luxurious dish with grilled steaks or chops and a juicy tomato salad.

- 6 ears corn
- 2 tablespoons butter or margarine
- 1 large red onion, chopped
- 1 red bell pepper, seeded and chopped
- 2 cups whipping cream
- 1 teaspoon sugar
   Salt and pepper

Pull off and discard husks and silk from corn; rinse corn. With a sharp knife, cut kernels from cobs and set aside.

   Melt butter in a wide frying pan over medium-high heat. Add onion and bell pepper and cook, stirring often, until vegetables are soft (about 10 minutes). Add corn, cream, and sugar. Cook, stirring constantly, until mixture is thickened (10 to 15 minutes). Season to taste with salt and pepper. Makes 6 servings.

Per serving: 359 calories, 5 g protein, 23 g carbohydrates, 30 g total fat, 99 mg cholesterol, 81 mg sodium

Grilled Vegetables

Pictured on facing page

Preparation time: About 20 minutes
Grilling time: 6 to 15 minutes

When you're serving the main course from the barbecue, why not grill the side dish as well? Bell peppers, onions, summer squash, and leeks all take well to this cooking method; brush them with olive oil and fresh herbs for added flavor.

- 2 to 4 red or yellow onions
- 2 to 4 crookneck squash, pattypan squash, or zucchini
- 2 to 4 slender leeks
- 2 to 4 red, yellow, or green bell peppers
- ½ cup olive oil or salad oil
- 2 tablespoons minced fresh herbs, such as oregano, thyme, rosemary, or tarragon (or a combination); or 2 teaspoons dry herbs
   Salt and pepper

Peel onions and cut in half lengthwise. Trim ends from squash and cut in half lengthwise. Trim and discard root ends and any tough or wilted leaves from leeks; split leeks in half lengthwise and rinse well. Leave bell peppers whole (or cut in half, if large).

   In a 4- to 6-quart pan, bring 2 quarts water to a boil over high heat. Add squash and leeks and boil for 2 minutes; drain, plunge into ice water, and drain again.

   In a small bowl, stir together oil and herbs. Brush vegetables all over with oil mixture, then place on a greased grill 4 to 6 inches above a solid bed of hot coals. Cook, turning and basting often with remaining oil mixture, until vegetables are tender and streaked with brown (6 to 8 minutes for squash and leeks, 10 to 15 minutes for onions and peppers). Season to taste with salt and pepper. Makes 6 to 8 servings.

Per serving: 184 calories, 2 g protein, 10 g carbohydrates, 16 g total fat, 0 mg cholesterol, 7 mg sodium

Colorful Grilled Vegetables (recipe on facing page)
cook alongside Grilled Fish Steaks (recipe on page 88).
Season the fish with a pat of Cilantro-Chili Butter
(recipe on page 149).

Sautéed Kale with Cannellini

Preparation time: About 10 minutes
Cooking time: About 25 minutes

Though it's often ignored at the market, nutritious kale is well worth trying. Here, the bold-flavored greens combine with cannellini and bacon in a robust accompaniment for barbecued ribs or chicken.

- 1½ pounds kale, tough stems removed
- 4 slices bacon, chopped
- 2 large onions, thinly sliced
  Salt and pepper
- 2 cans (about 15 oz. *each*) cannellini (white kidney beans), drained and rinsed

Rinse and drain kale; cut leaves crosswise into ½-inch strips and set aside.

In a wide frying pan, cook bacon over medium heat until crisp (about 8 minutes), stirring. Lift out, drain, and set aside.

Add onions to drippings in pan and cook, stirring, until soft (about 10 minutes). Add kale and cook, stirring, until wilted and bright green (3 to 4 minutes). Season to taste with salt and pepper. Transfer to a warm platter and keep warm.

Add cannellini to pan, reduce heat, and cook, stirring, until hot (about 4 minutes). Arrange cannellini alongside kale; sprinkle both with bacon. Makes 6 servings.

Per serving: 244 calories, 12 g protein, 28 g carbohydrates, 10 g total fat, 10 mg cholesterol, 323 mg sodium

Freezing & Reheating Bread

To freeze freshly baked bread or rolls, let cool completely; then wrap airtight in foil, package in a plastic bag, label, and place in the freezer for up to 3 months.

To serve, unwrap but leave partially covered; let thaw completely at room temperature before serving or reheating.

To reheat, place thawed bread on a baking sheet in a 350° oven. Heat rolls and small loaves of bread for about 10 minutes, large loaves for 15 minutes. If bread has a soft crust, protect it during reheating with a loose wrapping of foil; if bread is crusty, heat it uncovered.

Eggplant with Crispy Coating

Preparation time: About 10 minutes
Baking time: 20 to 25 minutes

Crunchy on the outside, soft in the center, and full of herbal flavor, these crumb-coated eggplant slices are delightful with pork chops or Turkey Scaloppine (page 128).

- 1 large eggplant (1¼ to 1½ lbs.)
- 2 eggs
- ½ cup fine dry bread crumbs or yellow cornmeal
- 1 teaspoon dry oregano
- ¼ cup grated Parmesan cheese
- 2 tablespoons olive oil or salad oil

Peel eggplant, if desired; then cut crosswise into ½-inch-thick slices. Set aside. In a shallow bowl, lightly beat eggs. In another shallow bowl, mix crumbs, oregano, and cheese.

Pour oil into a rimmed baking pan large enough to hold eggplant in a single layer; tilt pan to coat with oil. Dip each eggplant slice in eggs, drain briefly, and then coat with crumb mixture; shake off excess. Arrange eggplant slices in pan and bake in a 425° oven, turning once, until browned and very soft when pressed (20 to 25 minutes). Makes 4 to 6 servings.

Per serving: 160 calories, 6 g protein, 14 g carbohydrates, 9 g total fat, 89 mg cholesterol, 177 mg sodium

Trio of Sautéed Mushrooms

Preparation time: About 15 minutes
Cooking time: 15 to 20 minutes

If you've been longing to sample the enticing variety of mushrooms available in markets today, here's the perfect opportunity. The earthy flavors of cèpes and chanterelles deliciously enhance Pork Tenderloins with Stilton & Port (page 148)—or any roast pork or poultry.

- 1 **ounce *each* dried cèpes (also called porcini) and dried chanterelle mushrooms (or 2 oz. *total* of either)**
- 5 **tablespoons butter or margarine**
- 1½ **pounds fresh regular mushrooms, sliced**
- ¼ **teaspoon dry thyme**
  Salt and pepper

Soak dried mushrooms in very hot water to cover for 10 minutes. Drain in a colander, rinse well with cool water, and drain again. Set aside.

Melt 3 tablespoons of the butter in a wide frying pan over medium-high heat. Add fresh mushrooms and cook, stirring often, until mushrooms are soft and all liquid has evaporated (10 to 15 minutes).

Melt remaining 2 tablespoons butter in pan. Add cèpes, chanterelles, and thyme. Cook, stirring, until mushrooms are lightly browned (about 5 minutes). Season to taste with salt and pepper. Makes 6 servings.

Per serving: 139 calories, 3 g protein, 11 g carbohydrates, 10 g total fat, 26 mg cholesterol, 106 mg sodium

Minted Lettuce & Peas

Preparation time: About 10 minutes
Cooking time: About 2 minutes

To create a side-dish sensation, serve red leaf lettuce cups cradling tiny peas seasoned with lemon and mint.

- 1 **small head red leaf lettuce, separated into leaves, rinsed, and crisped**
- 2 **tablespoons butter or margarine**
- 1 **package (10 oz.) frozen tiny peas, thawed**
- ¼ **cup chopped fresh mint or 1½ tablespoons dry mint**
- 2 **teaspoons grated lemon peel**
  Salt and pepper

Set aside 6 large lettuce leaves; cut remaining lettuce into thin strips.

Melt butter in a wide frying pan over medium-high heat. Add peas and lettuce strips; cook, stirring, until lettuce is wilted (about 2 minutes). Stir in mint and lemon peel. Season to taste with salt and pepper.

To serve, place a whole lettuce leaf on each of 6 plates. Spoon pea mixture equally into center of each leaf. Makes 6 servings.

Per serving: 70 calories, 3 g protein, 6 g carbohydrates, 4 g total fat, 10 mg cholesterol, 105 mg sodium

*Peas in Pods (recipe on facing page) and Baked Potato Sticks
(recipe on page 168) are the perfect accompaniments for meaty
Oven-roasted Prime Rib Bones (recipe on page 140). To
complete a finger-food feast, offer ice cream cones for dessert.*

Roasted Onion Halves

Preparation time: About 5 minutes
Roasting time: 30 to 45 minutes

Golden roasted onions, their flavor accented with sweet-tart balsamic vinegar, are a simple, satisfying accompaniment for roast meat or poultry.

- 3 **large onions** (*each* **3 to 3½ inches in diameter**)
- ¼ **cup balsamic or red wine vinegar**
   Butter or margarine
   Salt and pepper

Cut unpeeled onions in half lengthwise. Pour vinegar into a 9- by 13-inch baking pan; place onions, cut sides down, in pan. Roast in a 350° oven until onions are soft when pressed (30 to 45 minutes). To eat, scoop onions from skins; add butter, salt, and pepper to taste. Makes 6 servings.

Per serving: 62 calories, 1 g protein, 6 g carbohydrates, 4 g total fat, 10 mg cholesterol, 41 mg sodium

Peas in Pods

Pictured on facing page

Preparation time: About 5 minutes
Cooking time: About 15 minutes

Preparing fresh peas doesn't get much easier than this—you just steam them, pods and all, then let diners shell their own at the table.

- 2 **pounds unshelled peas**
- 2 **tablespoons water**

Rinse peas; don't pat dry. Place peas in a 5-quart pan, add water, cover, and place over medium-high heat. Cook, stirring well every 5 minutes, until peas are tender to bite (about 15 minutes; shell a few to test). Pour into a warm serving bowl.

Shell peas at the table. Or, to eat straight from pods, hold a whole pod at one end and put it in your mouth. Bite lightly at the end you're holding, then pull pod through your teeth—peas pop into your mouth. Makes 4 servings.

Per serving: 70 calories, 5 g protein, 12 g carbohydrates, 0.3 g total fat, 0 mg cholesterol, 4 mg sodium

Sautéed Red Peppers with Basil

Preparation time: About 10 minutes
Cooking time: About 8 minutes

Successful vegetable gardeners (and their friends!) will appreciate this summertime special—just ripe red peppers, lightly sautéed and seasoned with aromatic fresh basil.

- 2 **tablespoons salad oil**
- 2 **large red bell peppers, seeded and cut into ½-inch-wide strips**
- 2 **tablespoons chopped fresh basil or 1 teaspoon dry basil**
   Salt and pepper
   Basil sprigs (optional)

Heat oil in a wide frying pan over medium heat. Add bell peppers and cook, stirring, until tender when pierced (about 8 minutes). Stir in chopped basil. Season to taste with salt and pepper. Serve; or, if made ahead, cover and let stand for up to 6 hours or refrigerate until next day.

To serve, reheat; or serve at room temperature or chilled. Garnish with basil sprigs, if desired. Makes 4 servings.

Per serving: 74 calories, 0.5 g protein, 3 g carbohydrates, 7 g total fat, 0 mg cholesterol, 2 mg sodium

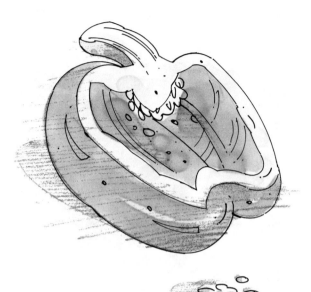

Sautéed Peppers & Pears

Preparation time: About 10 minutes
Cooking time: About 15 minutes

This fresh and vivid melange of sweet pears and red bell peppers makes a festive partner for ham, pork, or turkey. If you like, you can substitute sliced apples for the pears.

- 3 tablespoons butter or margarine
- 4 medium-size red or yellow bell peppers (or a combination), seeded and cut into ¼-inch-wide strips
- 3 medium-size firm-ripe pears or Golden Delicious apples, peeled, cored, and cut into ¼-inch-thick slices
- ¾ cup shredded jack or Münster cheese (optional)

Melt 1½ tablespoons of the butter in a wide frying pan over medium heat. Add bell peppers and cook, stirring often, until soft (about 10 minutes).

Melt remaining 1½ tablespoons butter in pan, then add pears. Cook, stirring often, until pears are tender when pierced (about 5 more minutes). Pour into a warm serving dish; immediately sprinkle with cheese, if desired. Makes 6 servings.

Per serving: 115 calories, 1 g protein, 16 g carbohydrates, 6 g total fat, 16 mg cholesterol, 60 mg sodium

Baked Potato Sticks

Pictured on page 166

Preparation time: About 5 minutes
Baking time: About 30 minutes

Reminiscent of giant-size French fries, these savory browned potato wedges are seasoned with garlic and oregano. (The oven-baking technique works well with sweet potatoes, too.)

- 2 large russet potatoes
- 2 to 3 tablespoons butter or margarine, melted
  Garlic salt
  Dry oregano

Scrub potatoes and cut each one lengthwise into eighths. Brush with butter; sprinkle with garlic salt and oregano. Arrange potato wedges, skin sides down, about 1 inch apart on a large baking sheet. Bake in a 425° oven until tender when pierced (about 30 minutes). Makes 4 servings.

Per serving: 144 calories, 2 g protein, 18 g carbohydrates, 7 g total fat, 19 mg cholesterol, 81 mg sodium

Baked Sweet Potato Sticks

Follow directions for **Baked Potato Sticks,** but substitute 2 large **sweet potatoes** or yams for russet potatoes. Omit garlic salt and oregano; instead, sprinkle potatoes with **ground nutmeg.** Decrease baking time to 25 minutes. Makes 4 servings.

Per serving: 272 calories, 3 g protein, 48 g carbohydrates, 8 g total fat, 19 mg cholesterol, 99 mg sodium

Spiced Spinach & Potatoes

Preparation time: About 10 minutes
Cooking time: 25 to 30 minutes

Subtly spiced and fragrant, this sturdy combination of spinach and diced potatoes makes a substantial meal when paired with simply cooked meat or chicken.

¼ **cup salad oil**
2 **large russet potatoes, peeled and cut into ½-inch cubes**
¾ **pound spinach, stems removed**
2 **cloves garlic, minced or pressed**
2 **teaspoons ground coriander**
½ **teaspoon ground ginger**
   About ½ cup water

Heat 3 tablespoons of the oil in a wide frying pan over medium-high heat. Add potatoes and cook, stirring occasionally, until browned (10 to 15 minutes). Meanwhile, rinse and drain spinach leaves; then cut crosswise into ½-inch-wide strips. Set aside.

Reduce heat to low. Add garlic, coriander, ginger, and remaining 1 tablespoon oil to potatoes; cook, stirring, until very fragrant (2 to 3 minutes). Pour in ½ cup of the water, cover, and simmer until potatoes are tender when pierced (about 8 minutes); add more water if needed to prevent sticking.

Add spinach to pan, increase heat to high, and cook, stirring, until leaves are wilted and almost all liquid has evaporated (about 2 minutes). Makes 4 servings.

Per serving: 242 calories, 4 g protein, 26 g carbohydrates, 14 g total fat, 0 mg cholesterol, 59 mg sodium

Best-ever Garlicky Potatoes

Preparation time: About 10 minutes
Baking time: About 23 minutes

We don't mean to brag, but we're sure you'll agree that these potatoes are absolutely irresistible. Choose an entrée you can bake in the same oven; breaded chicken breasts or Baked Pork Chops Dijon (page 152) are good choices.

1 **tablespoon olive oil**
1 **tablespoon butter or margarine**
3 **large red thin-skinned potatoes (about 1 lb. *total*), scrubbed and cut into eighths**
1 **medium-size onion, cut into eighths**
3 **cloves garlic, halved**
   Salt and pepper

Place oil and butter in a 9- by 13-inch baking pan and set in a 475° oven until butter is melted and sizzling (about 3 minutes).

Add potatoes, onion, and garlic to pan and stir well. Bake, stirring occasionally, until potatoes are golden brown and tender when pierced (about 20 minutes). Season to taste with salt and pepper. Makes 4 servings.

Per serving: 157 calories, 3 g protein, 23 g carbohydrates, 7 g total fat, 8 mg cholesterol, 39 mg sodium

Quick Ways with Vegetables

It's easy to dress up quick-cooked vegetables—just top them with minced parsley, grated cheese, or one of the seasoned butters you'll find in this book. Try Almond Browned Butter (page 100) or Lemon Butter (page 149), or choose an herb butter flavored with basil, chives, cilantro, oregano, mint, savory, or watercress (see pages 69 and 149). Pesto (page 169) also makes a quick, delicious topping for hot cooked vegetables.

Shredded Rutabagas

Preparation time: 5 to 10 minutes
Cooking time: About 5 minutes

Rutabagas are closely related to the familiar turnip—but they're denser in texture, sweeter in flavor, and yellow or pale orange in color. Enjoy them in an easy sauté, perhaps as an accompaniment to a crisp-skinned roast chicken.

- 3 tablespoons butter or margarine
- 2 cups coarsely shredded, firmly packed rutabagas
- 2 tablespoons water
- 1 to 1½ tablespoons firmly packed brown sugar
- 1 teaspoon soy sauce

Melt butter in a wide frying pan over medium-high heat. Add rutabagas, water, sugar, and soy sauce. Cover and cook, stirring often, until rutabagas are tender-crisp to bite (about 5 minutes). Makes 4 servings.

Per serving: 125 calories, 1 g protein, 11 g carbohydrates, 9 g total fat, 23 mg cholesterol, 192 mg sodium

Wilted Spinach with Parmesan & Pepper

Preparation time: About 10 minutes
Baking time: 10 to 12 minutes

If you're serving a baked or roasted entrée, it's convenient to cook the side dish in the oven, too. Here, you simply heat fresh spinach in a covered casserole, then top it with Parmesan cheese at the table.

- 8 cups firmly packed stemmed, rinsed, and drained spinach leaves
- 1 tablespoon butter or margarine
- ¼ cup grated or shredded Parmesan cheese
  Coarsely ground pepper

Place spinach (with water that clings to leaves) in a shallow 3-quart casserole; dot with butter. Cover and bake in a 450° oven until leaves are wilted (10 to 12 minutes). Lightly mix spinach with 2 forks to coat with butter. At the table, offer cheese and pepper to season spinach to taste. Makes 4 servings.

Per serving: 81 calories, 6 g protein, 5 g carbohydrates, 5 g total fat, 13 mg cholesterol, 242 mg sodium

Skillet Squash

Preparation time: About 10 minutes
Cooking time: 8 to 10 minutes

Here's an easy way to prepare zucchini—just slice, sauté, and season with herbs, onion, and parsley.

- 3 tablespoons olive oil, butter, or margarine
- 1 clove garlic, minced or pressed
- 6 medium-size zucchini, cut crosswise into ¼-inch-thick slices
- 1 tablespoon *each* minced parsley and thinly sliced green onion (including top)
- 1 teaspoon dry oregano
- ¼ teaspoon sugar
  Salt and pepper

Heat oil in a wide frying pan over medium-high heat. Add garlic; cook, stirring, for 2 to 3 minutes. Add zucchini and cook, stirring often, just until tender-crisp to bite (3 to 5 minutes). Stir in parsley, onion, oregano, and sugar. Season to taste with salt and pepper. Continue to cook, stirring, until zucchini and seasonings are well blended (1 to 2 more minutes). Makes 4 to 6 servings.

Per serving: 102 calories, 2 g protein, 6 g carbohydrates, 8 g total fat, 0 mg cholesterol, 6 mg sodium

*Flavored with cream, sherry, crisp almonds, and
tarragon, Almond Pilaf with Sherry (recipe on page 173)
is an elegant companion for Broiled Lamb Chops with
Papaya Chutney (recipe on page 156).*

Hashed-brown Zucchini

Preparation time: About 20 minutes
Cooking time: About 15 minutes

Great recipes are sometimes born from the reinvention of old favorites—and that's what happened when we made hash browns with shredded zucchini instead of potatoes. Serve with sausages for breakfast, with roast meat for dinner.

1½ pounds zucchini
½ teaspoon salt
2 eggs
6 tablespoons grated Parmesan cheese
1 clove garlic, minced or pressed
  About ¼ cup butter or margarine
  Tomato wedges (optional)

Coarsely shred zucchini (you should have about 4 cups) and combine with salt in a medium-size bowl. Let stand for about 15 minutes. Squeeze with your hands to press out moisture. Stir in eggs, cheese, and garlic.

Melt 2 tablespoons of the butter in a wide frying pan over medium-high heat. Mound about 2 tablespoons of the zucchini mixture in pan; flatten slightly to make a patty. Repeat until pan is filled, but don't crowd patties in pan. Cook patties, turning once, until golden on both sides (about 6 minutes). Lift out and arrange on a warm platter; keep warm. Repeat to cook remaining zucchini mixture, adding more butter as needed. Garnish with tomatoes, if desired. Makes 4 servings.

Per serving: 197 calories, 8 g protein, 6 g carbohydrates, 16 g total fat, 143 mg cholesterol, 428 mg sodium

Broiled Tomatoes Parmesan

Preparation time: About 5 minutes
Broiling time: 3 to 4 minutes

As a simple accompaniment to broiled meat or fish, serve juicy tomato halves topped with herbs and cheese.

6 medium-size tomatoes
  Pepper
  Dry basil
2 tablespoons grated Parmesan cheese
2 tablespoons butter or margarine

Cut tomatoes in half crosswise. Sprinkle cut surfaces with pepper and basil; then sprinkle evenly with cheese and dot evenly with butter. Place tomatoes, cut sides up, on rack of a broiler pan; broil about 6 inches below heat until lightly browned (3 to 4 minutes). Makes 6 servings.

Per serving: 65 calories, 2 g protein, 5 g carbohydrates, 5 g total fat, 12 mg cholesterol, 80 mg sodium

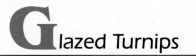

Glazed Turnips

Preparation time: About 5 minutes
Cooking time: 8 to 10 minutes

Enriched with butter and sweetened with just a bit of sugar, these thinly sliced turnips make a pleasing side dish for a meat loaf or other hearty, homestyle entrée.

2 cups thinly sliced turnips
2 tablespoons butter or margarine
2 tablespoons water
1 tablespoon sugar

In a wide frying pan, combine turnips, butter, water, and sugar. Cover and cook over medium-high heat, stirring often, until turnips are just tender when pierced (about 5 minutes). Uncover and continue to cook until glazed. Makes 4 servings.

Per serving: 80 calories, 0.6 g protein, 7 g carbohydrates, 6 g total fat, 16 mg cholesterol, 102 mg sodium

Hearty Grain Dishes

When you think of side dishes, you probably think first of vegetables— tiny green peas, crisp broccoli spears, tender fresh corn. But grains such as polenta and rice are superb partners for many main dishes, especially when you're looking for a particularly satisfying accompaniment to a simple entrée. Robust, bacon-dotted polenta is the perfect hearty complement for almost any meat or poultry meal. Our spicy, creamy Cheese & Chile Rice beautifully rounds out a steak and salad dinner; or try it with broiled chicken or crumb-coated fish fillets. And a rice and pasta pilaf is elegant along-side juicy chops or grilled turkey breast slices.

Bacon Polenta

Preparation time: About 10 minutes
Cooking time: About 15 minutes

5 slices bacon, chopped
⅓ cup finely chopped onion
2 large cloves garlic, minced or pressed
2¼ cups regular-strength chicken broth
¾ cup polenta or yellow cornmeal
Salt

In a 3-quart pan, cook bacon over medium heat until lightly browned (about 5 minutes), stirring. Add onion and garlic and cook, stirring, until onion is soft and bacon is well browned (about 5 more minutes). Discard all but 1 tablespoon of the drippings.

Add 1½ cups of the broth to pan and bring to a boil over high heat. Meanwhile, in a small bowl, mix polenta with remaining ¾ cup broth.

Using a long-handled spoon, stir polenta mixture into boiling broth (mixture will thicken and spatter). Reduce heat to low and cook, stirring constantly, for 5 minutes. Season to taste with salt. Makes 4 servings.

Per serving: 186 calories, 7 g protein, 22 g carbohydrates, 8 g total fat, 9 mg cholesterol, 699 mg sodium

Cheese & Chile Rice

Preparation time: About 10 minutes
Baking time: About 30 minutes

3 cups cooked long-grain white rice
1 can (4 oz.) diced green chiles
1 jar (2 oz.) diced pimentos, drained
1 cup sour cream
1 cup (4 oz.) shredded jack cheese
1 cup (4 oz.) shredded Cheddar cheese

In a large bowl, stir together rice, chiles, pimentos, sour cream, jack cheese, and ½ cup of the Cheddar cheese. Pour mixture into a greased shallow 1½-quart casserole; sprinkle with remaining ½ cup Cheddar cheese. Bake in a 350° oven until mixture is hot throughout and cheese is melted (about 30 minutes). Makes 6 servings.

Per serving: 390 calories, 14 g protein, 37 g carbohydrates, 20 g total fat, 53 mg cholesterol, 359 mg sodium

Almond Pilaf with Sherry

Pictured on page 171

Preparation time: About 5 minutes
Cooking time: About 30 minutes

½ cup slivered blanched almonds
½ cup 1-inch lengths of dry vermicelli
¼ cup butter or margarine
1 cup long-grain white rice
1¼ cups regular-strength chicken broth
¾ cup cream sherry
1½ teaspoons dry tarragon or 1 tablespoon chopped fresh tarragon
Tarragon sprigs (optional)

Toast almonds in a wide frying pan over medium heat until golden brown (about 4 minutes), stirring. Remove from pan and set aside. Add vermicelli to pan and stir until golden brown (about 2 minutes); remove from pan and set aside.

Add butter and rice to pan; cook, stirring, until rice is lightly toasted (about 3 minutes). Add broth, sherry, dry tarragon, and vermicelli. Bring mixture to a boil; reduce heat, cover, and simmer until rice is tender to bite (about 20 minutes). Sprinkle with almonds and garnish with tarragon sprigs, if desired. Makes 6 servings.

Per serving: 303 calories, 7 g protein, 38 g carbohydrates, 14 g total fat, 21 mg cholesterol, 290 mg sodium

*A showcase for glossy red Bartletts, Pear Fans with
Orange Syrup (recipe on page 176) are sophisticated in
their simplicity, appealing in their freshness. Try the
recipe with other pears, too.*

Desserts

Fresh fruit is the simplest sweet of all, so it's no surprise that ripe berries, juicy peaches, and other popular fruits play the starring role in nearly all our dessert recipes, Try your favorites dipped in silky chocolate sauce, layered with ice cream, topped with custard or clouds of meringue—or served almost plain, perhaps with just a chunk of cheese alongside. And on days when you crave something even sweeter than baked pears or citrus compote, choose our crisp-fried tortilla "cookies" or nutty graham-cracker treats.

Cheese with Fruit

For a simple, appealing dessert, serve fresh fruit and a selection of complementary cheeses. Arrange choice whole fruits in a basket, cheeses on a pretty tray; provide cheese cutters and small, sharp knives. Try blue, Gorgonzola, and Roquefort with apples, grapes, and pears; Brie with berries, papayas, mangoes, apples, and pears; Cheddar with pears and red-skinned apples; Jarlsberg and Gouda with apples, pears, and apricots; Swiss and Emmenthaler with pears; jack or teleme with apricots, melons, and plums.

Pear Fans with Orange Syrup

Pictured on page 174

Preparation time: About 20 minutes
Cooking time: About 1 minute

To show off perfectly ripe pears, present "fans" of slender slices atop a warm orange syrup. Rosy red Bartletts make a handsome dessert, but you can also use Anjou, Comice, or another favorite variety.

- ½ cup *each* sugar and orange juice
- ¼ cup butter or margarine
- 2 tablespoons lemon juice
- 1 teaspoon finely shredded orange or lemon peel
- 3 medium-size Bartlett or other pears
  Shredded orange or lemon peel (optional)

In a 1- to 2-quart pan, combine sugar, orange juice, butter, and 1 tablespoon of the lemon juice; cook over high heat, stirring, until butter is melted and sugar is dissolved. Stir in the 1 teaspoon orange peel, then divide orange syrup equally among 6 dessert plates.

Cut pears in half lengthwise. Remove core and blossom end from each half. Cut each pear half lengthwise into ¼-inch-thick slices, leaving stem end intact. Drizzle pear halves with remaining 1 tablespoon lemon juice. Place a pear half, cut side down, atop syrup on each plate. With flat of a knife, gently press down on each pear to fan out slices. Garnish with orange peel, if desired. Makes 6 servings.

Per serving: 192 calories, 0.6 g protein, 32 g carbohydrates, 8 g total fat, 21 mg cholesterol, 79 mg sodium

Grapefruit & Cherry Compote

Preparation time: About 20 minutes
Cooking time: About 10 minutes

This lively fruit dessert brings spicy meals to a refreshing conclusion. Enjoy it during summer, when cherries are in season—and again in winter, when imported cherries become available.

- 5 medium-size pink grapefruit (about 4¼ lbs. *total*)
- 1 pound dark sweet cherries, pitted
- ⅓ cup orange-flavored liqueur
- 2 tablespoons sugar
- 1½ tablespoons honey

With a sharp knife, cut peel (colored part only) from one of the grapefruit. Then cut peel into long, thin slivers, place in a 1½- to 2-quart pan, and add 1 cup water. Bring to a boil over high heat; drain. Repeat with 1 more cup water. Set drained peel aside in pan.

Cut peel and all white membrane from outsides of remaining 4 grapefruit. Holding fruit over a bowl, cut between membrane to release segments into bowl. Squeeze juice from membrane into bowl; discard membrane. Drain off juice and reserve. Add cherries, ¼ cup of the liqueur, and 1 tablespoon of the sugar to grapefruit segments. Mix gently.

Add reserved grapefruit juice, remaining 1 tablespoon sugar, and honey to drained grapefruit peel in pan. Bring to a boil over high heat; boil, stirring often, until syrup is reduced to about 2 tablespoons (about 5 minutes). Stir in remaining liqueur.

To serve, ladle fruit mixture into dessert bowls or goblets; top with peel and syrup. Makes 6 to 8 servings.

Per serving: 143 calories, 1 g protein, 31 g carbohydrates, 0.7 g total fat, 0 mg cholesterol, 0.3 mg sodium

Sherried Cream with Red Grapes

Preparation time: About 10 minutes
Cooking time: About 10 minutes

To make these fruit-and-pudding parfaits, fill your prettiest stemmed glasses with alternate layers of sherry-flavored custard and gleaming red grapes.

- ⅓ cup sugar
- 2 tablespoons cornstarch
- ⅛ teaspoon salt
- 2 cups milk
- ¼ cup cream sherry or apple juice
- 2 egg yolks
- 2 tablespoons butter or margarine
- 1 teaspoon vanilla
- 1½ cups seedless red grapes

In a 2-quart pan, stir together sugar, cornstarch, and salt. Gradually blend in milk and sherry. Bring to a boil over medium heat, stirring; continue to boil, stirring, for 1 minute. Remove from heat.

In a small bowl, beat egg yolks until blended. Stir some of the hot custard into egg yolks; then return mixture to pan and cook, stirring constantly, for 30 seconds. Remove from heat, add butter and vanilla, and stir until butter is melted.

Layer spoonfuls of custard and grapes alternately in 4 stemmed glasses. Let cool slightly, then cover and refrigerate until serving time or for up to 4 hours. Makes 4 servings.

Per serving: 266 calories, 6 g protein, 34 g carbohydrates, 12 g total fat, 139 mg cholesterol, 194 mg sodium

Sparkling Berries

Preparation time: About 5 minutes

Serve dessert and after-dinner drinks all in one: offer glasses of sparkling wine filled with your choice of juicy fresh berries.

- 2 cups hulled strawberries, fraises des bois, raspberries, or blackberries
  Chilled sparkling muscat wine

Divide berries equally among 4 stemmed glasses. Slowly fill each glass with wine. Sip wine first, then eat berries with a spoon. Makes 4 servings.

Per serving: 96 calories, 0.7 g protein, 8 g carbohydrates, 0.3 g total fat, 0 mg cholesterol, 8 mg sodium

Vanilla Cloud with Berries

Preparation time: About 15 minutes

A sweet, airy cheese whip sets off beautifully ripe berries. For a striking presentation, mound the berries and cheese mixture side by side in a bowl and garnish with mint sprigs.

- 1 large package (8 oz.) cream cheese, at room temperature
- ½ cup sugar
- 1 vanilla bean (4 to 6 inches long) or 1 teaspoon vanilla extract
- 2 cups sour cream or plain yogurt
- 8 cups blackberries, hulled strawberries, or raspberries
  Mint sprigs (optional)

In large bowl of an electric mixer, beat cream cheese and sugar until smoothly blended. Slit vanilla bean lengthwise and scrape seeds into bowl with tip of a knife (or add vanilla extract). Beat until smooth and fluffy. With mixer at high speed, gradually add sour cream, beating until smooth after each addition.

Mound berries in a wide bowl, keeping them to one side. Spoon cheese mixture beside fruit. Garnish with mint sprigs, if desired. To serve, spoon portions of fruit and cheese mixture into dessert bowls. Makes 8 to 10 servings.

Per serving: 282 calories, 4 g protein, 24 g carbohydrates, 20 g total fat, 50 mg cholesterol, 103 mg sodium

Warm Fruit Gratin with Zabaglione

Preparation time: About 10 minutes
Cooking time: 4 to 6 minutes

As simple as it's delicious, Italian *zabaglione* is nothing more than a warm, golden froth of eggs, wine, and sugar. Here, summer fruits are covered with zabaglione and a dusting of powdered sugar and almonds, then broiled just until the topping is browned.

  About 5 cups fruit, such as blueberries, hulled strawberries, or sliced peaches (or a combination)
3 **eggs**
6 **tablespoons granulated sugar**
2 **tablespoons fruity white wine, such as Johannisberg Riesling**
2 **tablespoons powdered sugar**
2 **tablespoons sliced almonds**

Divide fruit evenly among 4 to 6 shallow, wide-rimmed ovenproof bowls. Position broiler rack so tops of bowls will be about 4 inches below heat. Set bowls aside.

In a round-bottomed zabaglione pan or in the top of a double boiler, beat eggs, granulated sugar, and wine until frothy. Place container over a pan of simmering water and beat egg mixture rapidly until tripled in volume (3 to 5 minutes); then immediately pour evenly over fruit. Dust with powdered sugar, sprinkle with almonds, and broil until golden brown (about 1 minute). Makes 4 to 6 servings.

Per serving: 174 calories, 5 g protein, 29 g carbohydrates, 5 g total fat, 128 mg cholesterol, 40 mg sodium

Spirited Chocolate Fondue

Pictured on facing page

Preparation time: About 15 minutes
Cooking time: About 10 minutes

Chocolate fondue quickly turns your favorite fresh fruit (or ladyfingers or cubes of pound cake) into a luxurious close to a light meal. A splash of orange liqueur gives this version a spirited kick.

1 **pound bittersweet, semisweet, or milk chocolate (or a combination of all 3 kinds), coarsely chopped**
1 **cup whipping cream**
¼ **cup orange-flavored liqueur**
1 **pound mixed fruit, such as hulled strawberries, cubed melon, banana slices, and pear slices**
  Lemon juice (if using bananas and pears)

In a medium-size metal bowl or in the top of a double boiler, combine chocolate and cream. Place container over a pan of simmering water and stir chocolate mixture just until chocolate is melted and mixture is smooth (about 10 minutes). Stir in liqueur. Transfer chocolate mixture to a chafing dish or fondue pot and set over low heat.

If using bananas or pears, brush with lemon juice to prevent darkening. Arrange fruit in separate groups on a platter alongside fondue. Offer skewers for dipping fruit into chocolate. Makes 8 to 10 servings.

Per serving: 353 calories, 5 g protein, 33 g carbohydrates, 28 g total fat, 29 mg cholesterol, 12 mg sodium

*A sweet indulgence that you can assemble at the last
minute, rich and silken Spirited Chocolate Fondue
(recipe on facing page) brings any dinner party to
a delightful conclusion.*

Fresh Peach Sundaes with Hot Chocolate Sauce

Preparation time: About 10 minutes
Cooking time: About 5 minutes

Here's an especially simple way to enjoy fresh peaches—put a juicy peach half in a sherbet glass, top with a big scoop of ice cream, and spoon hot homemade dark chocolate sauce over all.

4 ounces semisweet chocolate, coarsely chopped
6 tablespoons whipping cream
2 large ripe peaches
About 1 pint vanilla ice cream

In a 1-quart pan, combine chocolate and cream. Stir constantly over low heat until chocolate is melted and sauce is smooth; keep warm.

Peel, halve, and pit peaches; place each half in a sherbet glass and top with a scoop of ice cream. Drizzle warm chocolate sauce evenly over ice cream, then serve. Makes 4 servings.

Per serving: 379 calories, 5 g protein, 42 g carbohydrates, 24 g total fat, 55 mg cholesterol, 66 mg sodium

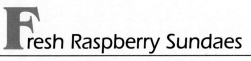

Fresh Raspberry Sundaes

Preparation time: About 10 minutes
Cooking time: 8 to 10 minutes

If you're lucky enough to have a good supply of fresh raspberries, turn a few cups of them into a ruby-red, tart-sweet sauce for toasted almond or other favorite ice cream.

½ cup sugar
1 tablespoon cornstarch
2 cups raspberries
1 tablespoon lemon juice
¼ teaspoon ground cinnamon
About 1 pint toasted almond ice cream

In a 2-quart pan, stir together sugar and cornstarch. Add 1 cup of the raspberries to cornstarch mixture and crush them with a spoon; then place pan over medium heat and cook, stirring, until sauce boils and thickens. Remove from heat; stir in remaining 1 cup berries, lemon juice, and cinnamon. Let cool.

Scoop ice cream into 4 sherbet glasses; top with raspberry sauce. Makes 4 servings.

Per serving: 281 calories, 3 g protein, 50 g carbohydrates, 9 g total fat, 30 mg cholesterol, 59 mg sodium

Gingered Papaya Sundaes

Preparation time: About 10 minutes
Cooking time: 2 to 4 minutes

For a wonderful finale to an Oriental meal, offer this ginger-sparked combination of gently heated papaya slices and cold vanilla ice cream.

1 firm-ripe papaya
2 or 3 large limes
2 tablespoons butter or margarine
2 tablespoons thinly slivered candied or crystallized ginger
1 tablespoon firmly packed brown sugar
About 1 pint vanilla ice cream

Peel papaya and cut in half lengthwise; scoop out seeds. Cut papaya halves crosswise into ½-inch-thick slices.

Pare a strip or two of peel (colored part only) from one lime; cut into enough thin slivers to make ½ teaspoon (or remove peel with a zesting tool). Squeeze enough fruit to make 2 tablespoons juice. Cut remaining lime into thin slices; set aside.

Melt butter in a wide frying pan over medium heat. Add papaya, ginger, and sugar. Cook until hot, gently turning papaya slices (2 to 4 minutes). Stir in lime peel and lime juice. Spoon papaya mixture into 4 shallow dessert bowls and moisten with pan juices. Top each portion with a scoop of ice cream and a few lime slices. Makes 4 servings.

Per serving: 257 calories, 3 g protein, 34 g carbohydrates, 13 g total fat, 45 mg cholesterol, 125 mg sodium

erry Slush

Preparation time: About 5 minutes

Nothing but berries, cream, and a little sugar goes into this refreshing dessert. It's a perfect choice for hot-weather dining.

About ⅓ cup whipping cream or half-and-half
3 cups frozen unsweetened blackberries
or raspberries
3 to 4 tablespoons sugar

Pour ⅓ cup of the cream into a food processor or blender. With motor running, add berries, about ¼ cup at a time; continue to process until smoothly blended. (If you're using a blender, you may need to add 2 to 4 tablespoons more cream.)

Stir in sugar, then spoon mixture into 4 glasses. Serve immediately; or, for a thicker consistency, place in the freezer for a few minutes. Makes 4 servings.

Per serving: 156 calories, 1 g protein, 25 g carbohydrates, 7 g total fat, 22 mg cholesterol, 7 mg sodium

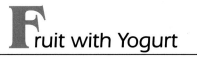ruit with Yogurt

Preparation time: About 5 minutes
Cooking time: 2 to 4 minutes

This hot-and-cold dessert makes a good breakfast treat as well. Start with yogurt and your choice of fruit, then spoon caramelized sugar syrup over all.

1 cup vanilla-flavored lowfat yogurt
4 small apricots, halved and pitted; or
6 to 8 large strawberries, hulled; or 2 small
peaches, peeled, halved, and pitted
1½ tablespoons sugar

Spoon half the yogurt into each of 2 small, shallow bowls. Set 4 apricot halves, 3 or 4 strawberries, or 2 peach halves atop each portion of yogurt.

Place sugar in a 6-inch frying pan. Set over medium heat and shake pan to mix sugar as it begins to liquefy and caramelize. When sugar is liquid and amber (do not let sugar scorch), let cool just until thickened to the consistency of light syrup (about 1 minute); then drizzle over fruit and yogurt. Makes 2 servings.

Per serving: 158 calories, 6 g protein, 31 g carbohydrates, 2 g total fat, 6 mg cholesterol, 76 mg sodium

uff Pastry Prune Pies

Preparation time: About 10 minutes,
plus 25 minutes to thaw patty shells
Baking time: About 15 minutes

Widely praised for their sweet flavor and nutritional virtues, prunes are nonetheless far more likely to show up at breakfast time than for dessert. But these little pies—featuring marzipan, tender prunes, and crisp almonds on a flaky crust—are definitely deserving of a place on the pastry cart. If you like, you can even add a scoop of ice cream.

1 package (about 10 oz.) frozen patty shells
¾ cup (about 8 oz.) marzipan or almond paste
18 moist-pack pitted prunes
⅓ cup sliced almonds
Vanilla ice cream (optional)

Let patty shells thaw at room temperature, then place well apart on a large baking sheet. With your fingers, press each shell into a 4-inch-diameter round. Press 2 tablespoons of the marzipan over top of each pastry. Firmly press 3 prunes into marzipan atop each pastry; sprinkle with almonds. Bake in a 400° oven until golden brown (about 15 minutes). Top with ice cream, if desired; serve warm. Makes 6 servings.

Per serving: 444 calories, 6 g protein, 67 g carbohydrates, 17 g total fat, 0 mg cholesterol, 230 mg sodium

This soufflélike cloud of eggs and sugar may look difficult to make, but it's actually quite easy to put together. And Salzburger Nockerln (recipe on facing page) is easy on the waistline, too.

Berries under Meringue

Preparation time: 10 to 15 minutes
Cooking time: About 10 minutes

Are you looking for a dressy presentation for ripe berries? You've just found it! Warmed, liqueur-spiked strawberries, raspberries, or blackberries are encircled by a gingery fresh orange sauce and crowned with a sweet meringue cloud.

    Orange-Ginger Sauce (recipe follows)
2 cups hulled strawberries, raspberries, or blackberries
2 tablespoons black currant-, raspberry-, or orange-flavored liqueur
3 egg whites
¼ teaspoon cream of tartar
½ cup granulated sugar
1 teaspoon vanilla
1 tablespoon powdered sugar

Prepare Orange-Ginger Sauce; set aside.

    Place berries close together in a single layer in center of a 10- to 12-inch ovenproof rimmed platter. Spoon liqueur over berries.

    In large bowl of an electric mixer, beat egg whites and cream of tartar at high speed until frothy. Gradually add granulated sugar, beating until meringue holds stiff peaks. Beat in vanilla.

    Spoon meringue over berries, mounding it so a 1- to 2-inch-wide border of berries remains uncovered. Sift powdered sugar evenly over meringue. Broil 6 inches below heat until lightly browned (about 3 minutes). Pour Orange-Ginger Sauce around berries on platter; serve warm. Makes 6 servings.

Orange-Ginger Sauce. In a 1- to 1½-quart pan, stir together ½ cup **sugar** and 1½ tablespoons **cornstarch.** Blend in 1 cup **orange juice** and 3 thin, quarter-size slices **fresh ginger.** Bring to a boil over high heat, stirring constantly. Remove from heat and discard ginger; stir in 3 tablespoons **lemon juice.** Serve warm (reheat, if necessary).

Per serving: 206 calories, 2 g protein, 48 g carbohydrates, 0.2 g total fat, 0 mg cholesterol, 30 mg sodium

Storing Coffee

Heat and moisture cause coffee to go stale quickly, so store both beans and ground coffee airtight—preferably in glass jars with tight screw-on lids—in the refrigerator or freezer. When you want to brew coffee, just remove the amount you need; there's no need to thaw it or bring it to room temperature before using. Buy coffee in small quantities, since it loses its freshness after about a month even if stored properly.

Salzburger Nockerln

Pictured on facing page

Preparation time: About 15 minutes
Baking time: 10 to 12 minutes

Light, billowy, and easy to prepare, this Austrian specialty is a dramatic after-dinner offering. Serve it warm and golden from the oven, sprinkled with shavings of semisweet chocolate.

1 ounce semisweet chocolate
4 eggs, separated
¼ cup sugar
4 teaspoons all-purpose flour
1 tablespoon butter or margarine

Using a vegetable peeler, shave chocolate firmly. Set shavings aside.

    In large bowl of an electric mixer, beat egg whites until they hold soft peaks. Gradually add sugar, continuing to beat until mixture is very stiff. Set aside.

    Place egg yolks in a small bowl and beat with electric mixer at high speed until very light in color and slightly thickened. Gradually add flour, beating until mixture is thick and well blended. Fold yolk mixture into beaten whites, blending lightly but thoroughly.

    Melt butter in a shallow 2-quart oval or rectangular ovenproof pan directly over medium heat. Heap egg mixture atop butter in pan, making 6 equal mounds. Bake in a 350° oven until top is pale brown (10 to 12 minutes). Sprinkle with chocolate. Makes 6 servings.

Per serving: 129 calories, 5 g protein, 13 g carbohydrates, 7 g total fat, 147 mg cholesterol, 62 mg sodium

Peach Brûlée

Preparation time: About 15 minutes
Broiling time: About 3 minutes

Crème brûlée, a classic French custard, has a delicious crackly topping of caramelized sugar. Here, a similar cooked sugar crust crowns blueberry-filled peaches.

About 3 tablespoons butter or margarine
2 **tablespoons lemon juice**
3 **large ripe peaches, peeled, halved, and pitted**
½ **cup blueberries**
6 **tablespoons firmly packed brown sugar**
⅓ **to ½ cup sour cream**

Melt 2 tablespoons of the butter in a small pan; mix in lemon juice. Coat peach halves with butter mixture and place, cut sides up, on a large baking sheet. Fill each peach half with 1 tablespoon of the blueberries. Set remaining 2 tablespoons berries aside.

Line another large baking sheet with foil; butter foil generously. Push about 1 tablespoon of the sugar through a wire sieve onto foil, making an even layer about 3 inches square. Repeat with remaining sugar to make 5 more squares. Broil sugar about 6 inches below heat just until melted (1 to 2 minutes). Let cool until set, but still pliable (about 30 seconds).

With a wide spatula, set a sugar square atop each peach half. Broil about 6 inches below heat just until sugar crust drapes around peach half (10 to 30 seconds). Transfer peach halves to dessert plates; garnish with sour cream and remaining 2 tablespoons berries. Makes 6 servings.

Per serving: 176 calories, 1 g protein, 25 g carbohydrates, 9 g total fat, 22 mg cholesterol, 72 mg sodium

Cider-poached Apples with Yogurt

Preparation time: About 10 minutes
Cooking time: About 30 minutes

Instead of baking apples, poach them in cider that's been reduced to a fragrant amber sauce. Crunchy pecans and cool yogurt add appetizing contrast.

4 **cups cider or apple juice**
4 **medium-size McIntosh or Golden Delicious apples**
½ **to ¾ cup plain or vanilla-flavored yogurt**
½ **cup chopped pecans**

In a 2- to 3-quart pan, boil cider over high heat until reduced to 1 cup (about 15 minutes). Meanwhile, core apples. Add apples to cider and return to a boil. Reduce heat, cover, and simmer until apples are tender when pierced (12 to 15 minutes). Transfer apples to dessert bowls; top with cider sauce, yogurt, and pecans. Makes 4 servings.

Per serving: 310 calories, 3 g protein, 54 g carbohydrates, 11 g total fat, 5 mg cholesterol, 24 mg sodium

Baked Pears with Anise Seeds

Preparation time: About 10 minutes
Baking time: About 25 minutes

Anise seeds add a spicy dimension to these tender baked pears. Accompany with a late-harvest Riesling for a special occasion.

4 **medium-size firm-ripe Comice or Anjou pears, peeled**
2 **tablespoons butter or margarine**
¼ **cup *each* hot water and firmly packed brown sugar**
¼ **teaspoon anise seeds**

Set pears upright in a shallow baking pan just large enough to hold them side by side. Melt butter in a small pan; remove from heat and stir in water, sugar, and anise seeds. Pour over pears. Bake in a 375° oven, basting occasionally with pan juices, until pears are tender when pierced (about 25 minutes). Transfer pears to dessert bowls and drizzle with pan juices. Makes 4 servings.

Per serving: 200 calories, 0.7 g protein, 38 g carbohydrates, 6 g total fat, 16 mg cholesterol, 63 mg sodium

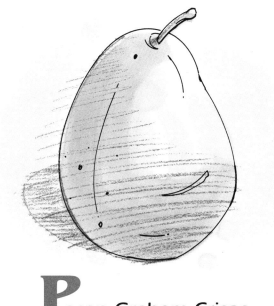

Pecan Graham Crisps

Preparation time: About 20 minutes
Cooking time: About 10 minutes

Chewy toffee and chocolate chips top graham crackers in this easy-to-make confection. Serve with milk, coffee, or tea whenever you crave a simple homemade sweet. (You'll need a candy thermometer to make the toffee.)

- 12   whole graham crackers (*each 2½ by 4¾ inches*)
- 1   cup (½ lb.) butter or margarine
- 1¼   cups firmly packed light brown sugar
- 1   cup finely chopped pecans or walnuts
- 1   teaspoon vanilla
- 1   cup (6 oz.) semisweet or milk chocolate chips

Place crackers side by side in a single layer in a rimmed 10- by 15-inch baking pan. Set aside.

Melt butter in a 1- to 2-quart pan over medium heat. Stir in sugar and pecans; bring to a boil, stirring often. Continue to boil until mixture registers 238°F on a candy thermometer (4 to 5 minutes). Remove from heat, stir in vanilla, and immediately pour over crackers, spreading to cover completely.

Bake in a 375° oven until very bubbly (about 5 minutes). Remove from oven and immediately sprinkle with chocolate chips. Let stand until chocolate is melted (2 to 3 minutes); then carefully spread chocolate over topping. Cut into 24 squares; then cut each square in half diagonally. Let cool for at least 10 minutes before eating. Makes 48 crisps.

Per crisp: 103 calories, 0.7 g protein, 11 g carbohydrates, 7 g total fat, 10 mg cholesterol, 65 mg sodium

Pears, Pepper & Cheese

Preparation time: About 5 minutes

Fruit and cheese are classic dessert partners. We suggest serving your favorite ripe pears with a rich blue-veined cheese and—for a nippy accent—a sprinkling of freshly ground pepper.

- 4   medium-size firm-ripe pears
- 8   ounces buttery blue-veined cheese, such as dolce Gorgonzola or Cambozola (from Bavaria); or double- or triple-cream cheese, such as St. André, l'Explorateur, or Boursault
     Peppermill with whole black peppercorns; or fresh coarse-ground black pepper

Present pears, a chunk of cheese, and peppermill on a plate or board. To eat, slice off a piece of fruit, top with a portion of cheese, and sprinkle lightly with pepper. Makes 4 servings.

Per serving: 297 calories, 9 g protein, 26 g carbohydrates, 19 g total fat, 52 mg cholesterol, 480 mg sodium

Tortilla Crisps

Preparation time: About 15 minutes
Cooking time: About 15 minutes

To make these quick "cookies," just coat crisp-fried flour tortilla wedges with cinnamon sugar. Serve with bowls of ice cream or alongside cups of coffee or hot chocolate.

- ⅓   cup sugar
- 1½   teaspoons ground cinnamon
- 10   to 12 flour tortillas (*each 7 to 8 inches in diameter*)
     Salad oil

In a small bowl, stir together sugar and cinnamon; set aside. Stack tortillas, then cut stack into 6 wedges.

In a wide frying pan, heat ½ inch oil over medium-high heat to 350°F on a deep-frying thermometer. Add tortilla wedges, about 6 at a time (do not crowd pan); cook until golden and puffy (about 30 seconds on each side).

Drain on paper towels. As tortilla wedges are cooked, lightly sprinkle with cinnamon-sugar mixture. Makes 60 to 72 crisps.

Per crisp: 27 calories, 0.5 g protein, 5 g carbohydrates, 0.7 g total fat, 0 mg cholesterol, 33 mg sodium

Index

Broiled Swordfish with Tomato-Olive Confetti (recipe on page 89)

Linguine with Prosciutto & Olives (recipe on page 82)